STAR WARS®

LEGACY

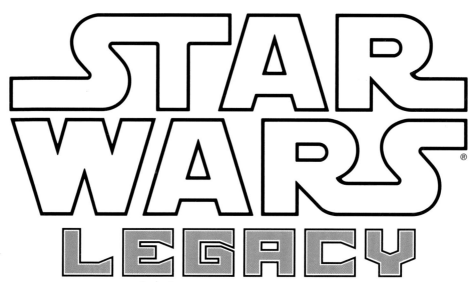

VOLUME II

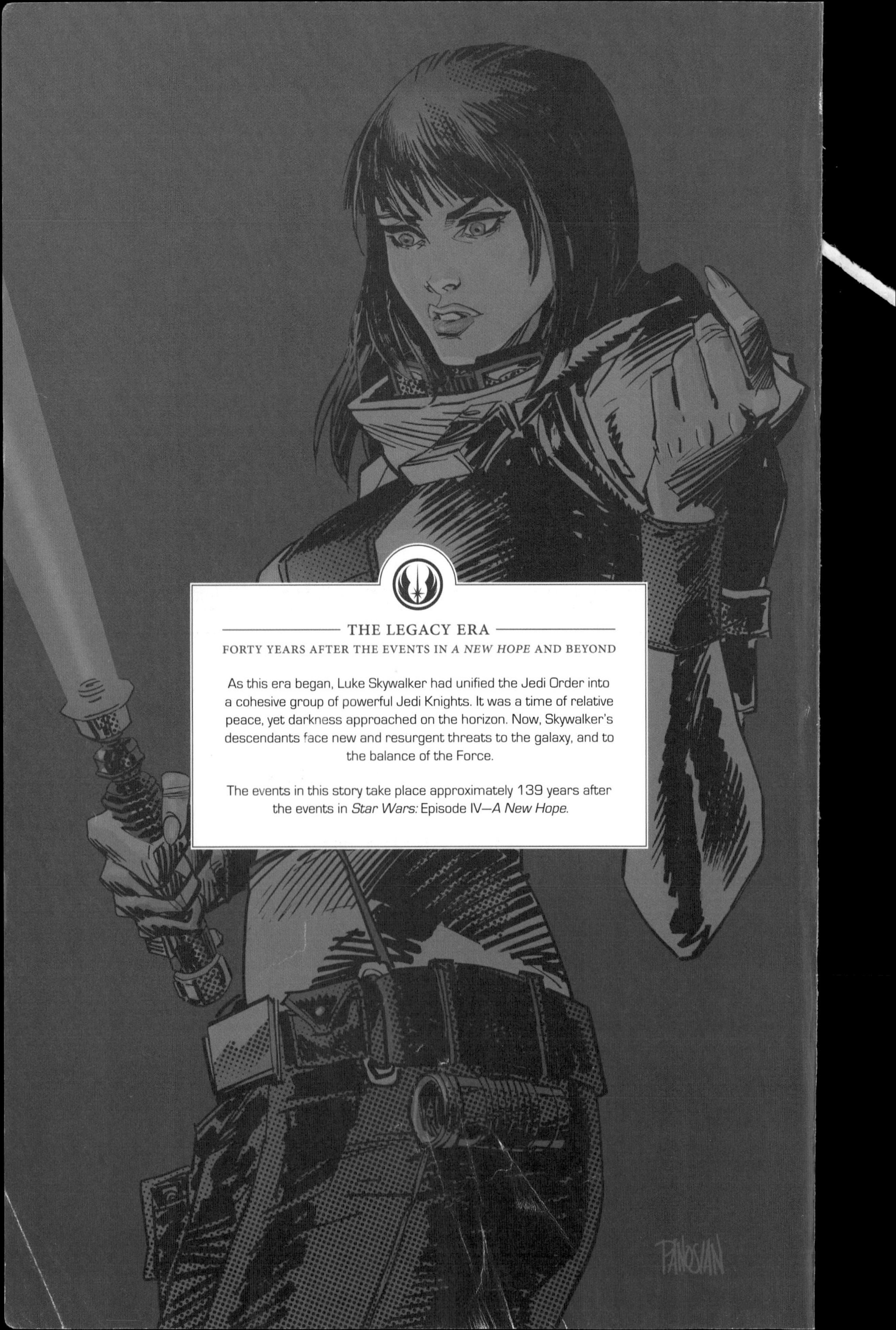
PANOSIAN

THE LEGACY ERA

FORTY YEARS AFTER THE EVENTS IN *A NEW HOPE* AND BEYOND

As this era began, Luke Skywalker had unified the Jedi Order into a cohesive group of powerful Jedi Knights. It was a time of relative peace, yet darkness approached on the horizon. Now, Skywalker's descendants face new and resurgent threats to the galaxy, and to the balance of the Force.

The events in this story take place approximately 139 years after the events in *Star Wars:* Episode IV—*A New Hope*.

PANOSYAN

At her trial for the murder of an Imperial Knight, Ania Solo was proven innocent with evidence brought by her friend, Imperial Knight Jao Assam.

Unfortunately, Jao's appearance in court led to his arrest for deserting the Knights—a crime which carries the death penalty. Empress Fel, the only one with the authority to stay the sentence, refuses to do so.

While Ania, Sauk, and assassin droid AG-37 are doing their best to bring about Jao's release, the Sith Darth Wredd—for whom Ania and her friends have been searching—is furthering his plans . . . plans that include Jao!

BOOK 4

EMPIRE OF ONE

STAR WARS® LEGACY

VOLUME II

SCRIPT
CORINNA BECHKO GABRIEL HARDMAN

ART
BRIAN ALBERT THIES
GABRIEL HARDMAN (PAGES 73–74)

COLORS
JORDAN BOYD

LETTERING
MICHAEL HEISLER

FRONT COVER ART
AGUSTIN ALESSIO

DARK HORSE BOOKS LUCAS BOOKS

PRESIDENT AND PUBLISHER
MIKE RICHARDSON

COLLECTION DESIGNER
JIMMY PRESLER

EDITOR
RANDY STRADLEY

ASSISTANT EDITOR
FREDDYE LINS

NEIL HANKERSON EXECUTIVE VICE PRESIDENT TOM WEDDLE CHIEF FINANCIAL OFFICER RANDY STRADLEY VICE PRESIDENT OF PUBLISHING MICHAEL MARTENS VICE PRESIDENT OF BOOK TRADE SALES ANITA NELSON VICE PRESIDENT OF BUSINESS AFFAIRS SCOTT ALLIE EDITOR IN CHIEF MATT PARKINSON VICE PRESIDENT OF MARKETING DAVID SCROGGY VICE PRESIDENT OF PRODUCT DEVELOPMENT DALE LaFOUNTAIN VICE PRESIDENT OF INFORMATION TECHNOLOGY DARLENE VOGEL SENIOR DIRECTOR OF PRINT, DESIGN, AND PRODUCTION KEN LIZZI GENERAL COUNSEL DAVEY ESTRADA EDITORIAL DIRECTOR CHRIS WARNER SENIOR BOOKS EDITOR DIANA SCHUTZ EXECUTIVE EDITOR CARY GRAZZINI DIRECTOR OF PRINT AND DEVELOPMENT LIA RIBACCHI ART DIRECTOR CARA NIECE DIRECTOR OF SCHEDULING TIM WIESCH DIRECTOR OF INTERNATIONAL LICENSING MARK BERNARDI DIRECTOR OF DIGITAL PUBLISHING

SPECIAL THANKS TO JENNIFER HEDDLE, LELAND CHEE, TROY ALDERS, CAROL ROEDER, JANN MOORHEAD, AND DAVID ANDERMAN AT LUCAS LICENSING.

ART ON PAGES 2 AND 6 BY DAN PANOSIAN

This volume collects issues #16–#18 of the Dark Horse comic-book series *Star Wars: Legacy Volume II*, and #0½ of the Dark Horse comic-book series *Star Wars: Legacy*.

Published by Dark Horse Books
A division of Dark Horse Comics, Inc.
10956 SE Main Street, Milwaukie, OR 97222

DarkHorse.com StarWars.com

International Licensing: 503-905-2377

To find a comics shop in your area, call the Comic Shop Locator Service toll-free at 1-888-266-4226.

Library of Congress Cataloging-in-Publication Data

Bechko, Corinna, 1973- author.
Star wars legacy. Volume II, Book 4, Empire of one / script, Corinna Bechko, Gabriel Hardman ; art, Brian Albert Theis, Gabriel Hardman, pages 73-74 ; colors, Jordan Boyd ; lettering, Michael Heisler ; front cover art, Agustin Alessio.
pages cm
Summary: "Empress Fel enlists Ania Solo to rescue Imperial Knight Jao from the Sith Darth Wredd, but they are unaware they are headed into a showdown with a lot of Sith"– Provided by publisher.
ISBN 978-1-61655-553-5 (paperback)
1. Graphic novels. [1. Graphic novels. 2. Science fiction.] I. Hardman, Gabriel, author. II. Theis, Brian Albert, illustrator. III. Alessio, Agustin, illustrator. IV. Title. V. Title: Empire of one.

PZ7.7.B425St 2014
741.5'973-dc23

2014025748

First edition: October 2014
ISBN 978-1-61655-553-5

1 3 5 7 9 10 8 6 4 2
Printed in Canada

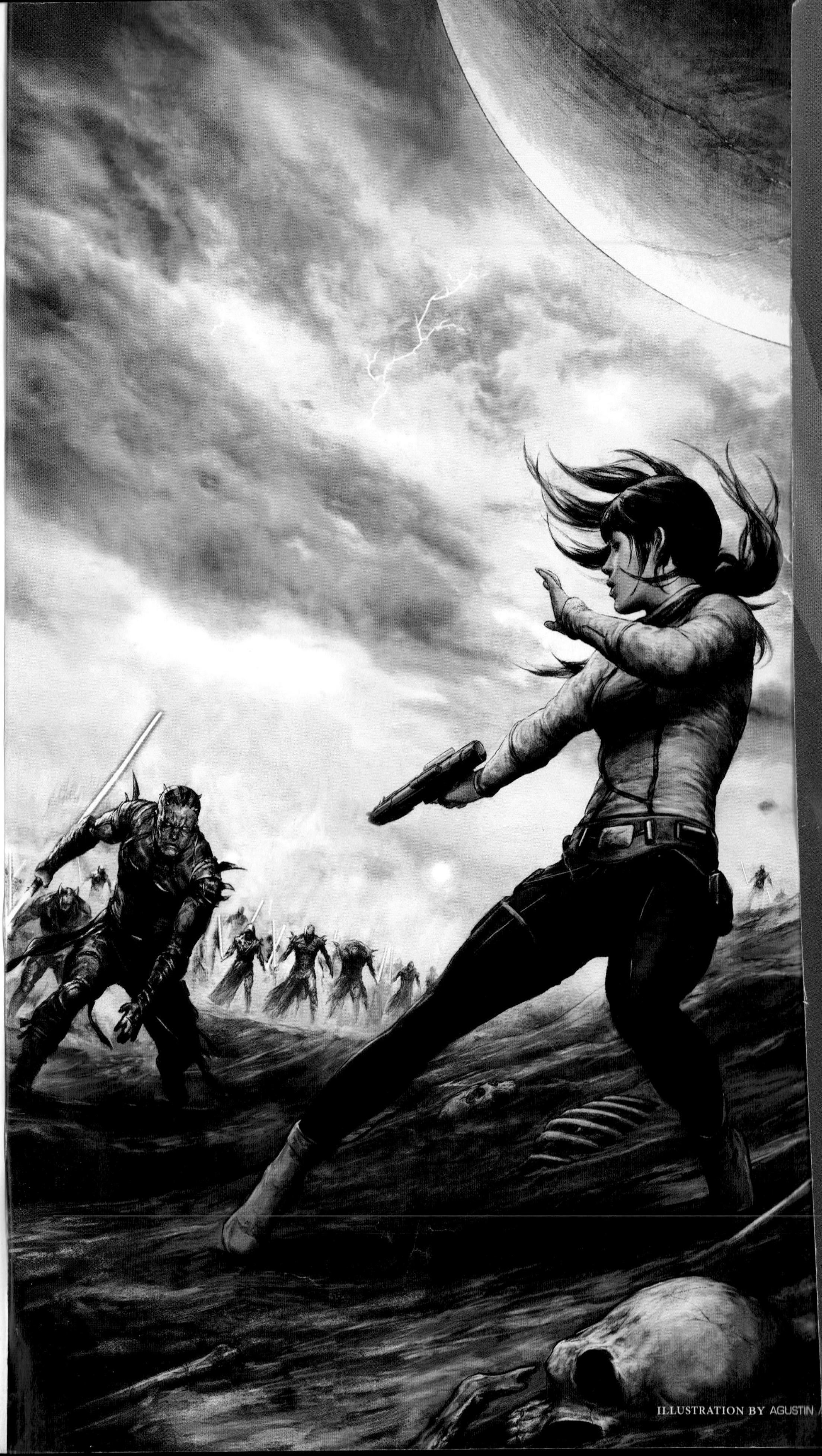
ILLUSTRATION BY AGUSTIN A

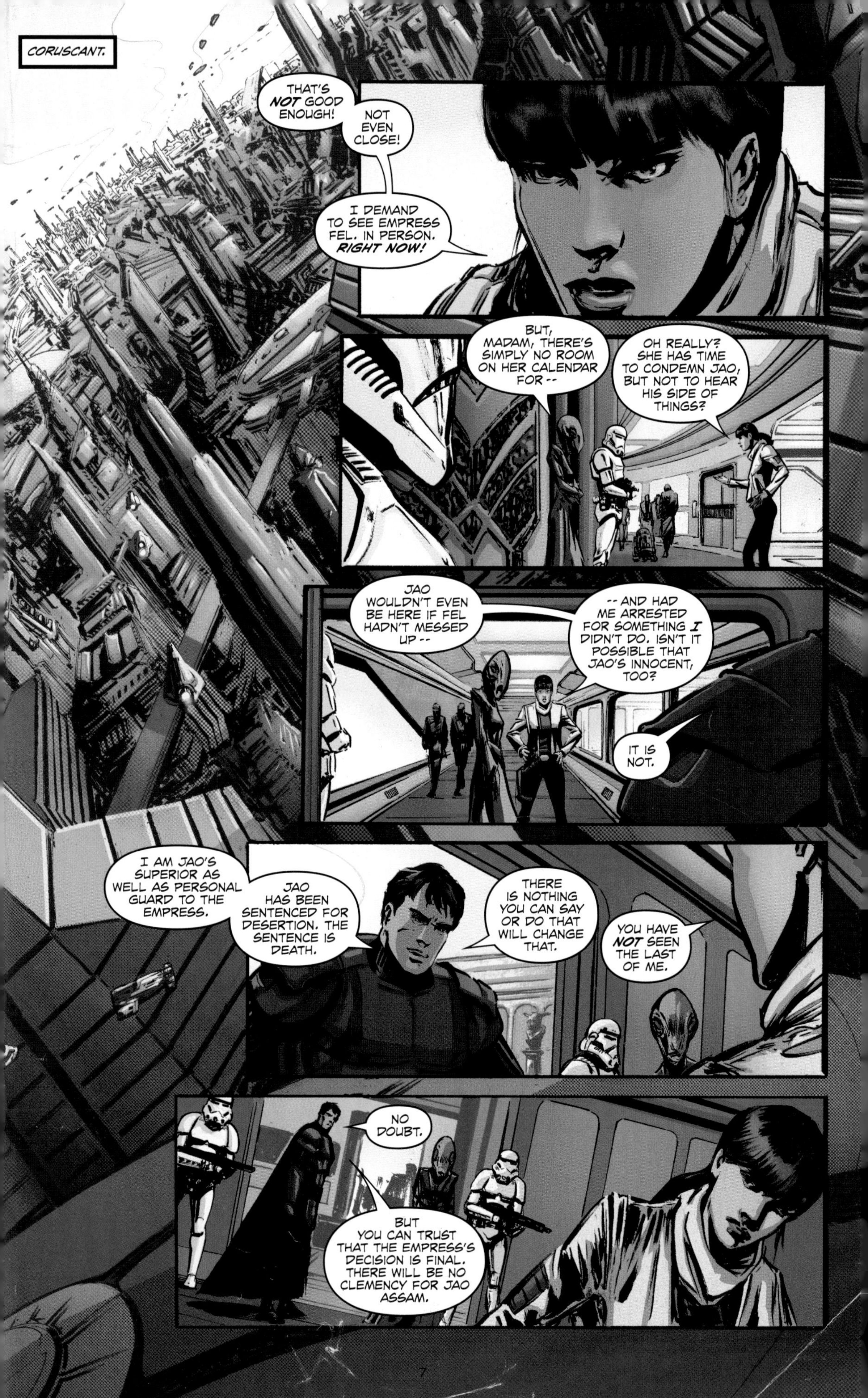
CORUSCANT.
THAT'S NOT GOOD ENOUGH!
NOT EVEN CLOSE!
I DEMAND TO SEE EMPRESS FEL. IN PERSON. RIGHT NOW!
BUT, MADAM, THERE'S SIMPLY NO ROOM ON HER CALENDAR FOR --
OH REALLY? SHE HAS TIME TO CONDEMN JAO, BUT NOT TO HEAR HIS SIDE OF THINGS?
JAO WOULDN'T EVEN BE HERE IF FEL HADN'T MESSED UP --
-- AND HAD ME ARRESTED FOR SOMETHING I DIDN'T DO. ISN'T IT POSSIBLE THAT JAO'S INNOCENT, TOO?
IT IS NOT.
I AM JAO'S SUPERIOR AS WELL AS PERSONAL GUARD TO THE EMPRESS.
JAO HAS BEEN SENTENCED FOR DESERTION. THE SENTENCE IS DEATH.
THERE IS NOTHING YOU CAN SAY OR DO THAT WILL CHANGE THAT.
YOU HAVE NOT SEEN THE LAST OF ME.
NO DOUBT.
BUT YOU CAN TRUST THAT THE EMPRESS'S DECISION IS FINAL. THERE WILL BE NO CLEMENCY FOR JAO ASSAM.

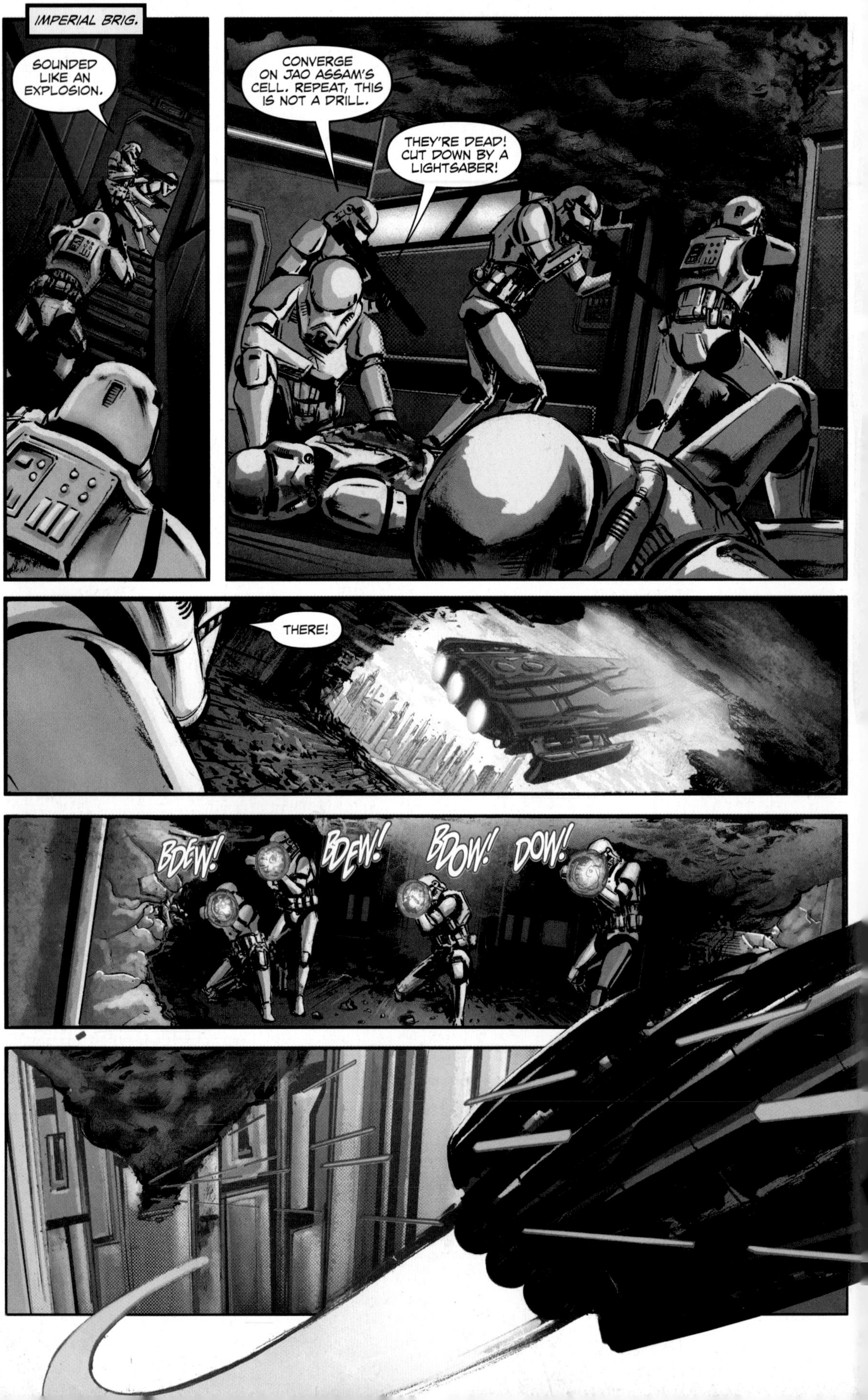
IMPERIAL BRIG.
SOUNDED LIKE AN EXPLOSION.
CONVERGE ON JAO ASSAM'S CELL. REPEAT, THIS IS NOT A DRILL.
THEY'RE DEAD! CUT DOWN BY A LIGHTSABER!
THERE!
BDEW!
BDEW!
BDOW!
DOW!

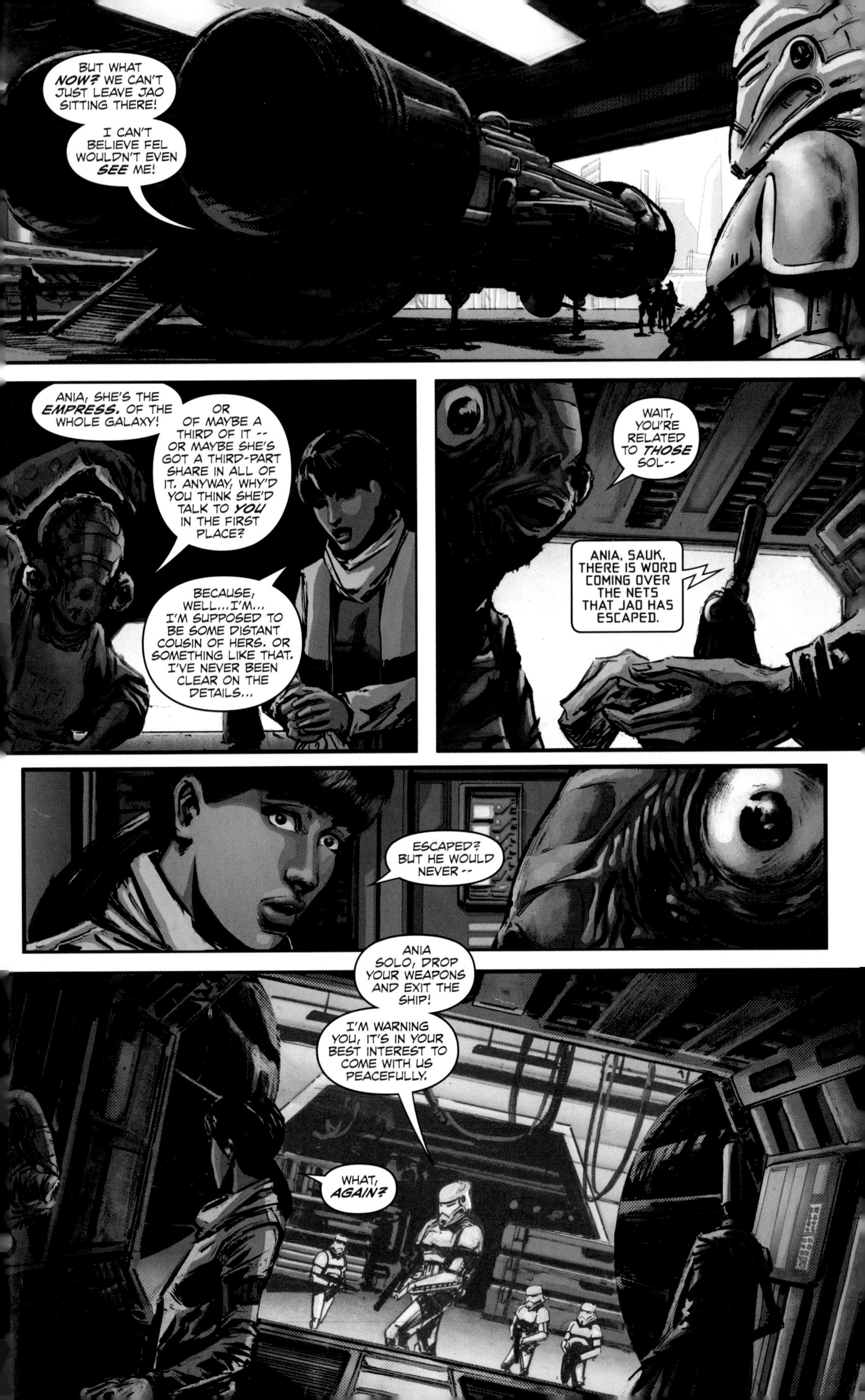
BUT WHAT NOW? WE CAN'T JUST LEAVE JAO SITTING THERE!
I CAN'T BELIEVE FEL WOULDN'T EVEN SEE ME!
ANIA, SHE'S THE EMPRESS. OF THE WHOLE GALAXY!
OR OF MAYBE A THIRD OF IT -- OR MAYBE SHE'S GOT A THIRD-PART SHARE IN ALL OF IT. ANYWAY, WHY'D YOU THINK SHE'D TALK TO YOU IN THE FIRST PLACE?
BECAUSE, WELL...I'M... I'M SUPPOSED TO BE SOME DISTANT COUSIN OF HERS. OR SOMETHING LIKE THAT. I'VE NEVER BEEN CLEAR ON THE DETAILS...
WAIT, YOU'RE RELATED TO THOSE SOL--
ANIA, SAUK, THERE IS WORD COMING OVER THE NETS THAT JAO HAS ESCAPED.
ESCAPED? BUT HE WOULD NEVER --
ANIA SOLO, DROP YOUR WEAPONS AND EXIT THE SHIP!
I'M WARNING YOU, IT'S IN YOUR BEST INTEREST TO COME WITH US PEACEFULLY.
WHAT, AGAIN?

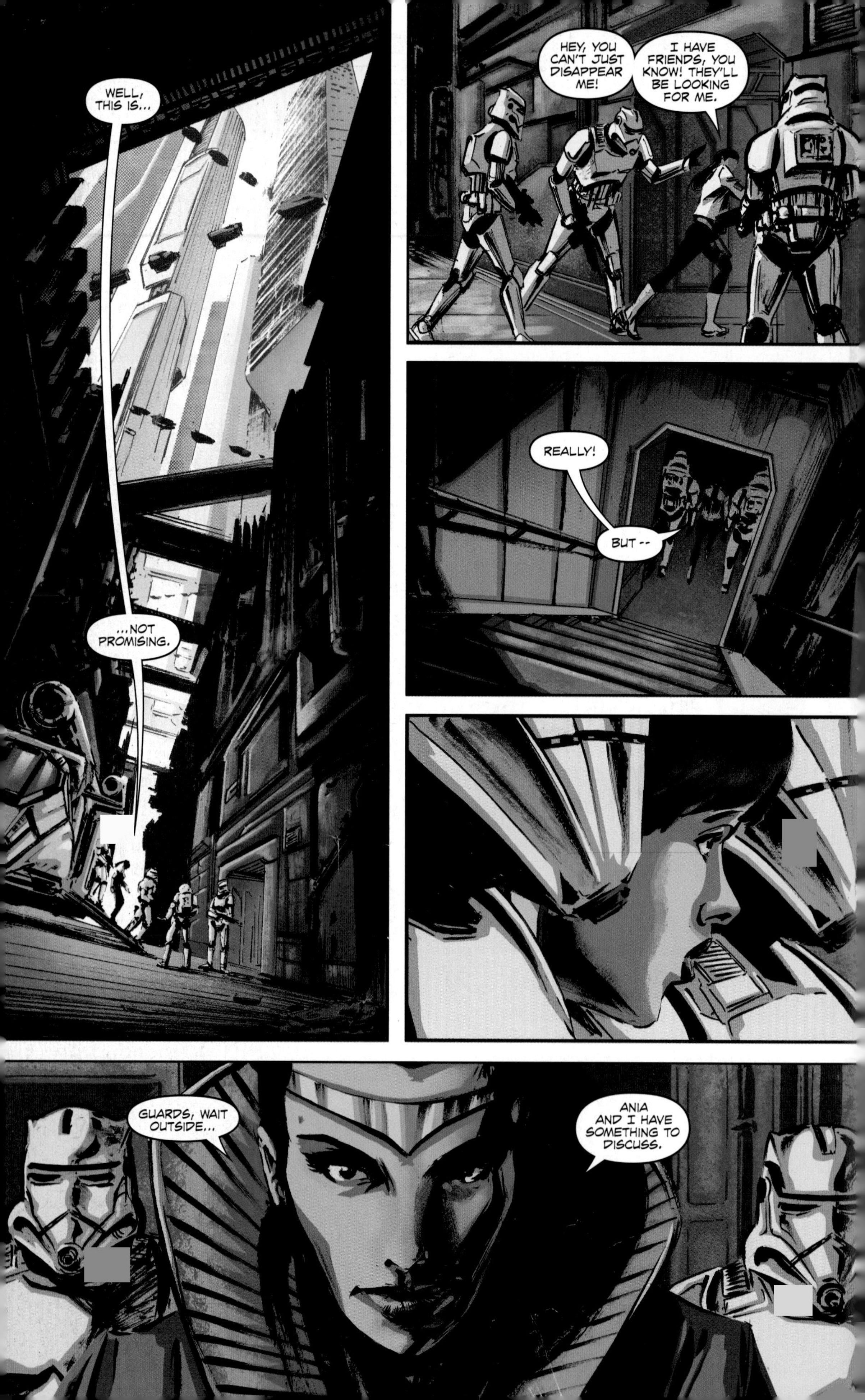
WELL, THIS IS...
...NOT PROMISING.
HEY, YOU CAN'T JUST DISAPPEAR ME!
I HAVE FRIENDS, YOU KNOW! THEY'LL BE LOOKING FOR ME.
REALLY!
BUT --
GUARDS, WAIT OUTSIDE...
ANIA AND I HAVE SOMETHING TO DISCUSS.

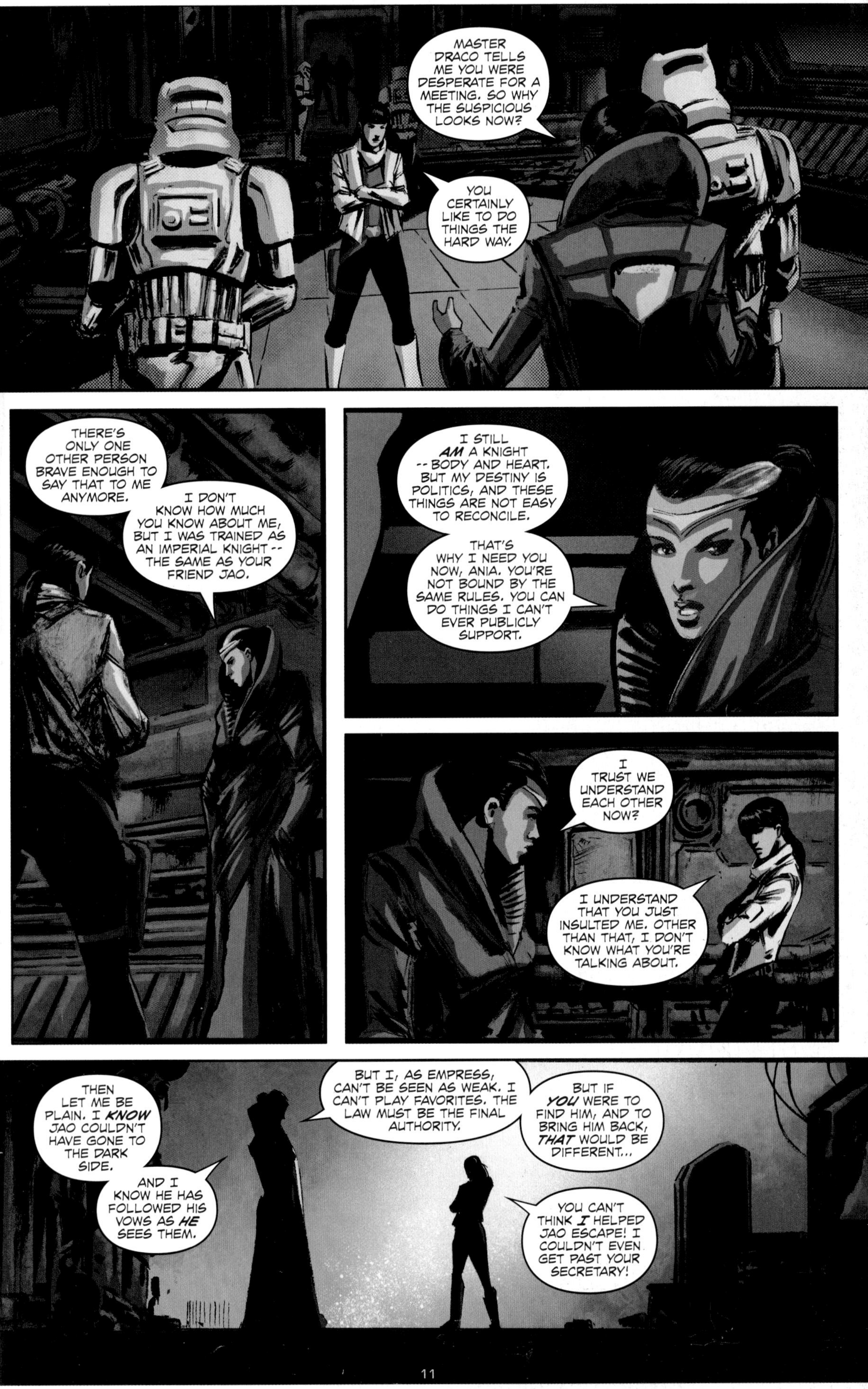
MASTER DRACO TELLS ME YOU WERE DESPERATE FOR A MEETING. SO WHY THE SUSPICIOUS LOOKS NOW?
YOU CERTAINLY LIKE TO DO THINGS THE HARD WAY.
THERE'S ONLY ONE OTHER PERSON BRAVE ENOUGH TO SAY THAT TO ME ANYMORE.
I DON'T KNOW HOW MUCH YOU KNOW ABOUT ME, BUT I WAS TRAINED AS AN IMPERIAL KNIGHT -- THE SAME AS YOUR FRIEND JAO.
I STILL **AM** A KNIGHT -- BODY AND HEART. BUT MY DESTINY IS POLITICS, AND THESE THINGS ARE NOT EASY TO RECONCILE.
THAT'S WHY I NEED YOU NOW, ANIA. YOU'RE NOT BOUND BY THE SAME RULES. YOU CAN DO THINGS I CAN'T EVER PUBLICLY SUPPORT.
I TRUST WE UNDERSTAND EACH OTHER NOW?
I UNDERSTAND THAT YOU JUST INSULTED ME. OTHER THAN THAT, I DON'T KNOW WHAT YOU'RE TALKING ABOUT.
THEN LET ME BE PLAIN. I ***KNOW*** JAO COULDN'T HAVE GONE TO THE DARK SIDE.
AND I KNOW HE HAS FOLLOWED HIS VOWS AS ***HE*** SEES THEM.
BUT I, AS EMPRESS, CAN'T BE SEEN AS WEAK. I CAN'T PLAY FAVORITES. THE LAW MUST BE THE FINAL AUTHORITY.
BUT IF ***YOU*** WERE TO FIND HIM, AND TO BRING HIM BACK, ***THAT*** WOULD BE DIFFERENT...
YOU CAN'T THINK ***I*** HELPED JAO ESCAPE! I COULDN'T EVEN GET PAST YOUR SECRETARY!

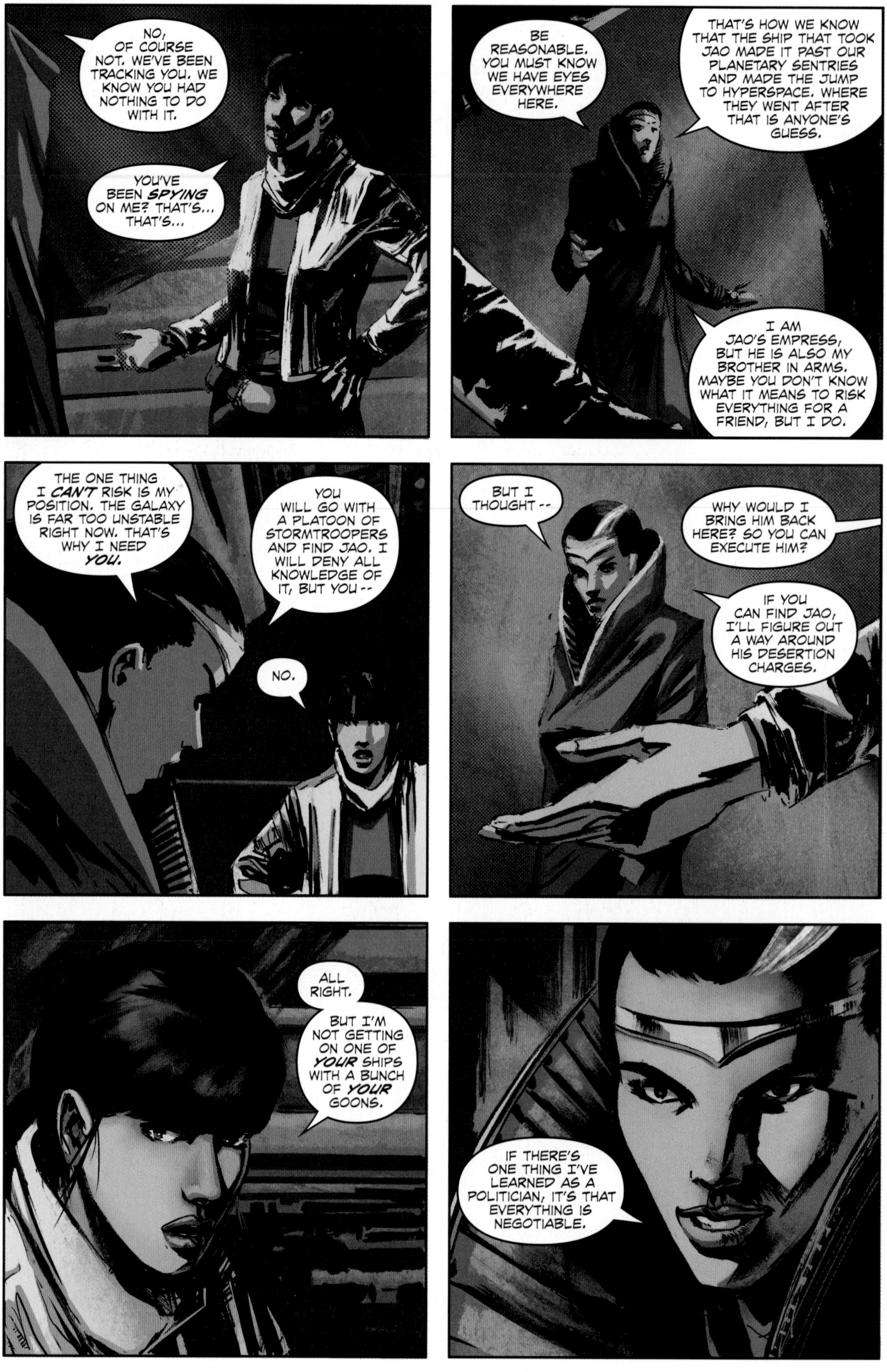
NO, OF COURSE NOT. WE'VE BEEN TRACKING YOU. WE KNOW YOU HAD NOTHING TO DO WITH IT.
YOU'VE BEEN SPYING ON ME? THAT'S... THAT'S...
BE REASONABLE. YOU MUST KNOW WE HAVE EYES EVERYWHERE HERE.
THAT'S HOW WE KNOW THAT THE SHIP THAT TOOK JAO MADE IT PAST OUR PLANETARY SENTRIES AND MADE THE JUMP TO HYPERSPACE. WHERE THEY WENT AFTER THAT IS ANYONE'S GUESS.
I AM JAO'S EMPRESS, BUT HE IS ALSO MY BROTHER IN ARMS. MAYBE YOU DON'T KNOW WHAT IT MEANS TO RISK EVERYTHING FOR A FRIEND, BUT I DO.
THE ONE THING I CAN'T RISK IS MY POSITION. THE GALAXY IS FAR TOO UNSTABLE RIGHT NOW. THAT'S WHY I NEED YOU.
YOU WILL GO WITH A PLATOON OF STORMTROOPERS AND FIND JAO. I WILL DENY ALL KNOWLEDGE OF IT, BUT YOU --
NO.
BUT I THOUGHT --
WHY WOULD I BRING HIM BACK HERE? SO YOU CAN EXECUTE HIM?
IF YOU CAN FIND JAO, I'LL FIGURE OUT A WAY AROUND HIS DESERTION CHARGES.
ALL RIGHT.
BUT I'M NOT GETTING ON ONE OF YOUR SHIPS WITH A BUNCH OF YOUR GOONS.
IF THERE'S ONE THING I'VE LEARNED AS A POLITICIAN, IT'S THAT EVERYTHING IS NEGOTIABLE.

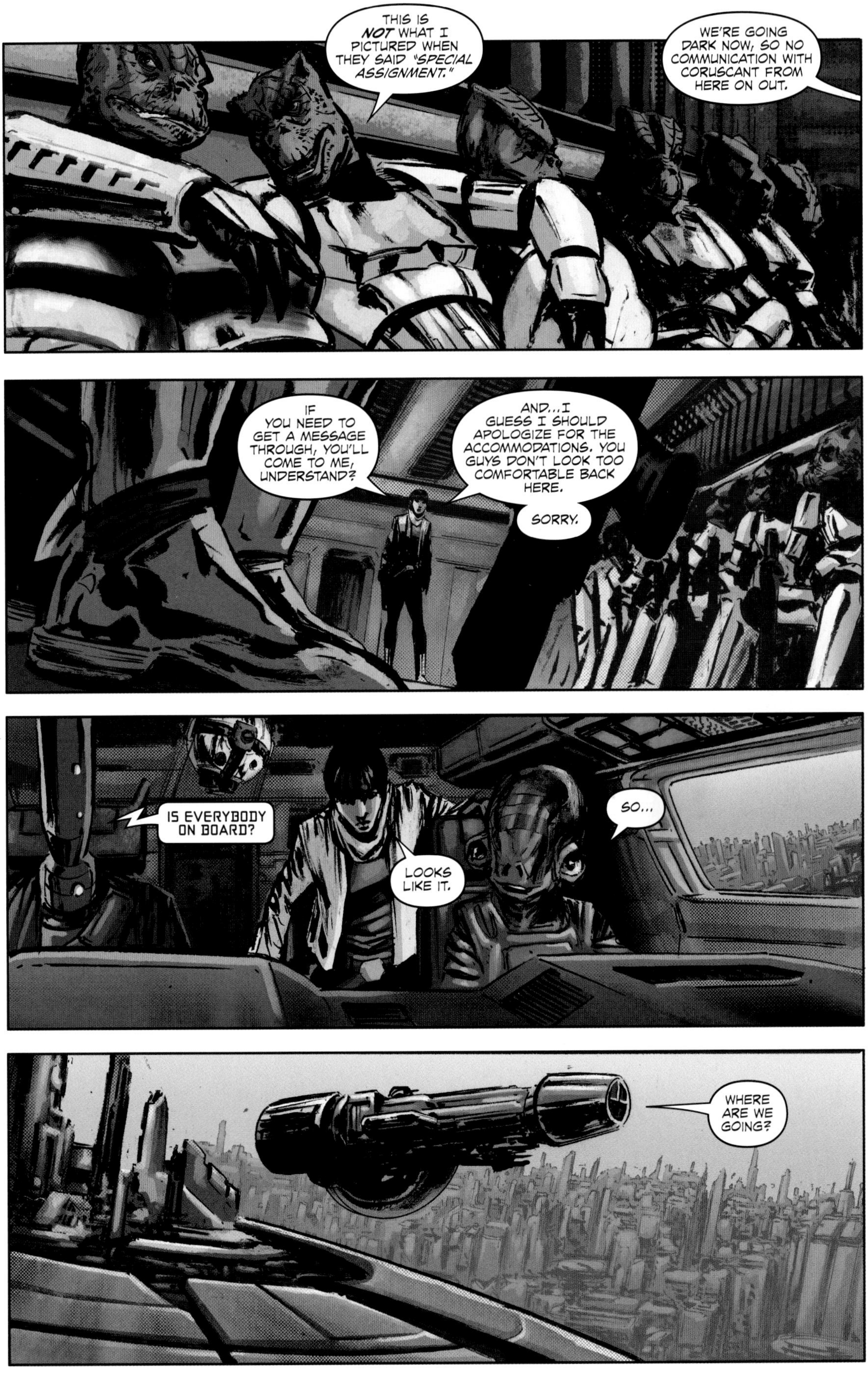
THIS IS NOT WHAT I PICTURED WHEN THEY SAID "SPECIAL ASSIGNMENT."
WE'RE GOING DARK NOW, SO NO COMMUNICATION WITH CORUSCANT FROM HERE ON OUT.
IF YOU NEED TO GET A MESSAGE THROUGH, YOU'LL COME TO ME, UNDERSTAND?
AND...I GUESS I SHOULD APOLOGIZE FOR THE ACCOMMODATIONS. YOU GUYS DON'T LOOK TOO COMFORTABLE BACK HERE.
SORRY.
IS EVERYBODY ON BOARD?
LOOKS LIKE IT.
SO...
WHERE ARE WE GOING?

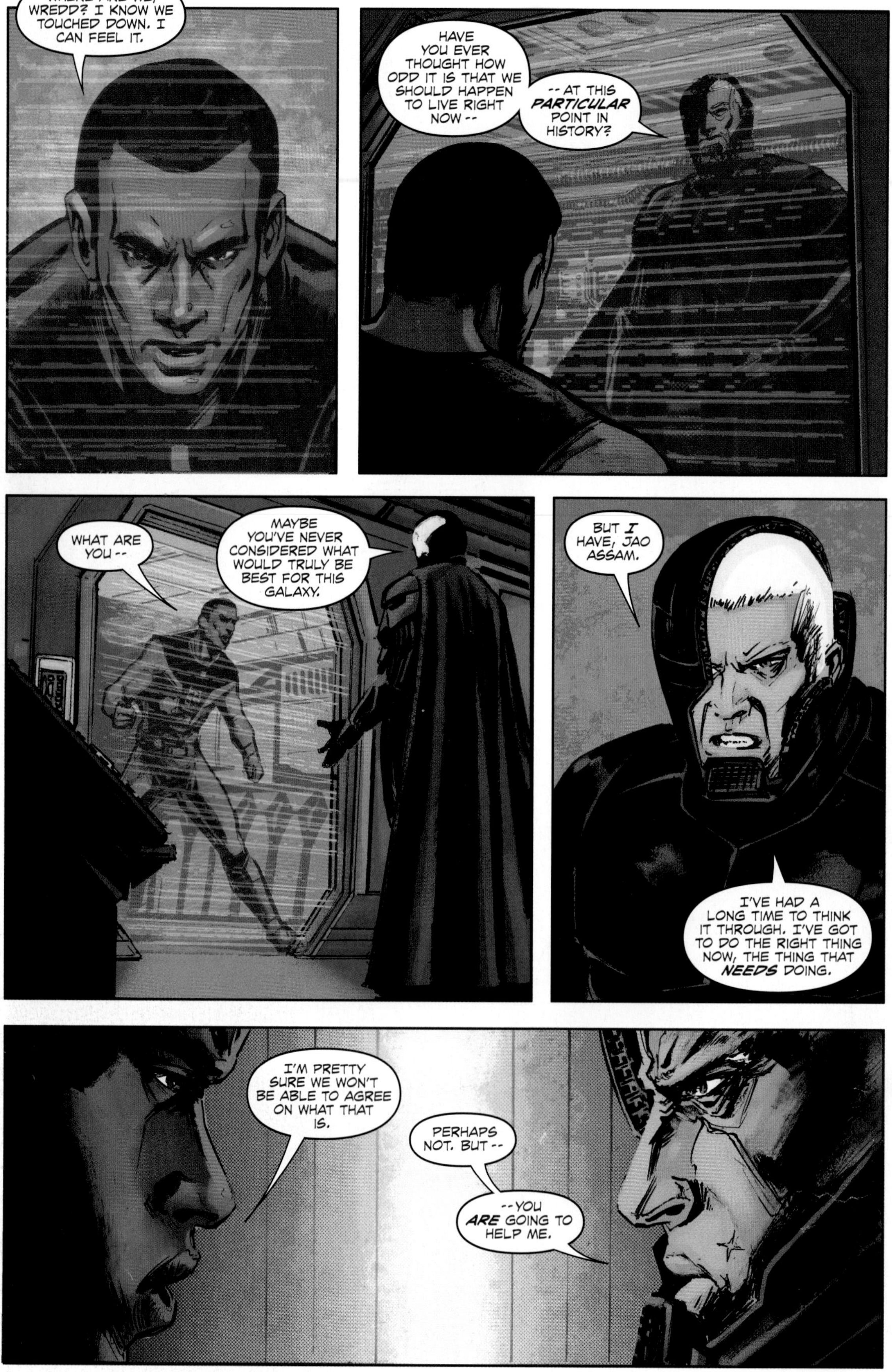
WHERE ARE WE, WREDD? I KNOW WE TOUCHED DOWN. I CAN FEEL IT.
HAVE YOU EVER THOUGHT HOW ODD IT IS THAT WE SHOULD HAPPEN TO LIVE RIGHT NOW --
-- AT THIS *PARTICULAR* POINT IN HISTORY?
WHAT ARE YOU --
MAYBE YOU'VE NEVER CONSIDERED WHAT WOULD TRULY BE BEST FOR THIS GALAXY.
BUT *I* HAVE, JAO ASSAM.
I'VE HAD A LONG TIME TO THINK IT THROUGH. I'VE GOT TO DO THE RIGHT THING NOW, THE THING THAT *NEEDS* DOING.
I'M PRETTY SURE WE WON'T BE ABLE TO AGREE ON WHAT THAT IS.
PERHAPS NOT. BUT --
-- YOU *ARE* GOING TO HELP ME.

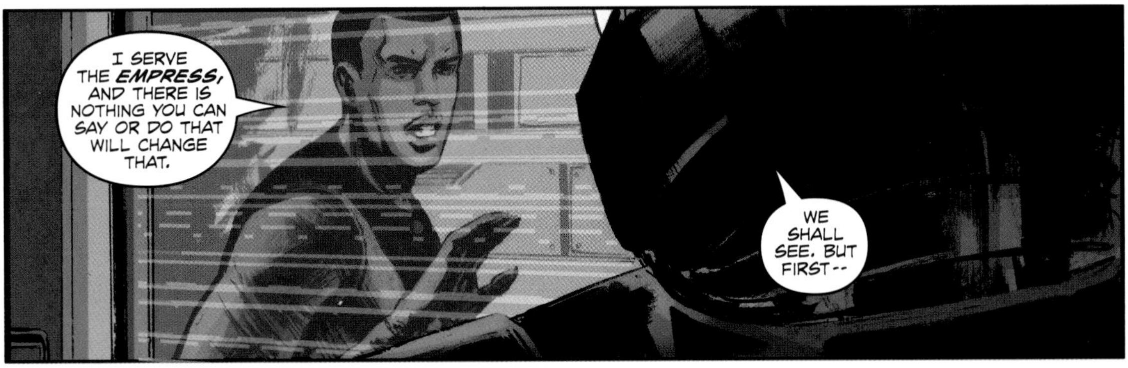
I SERVE THE *EMPRESS,* AND THERE IS NOTHING YOU CAN SAY OR DO THAT WILL CHANGE THAT.
WE SHALL SEE. BUT FIRST--

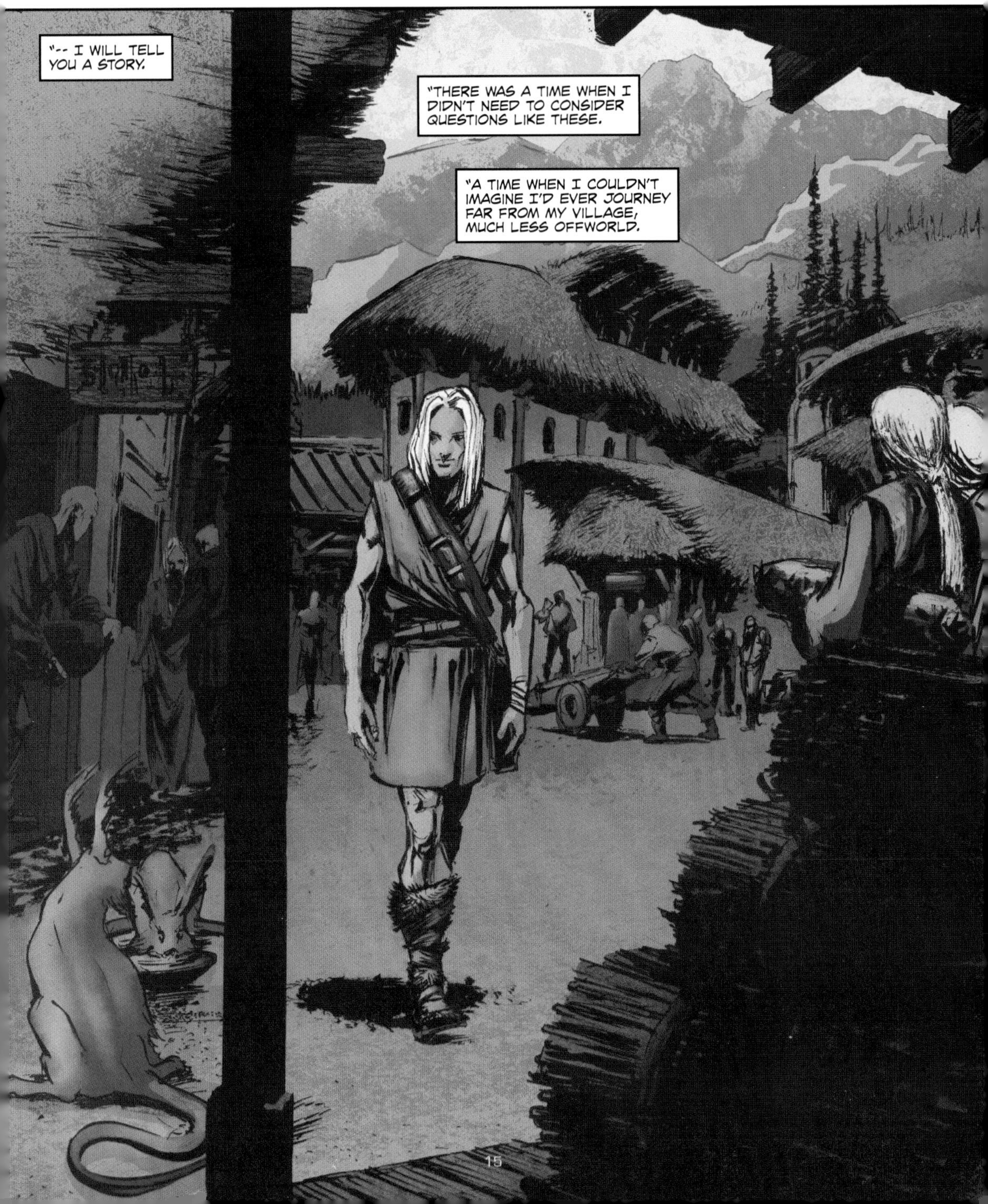
"-- I WILL TELL YOU A STORY.
"THERE WAS A TIME WHEN I DIDN'T NEED TO CONSIDER QUESTIONS LIKE THESE.
"A TIME WHEN I COULDN'T IMAGINE I'D EVER JOURNEY FAR FROM MY VILLAGE, MUCH LESS OFFWORLD.

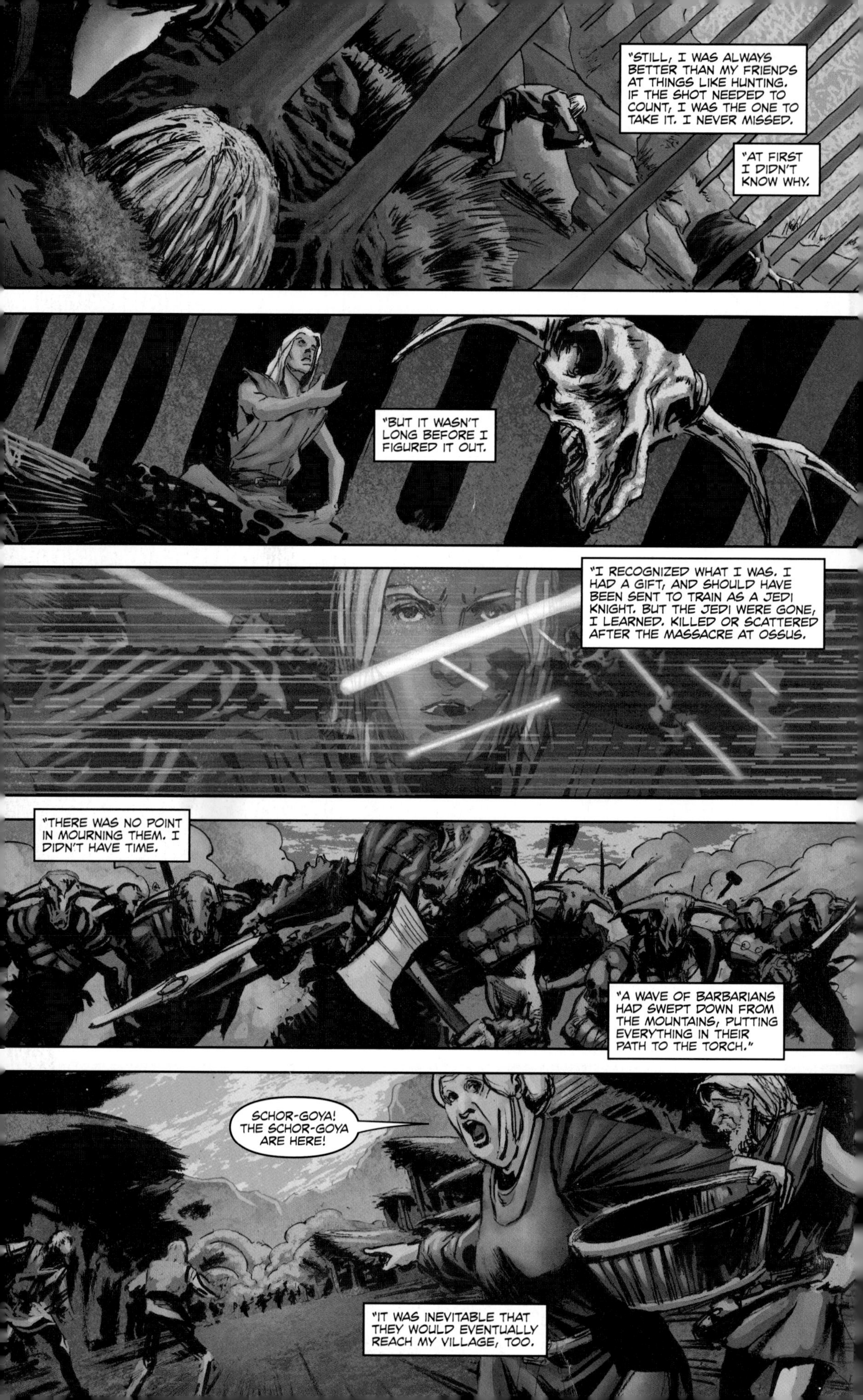
"STILL, I WAS ALWAYS BETTER THAN MY FRIENDS AT THINGS LIKE HUNTING. IF THE SHOT NEEDED TO COUNT, I WAS THE ONE TO TAKE IT. I NEVER MISSED.
"AT FIRST I DIDN'T KNOW WHY.
"BUT IT WASN'T LONG BEFORE I FIGURED IT OUT.
"I RECOGNIZED WHAT I WAS. I HAD A GIFT, AND SHOULD HAVE BEEN SENT TO TRAIN AS A JEDI KNIGHT. BUT THE JEDI WERE GONE, I LEARNED. KILLED OR SCATTERED AFTER THE MASSACRE AT OSSUS.
"THERE WAS NO POINT IN MOURNING THEM. I DIDN'T HAVE TIME.
"A WAVE OF BARBARIANS HAD SWEPT DOWN FROM THE MOUNTAINS, PUTTING EVERYTHING IN THEIR PATH TO THE TORCH."
SCHOR-GOYA! THE SCHOR-GOYA ARE HERE!
"IT WAS INEVITABLE THAT THEY WOULD EVENTUALLY REACH MY VILLAGE, TOO.

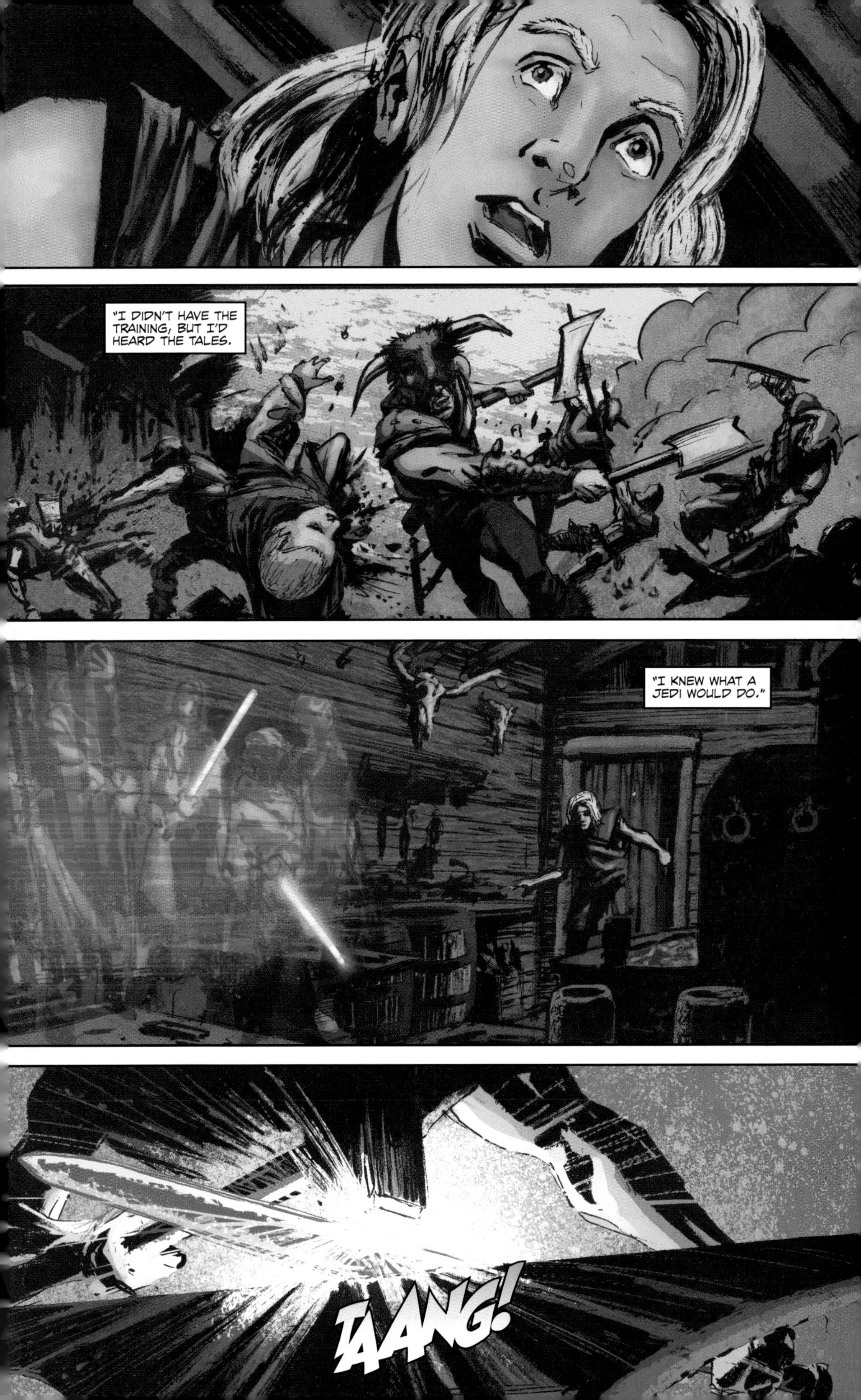

"I DIDN'T HAVE THE TRAINING, BUT I'D HEARD THE TALES.
"I KNEW WHAT A JEDI WOULD DO."
TAANG!

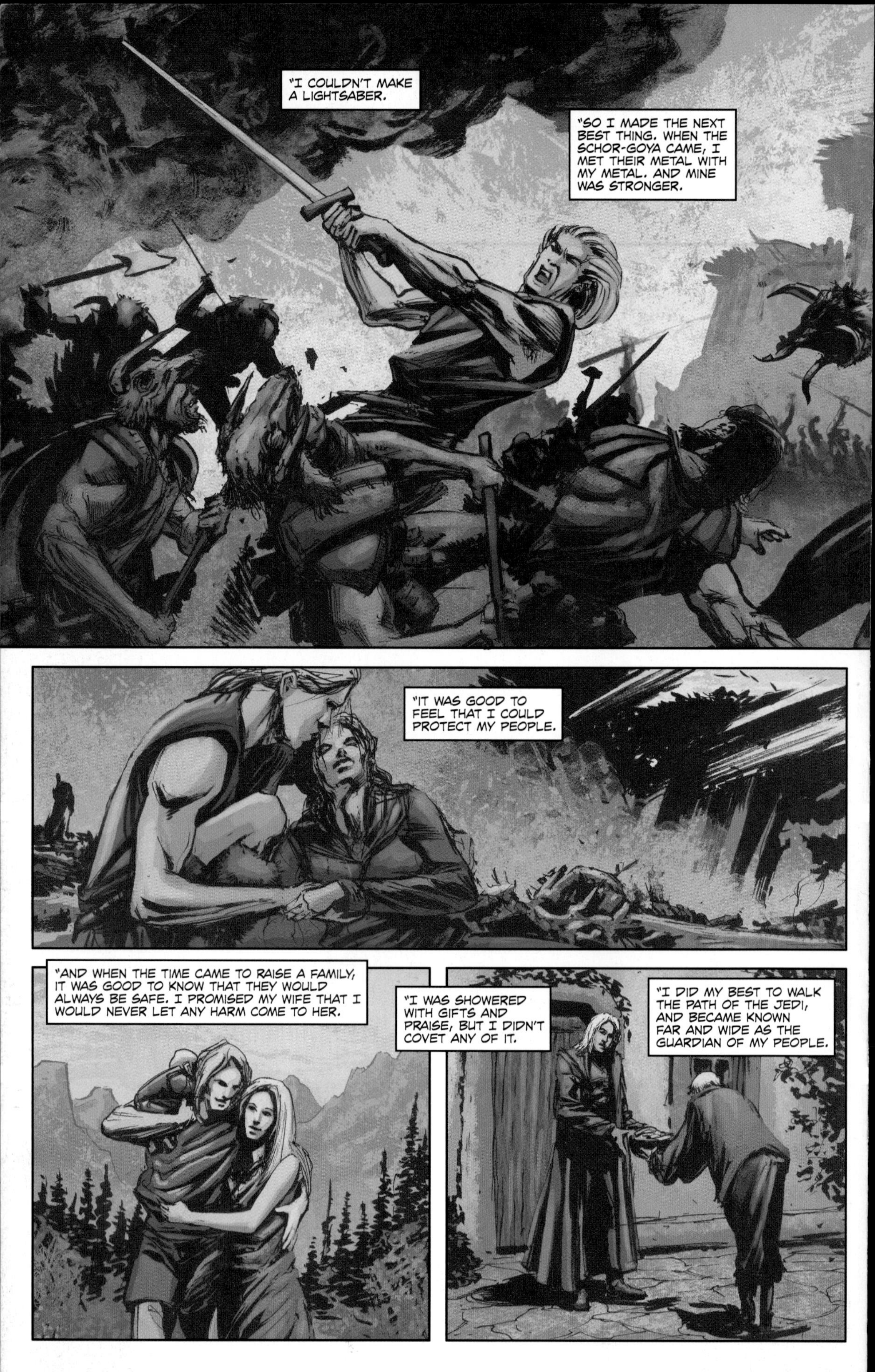
"I COULDN'T MAKE A LIGHTSABER.
"SO I MADE THE NEXT BEST THING. WHEN THE SCHOR-GOYA CAME, I MET THEIR METAL WITH MY METAL. AND MINE WAS STRONGER.
"IT WAS GOOD TO FEEL THAT I COULD PROTECT MY PEOPLE.
"AND WHEN THE TIME CAME TO RAISE A FAMILY, IT WAS GOOD TO KNOW THAT THEY WOULD ALWAYS BE SAFE. I PROMISED MY WIFE THAT I WOULD NEVER LET ANY HARM COME TO HER.
"I WAS SHOWERED WITH GIFTS AND PRAISE, BUT I DIDN'T COVET ANY OF IT.
"I DID MY BEST TO WALK THE PATH OF THE JEDI, AND BECAME KNOWN FAR AND WIDE AS THE GUARDIAN OF MY PEOPLE.

"IT NEVER OCCURRED TO ME THAT THERE MIGHT BE A THREAT I COULDN'T HANDLE.

"I KNEW NOTHING OF THE WAY OF THE SITH."

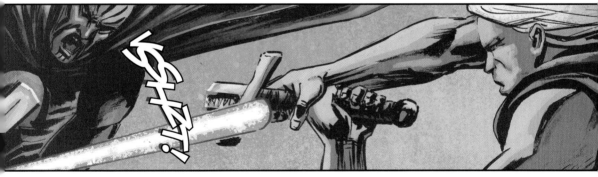

SHZT!

"MY COURAGE MADE ME STUPID.

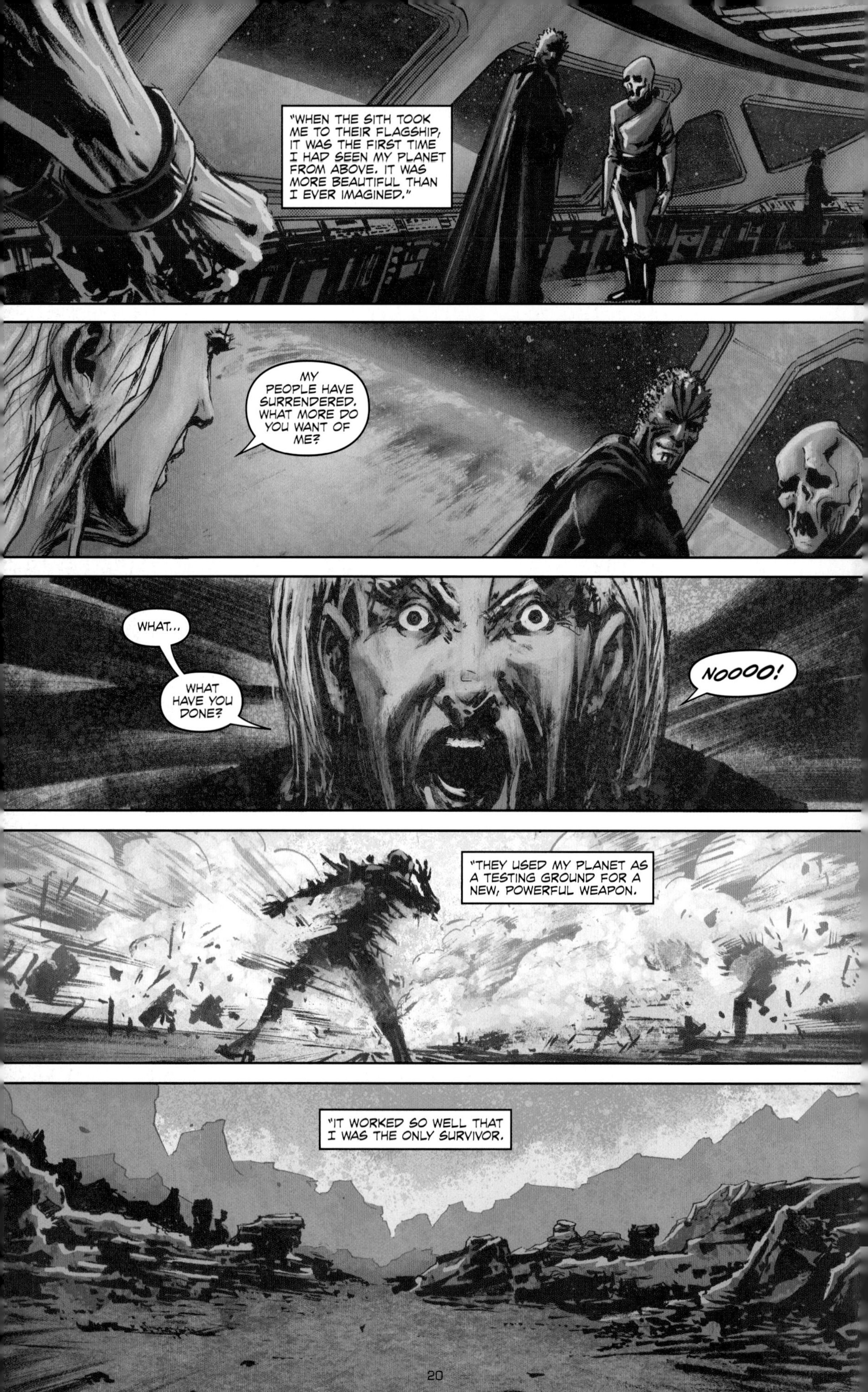
"WHEN THE SITH TOOK ME TO THEIR FLAGSHIP, IT WAS THE FIRST TIME I HAD SEEN MY PLANET FROM ABOVE. IT WAS MORE BEAUTIFUL THAN I EVER IMAGINED."
MY PEOPLE HAVE SURRENDERED. WHAT MORE DO YOU WANT OF ME?
WHAT...
WHAT HAVE YOU DONE?
NOOOO!
"THEY USED MY PLANET AS A TESTING GROUND FOR A NEW, POWERFUL WEAPON.
"IT WORKED SO WELL THAT I WAS THE ONLY SURVIVOR.

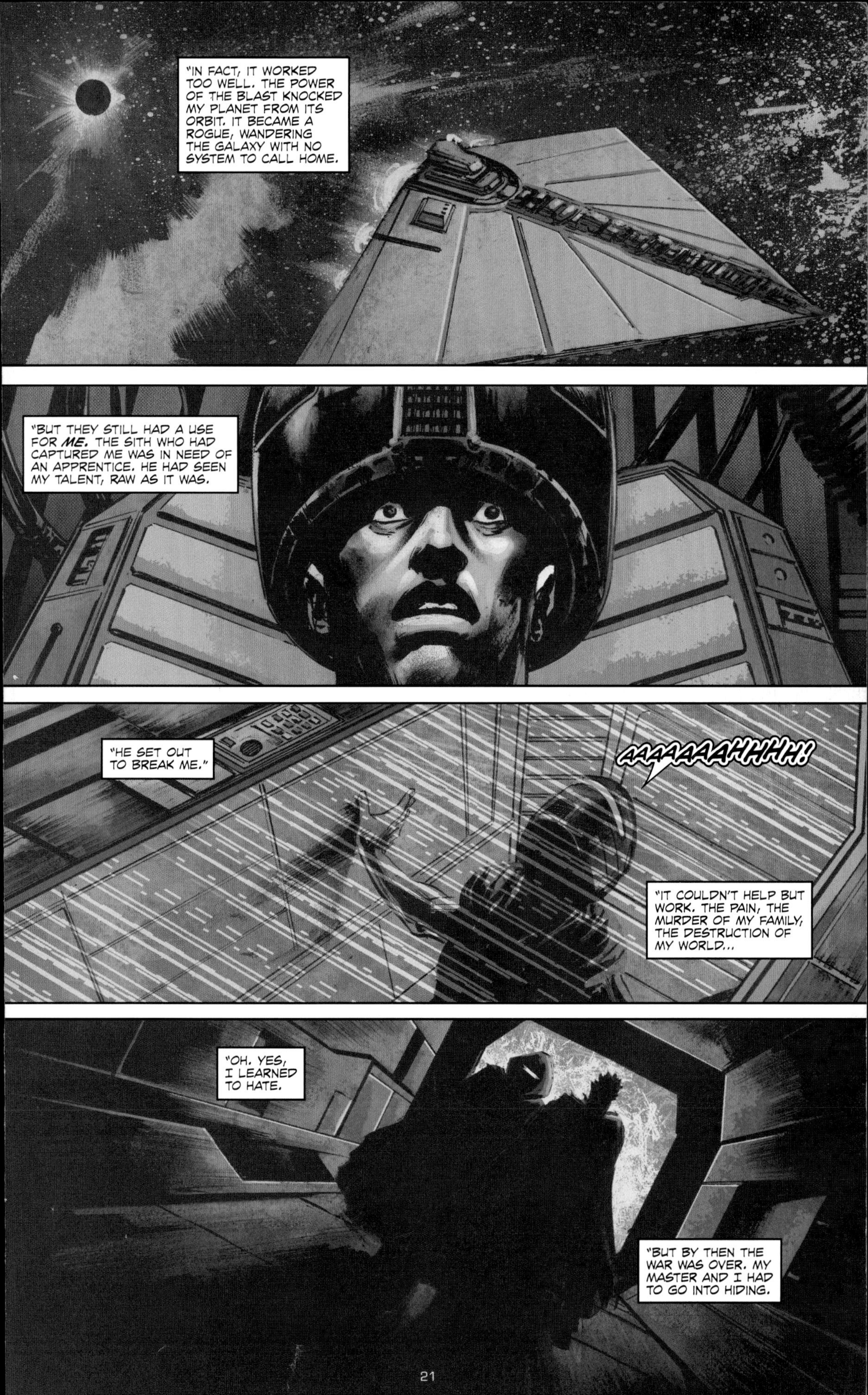
"IN FACT, IT WORKED TOO WELL. THE POWER OF THE BLAST KNOCKED MY PLANET FROM ITS ORBIT. IT BECAME A ROGUE, WANDERING THE GALAXY WITH NO SYSTEM TO CALL HOME.
"BUT THEY STILL HAD A USE FOR ME. THE SITH WHO HAD CAPTURED ME WAS IN NEED OF AN APPRENTICE. HE HAD SEEN MY TALENT, RAW AS IT WAS.
"HE SET OUT TO BREAK ME."
AAAAAAAHHHH!
"IT COULDN'T HELP BUT WORK. THE PAIN, THE MURDER OF MY FAMILY, THE DESTRUCTION OF MY WORLD...
"OH. YES, I LEARNED TO HATE.
"BUT BY THEN THE WAR WAS OVER. MY MASTER AND I HAD TO GO INTO HIDING.

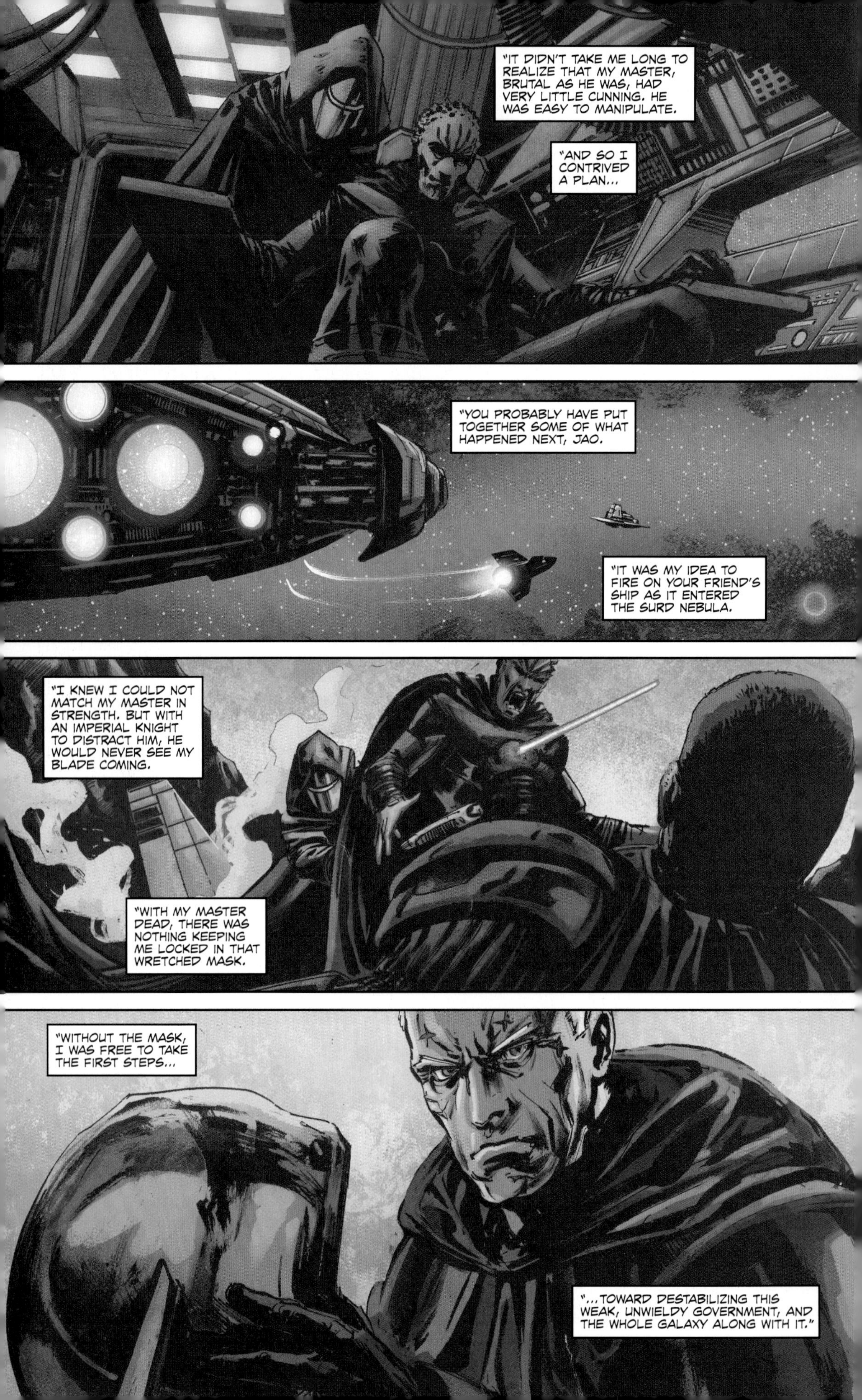
"IT DIDN'T TAKE ME LONG TO REALIZE THAT MY MASTER, BRUTAL AS HE WAS, HAD VERY LITTLE CUNNING. HE WAS EASY TO MANIPULATE.
"AND SO I CONTRIVED A PLAN...
"YOU PROBABLY HAVE PUT TOGETHER SOME OF WHAT HAPPENED NEXT, JAO.
"IT WAS MY IDEA TO FIRE ON YOUR FRIEND'S SHIP AS IT ENTERED THE SURD NEBULA.
"I KNEW I COULD NOT MATCH MY MASTER IN STRENGTH. BUT WITH AN IMPERIAL KNIGHT TO DISTRACT HIM, HE WOULD NEVER SEE MY BLADE COMING.
"WITH MY MASTER DEAD, THERE WAS NOTHING KEEPING ME LOCKED IN THAT WRETCHED MASK.
"WITHOUT THE MASK, I WAS FREE TO TAKE THE FIRST STEPS...
"...TOWARD DESTABILIZING THIS WEAK, UNWIELDY GOVERNMENT, AND THE WHOLE GALAXY ALONG WITH IT."

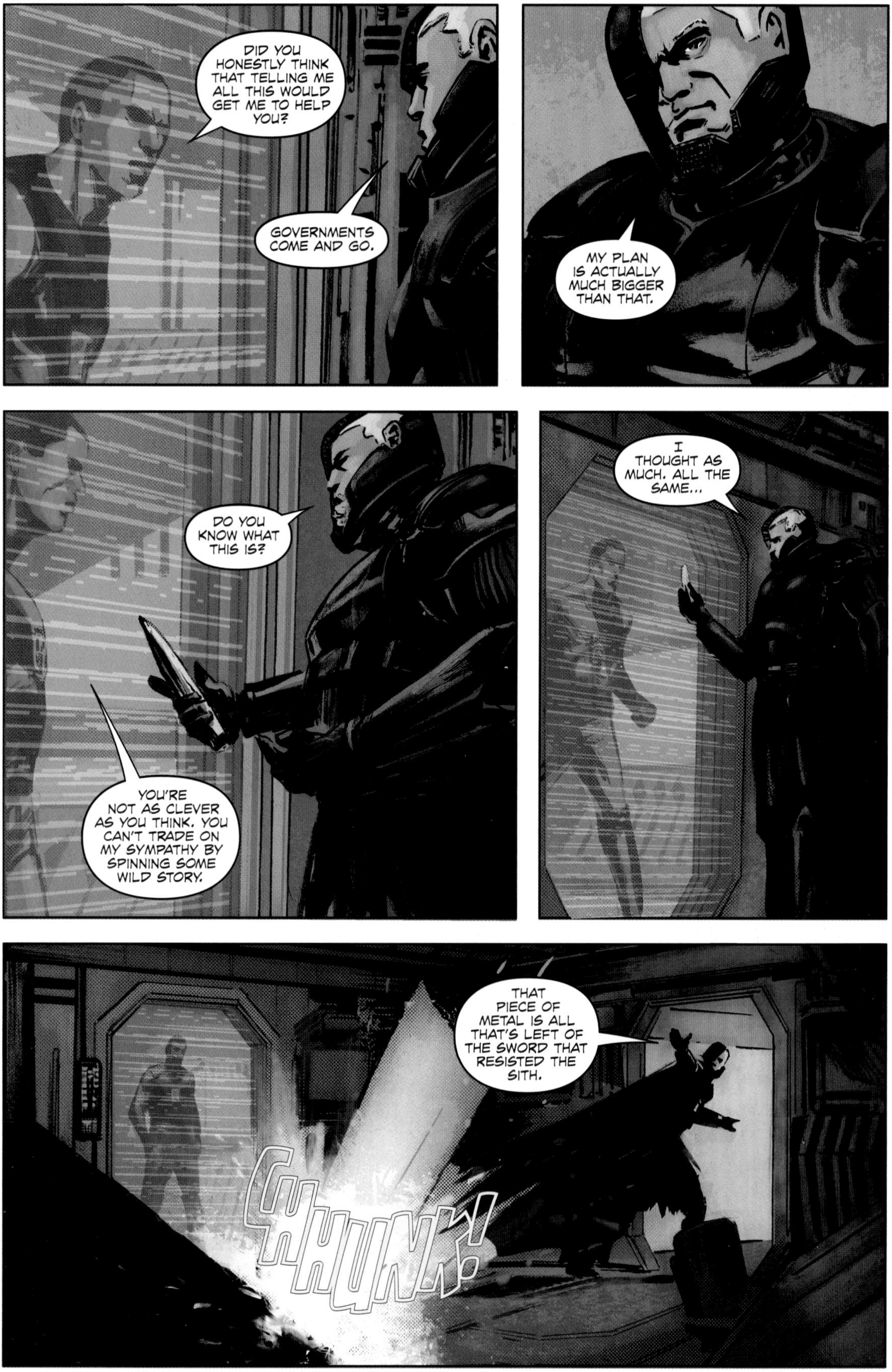
DID YOU HONESTLY THINK THAT TELLING ME ALL THIS WOULD GET ME TO HELP YOU?
GOVERNMENTS COME AND GO.
MY PLAN IS ACTUALLY MUCH BIGGER THAN THAT.
DO YOU KNOW WHAT THIS IS?
YOU'RE NOT AS CLEVER AS YOU THINK. YOU CAN'T TRADE ON MY SYMPATHY BY SPINNING SOME WILD STORY.
I THOUGHT AS MUCH. ALL THE SAME...
THAT PIECE OF METAL IS ALL THAT'S LEFT OF THE SWORD THAT RESISTED THE SITH.
CHHUNK!

LATER.

SKRIT

SKRIT
SKRIT

CHING!

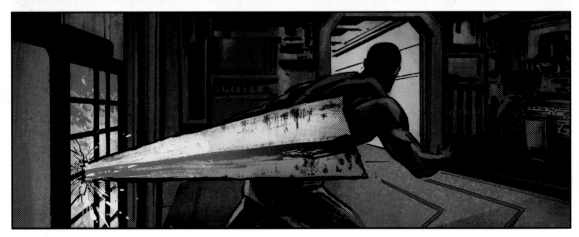

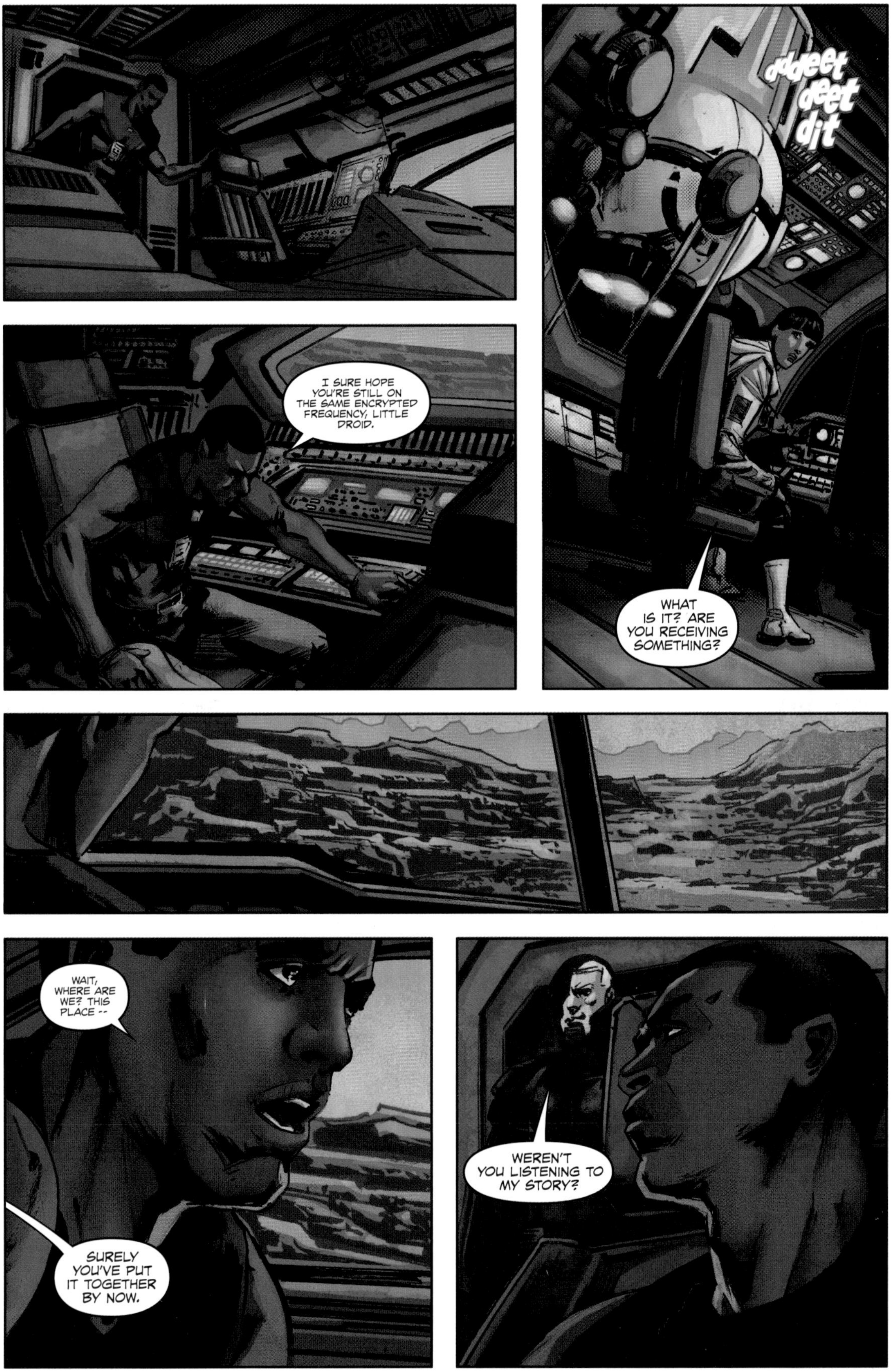
ddeet deet dit
I SURE HOPE YOU'RE STILL ON THE SAME ENCRYPTED FREQUENCY, LITTLE DROID.
WHAT IS IT? ARE YOU RECEIVING SOMETHING?
WAIT, WHERE ARE WE? THIS PLACE --
SURELY YOU'VE PUT IT TOGETHER BY NOW.
WEREN'T YOU LISTENING TO MY STORY?

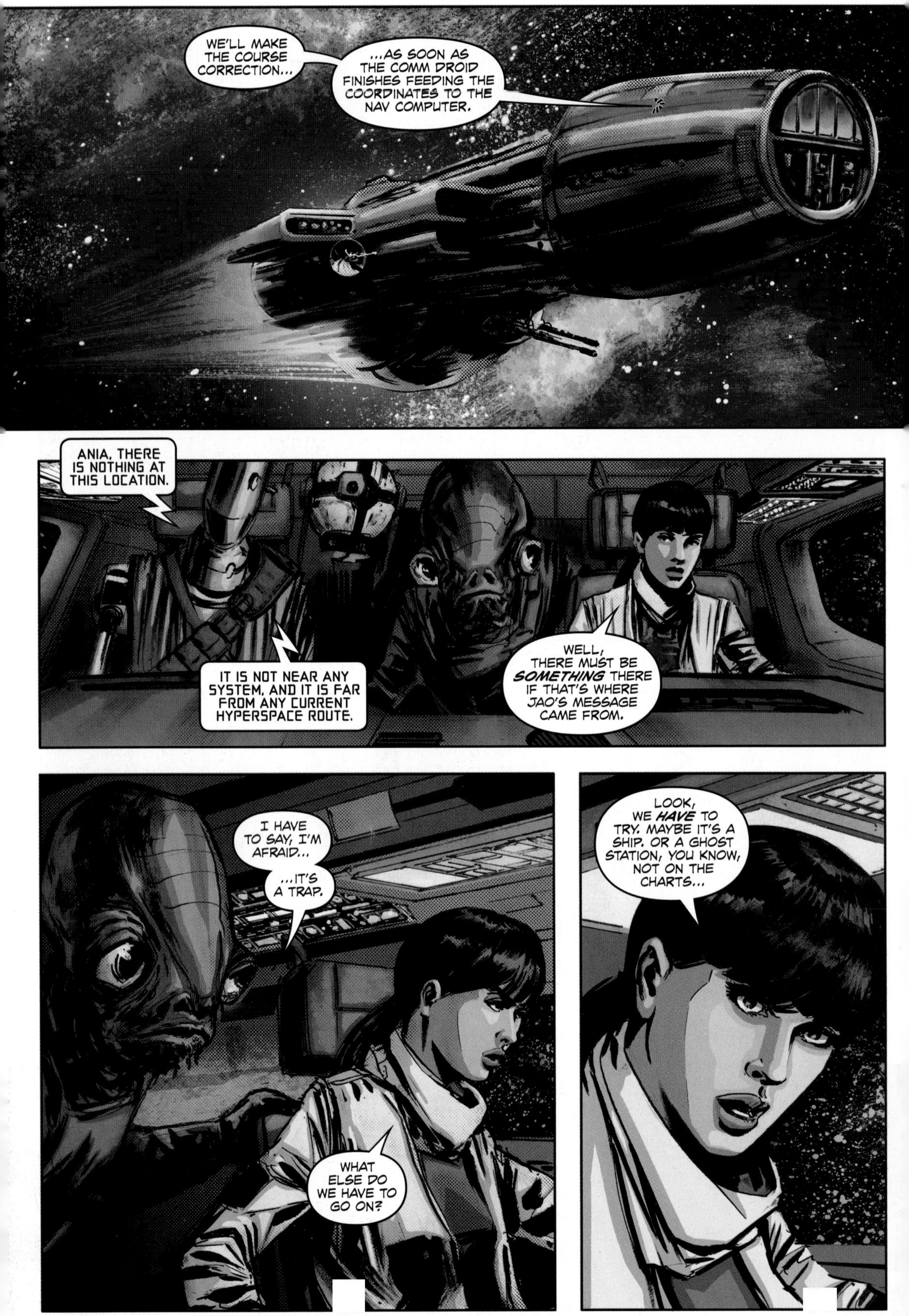
WE'LL MAKE THE COURSE CORRECTION...
...AS SOON AS THE COMM DROID FINISHES FEEDING THE COORDINATES TO THE NAV COMPUTER.
ANIA, THERE IS NOTHING AT THIS LOCATION.
IT IS NOT NEAR ANY SYSTEM, AND IT IS FAR FROM ANY CURRENT HYPERSPACE ROUTE.
WELL, THERE MUST BE SOMETHING THERE IF THAT'S WHERE JAO'S MESSAGE CAME FROM.
I HAVE TO SAY, I'M AFRAID...
...IT'S A TRAP.
WHAT ELSE DO WE HAVE TO GO ON?
LOOK, WE HAVE TO TRY. MAYBE IT'S A SHIP. OR A GHOST STATION, YOU KNOW, NOT ON THE CHARTS...

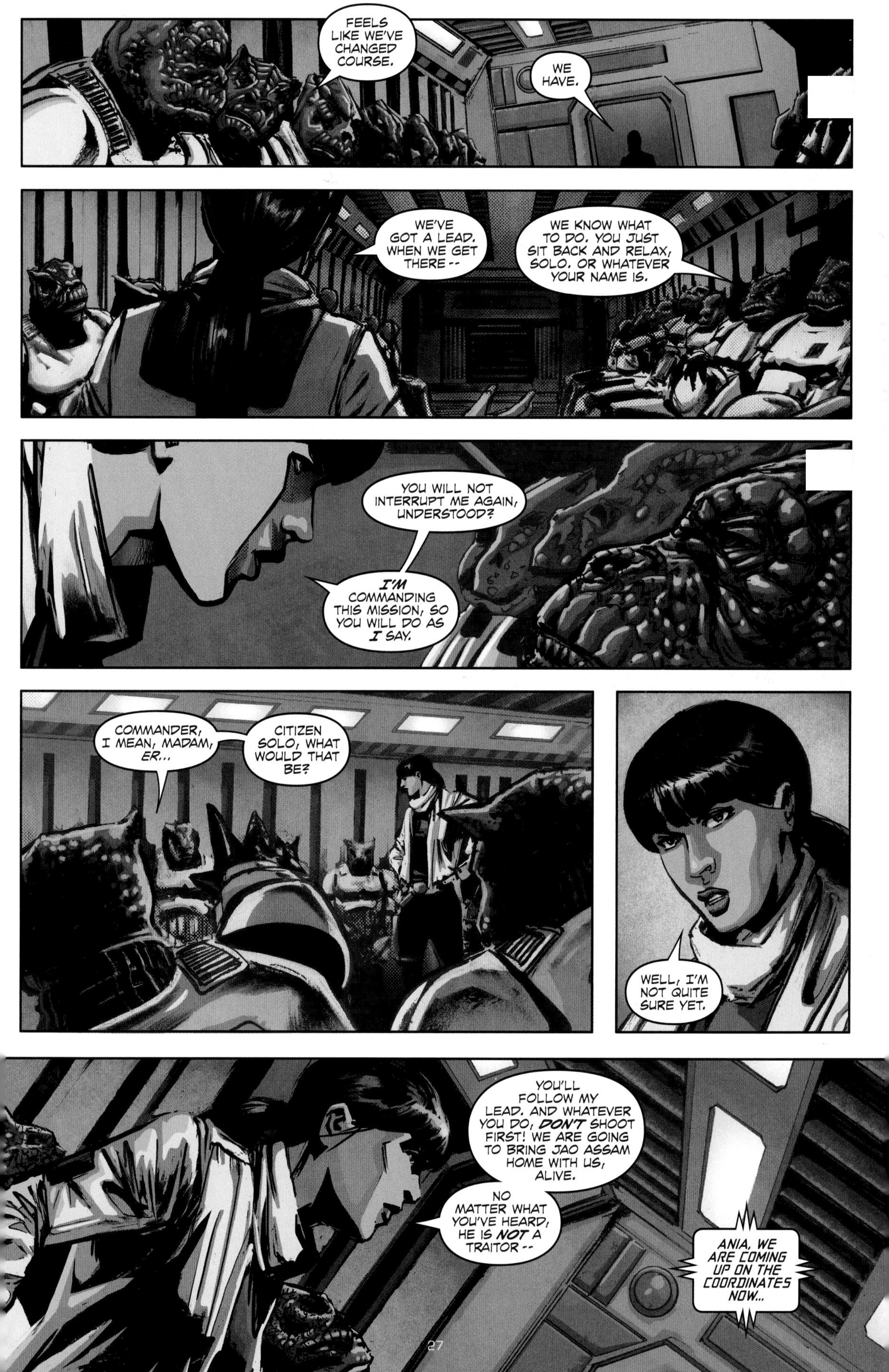
FEELS LIKE WE'VE CHANGED COURSE.
WE HAVE.
WE'VE GOT A LEAD. WHEN WE GET THERE --
WE KNOW WHAT TO DO. YOU JUST SIT BACK AND RELAX, SOLO. OR WHATEVER YOUR NAME IS.
YOU WILL NOT INTERRUPT ME AGAIN, UNDERSTOOD?
I'M COMMANDING THIS MISSION, SO YOU WILL DO AS I SAY.
COMMANDER, I MEAN, MADAM, ER...
CITIZEN SOLO, WHAT WOULD THAT BE?
WELL, I'M NOT QUITE SURE YET.
YOU'LL FOLLOW MY LEAD. AND WHATEVER YOU DO, DON'T SHOOT FIRST! WE ARE GOING TO BRING JAO ASSAM HOME WITH US, ALIVE.
NO MATTER WHAT YOU'VE HEARD, HE IS NOT A TRAITOR --
ANIA, WE ARE COMING UP ON THE COORDINATES NOW...

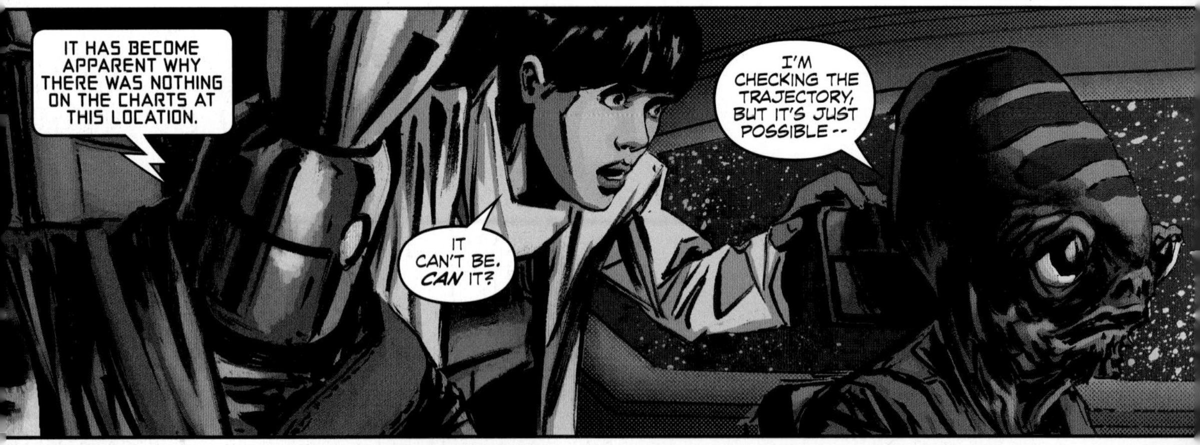
IT HAS BECOME APPARENT WHY THERE WAS NOTHING ON THE CHARTS AT THIS LOCATION.
IT CAN'T BE. *CAN* IT?
I'M CHECKING THE TRAJECTORY, BUT IT'S JUST POSSIBLE --

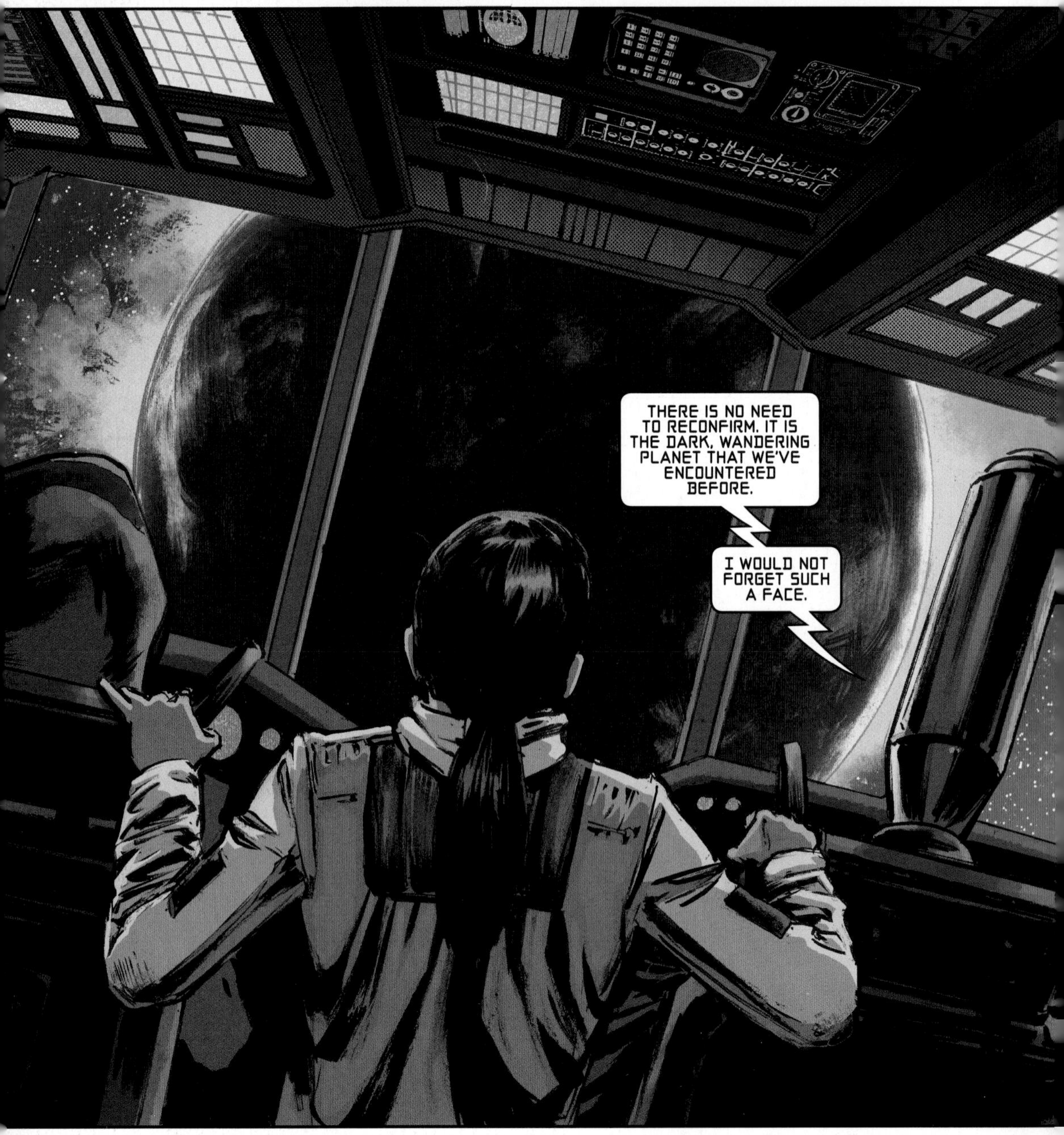
THERE IS NO NEED TO RECONFIRM. IT IS THE DARK, WANDERING PLANET THAT WE'VE ENCOUNTERED BEFORE.
I WOULD NOT FORGET SUCH A FACE.

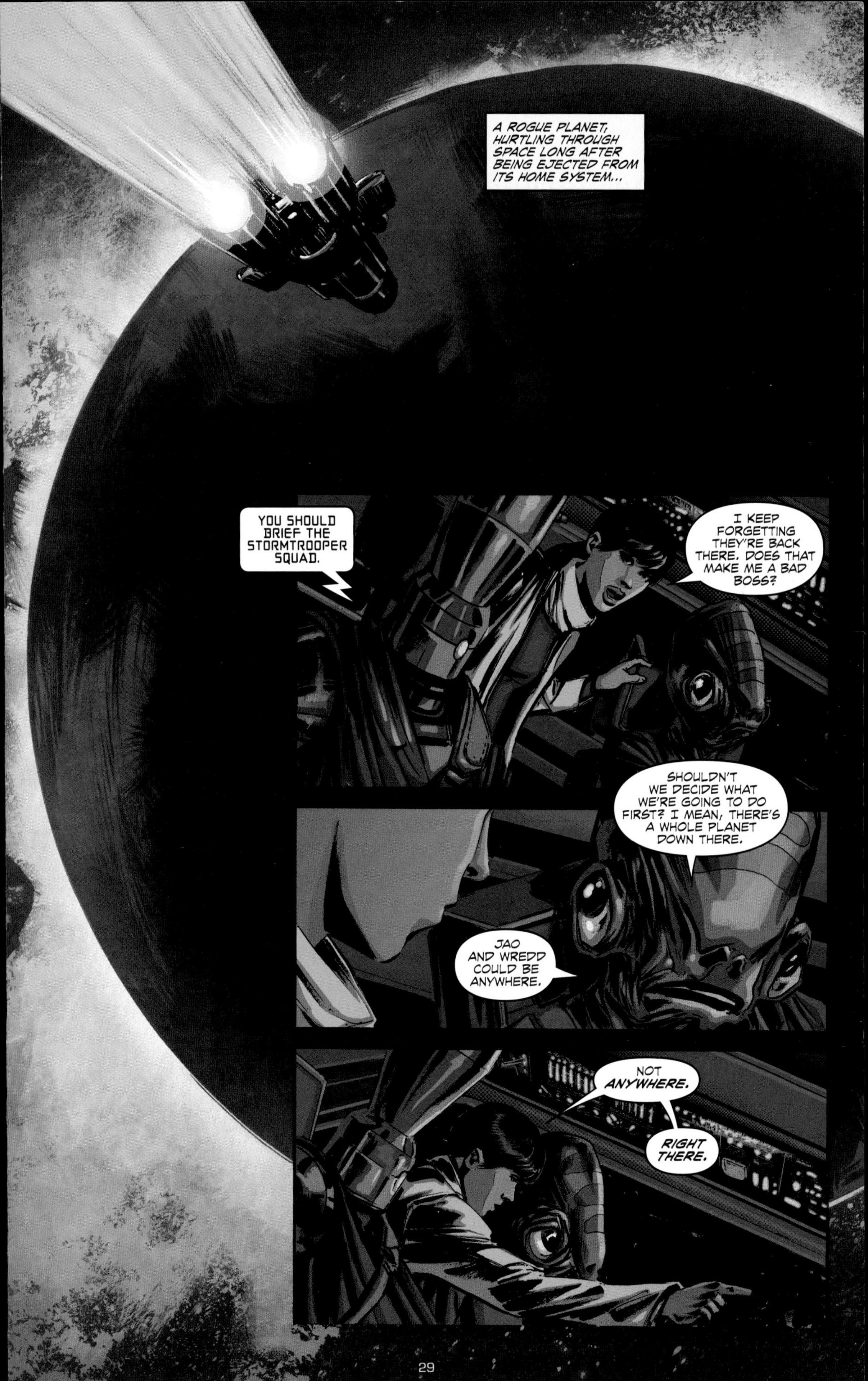
A ROGUE PLANET, HURTLING THROUGH SPACE LONG AFTER BEING EJECTED FROM ITS HOME SYSTEM...
YOU SHOULD BRIEF THE STORMTROOPER SQUAD.
I KEEP FORGETTING THEY'RE BACK THERE. DOES THAT MAKE ME A BAD BOSS?
SHOULDN'T WE DECIDE WHAT WE'RE GOING TO DO FIRST? I MEAN, THERE'S A WHOLE PLANET DOWN THERE.
JAO AND WREDD COULD BE ANYWHERE.
NOT *ANYWHERE.*
RIGHT THERE.

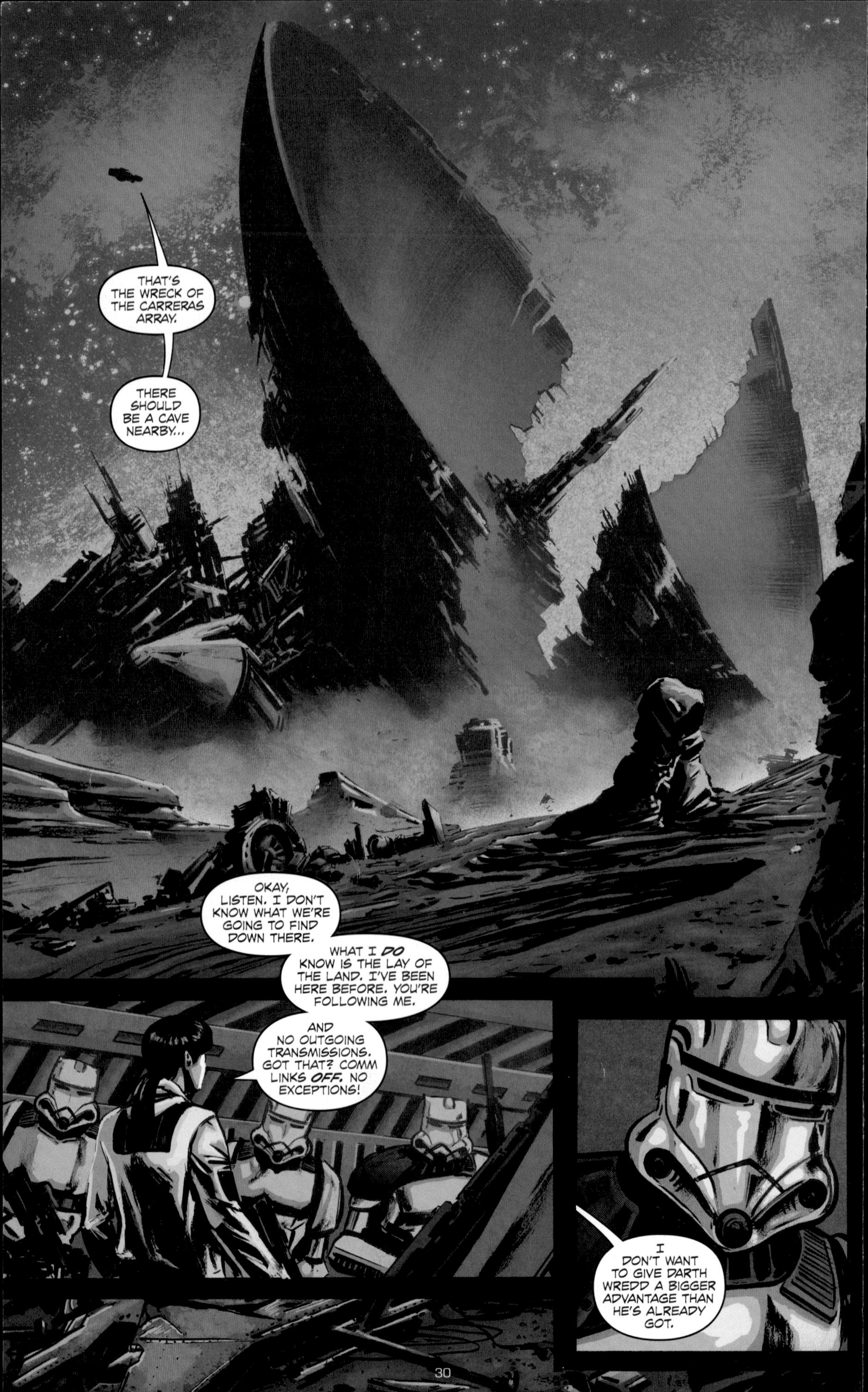
THAT'S THE WRECK OF THE CARRERAS ARRAY.
THERE SHOULD BE A CAVE NEARBY...
OKAY, LISTEN. I DON'T KNOW WHAT WE'RE GOING TO FIND DOWN THERE.
WHAT I DO KNOW IS THE LAY OF THE LAND. I'VE BEEN HERE BEFORE. YOU'RE FOLLOWING ME.
AND NO OUTGOING TRANSMISSIONS. GOT THAT? COMM LINKS OFF. NO EXCEPTIONS!
I DON'T WANT TO GIVE DARTH WREDD A BIGGER ADVANTAGE THAN HE'S ALREADY GOT.

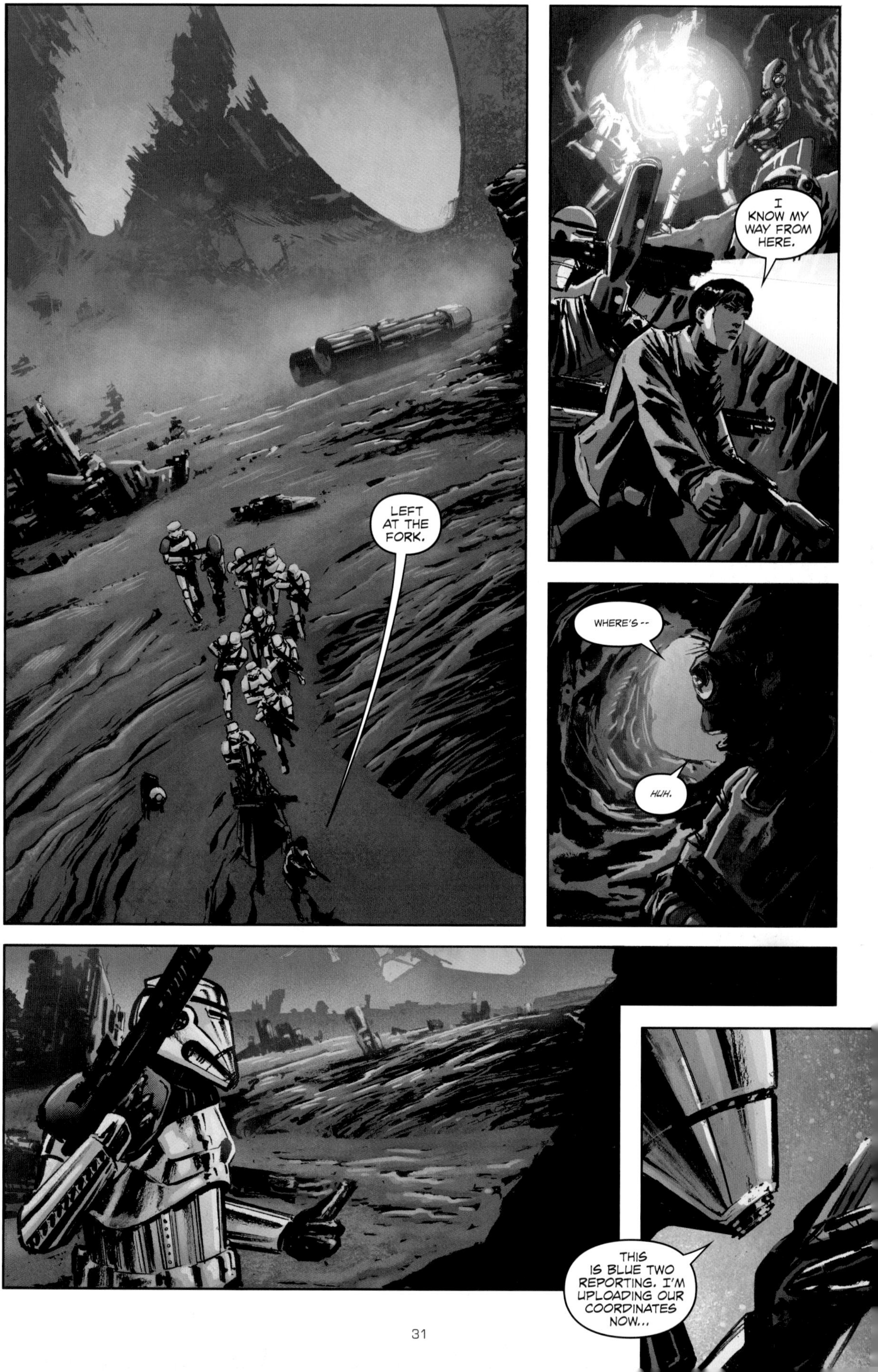
LEFT AT THE FORK.
I KNOW MY WAY FROM HERE.
WHERE'S --
HUH.
THIS IS BLUE TWO REPORTING. I'M UPLOADING OUR COORDINATES NOW...

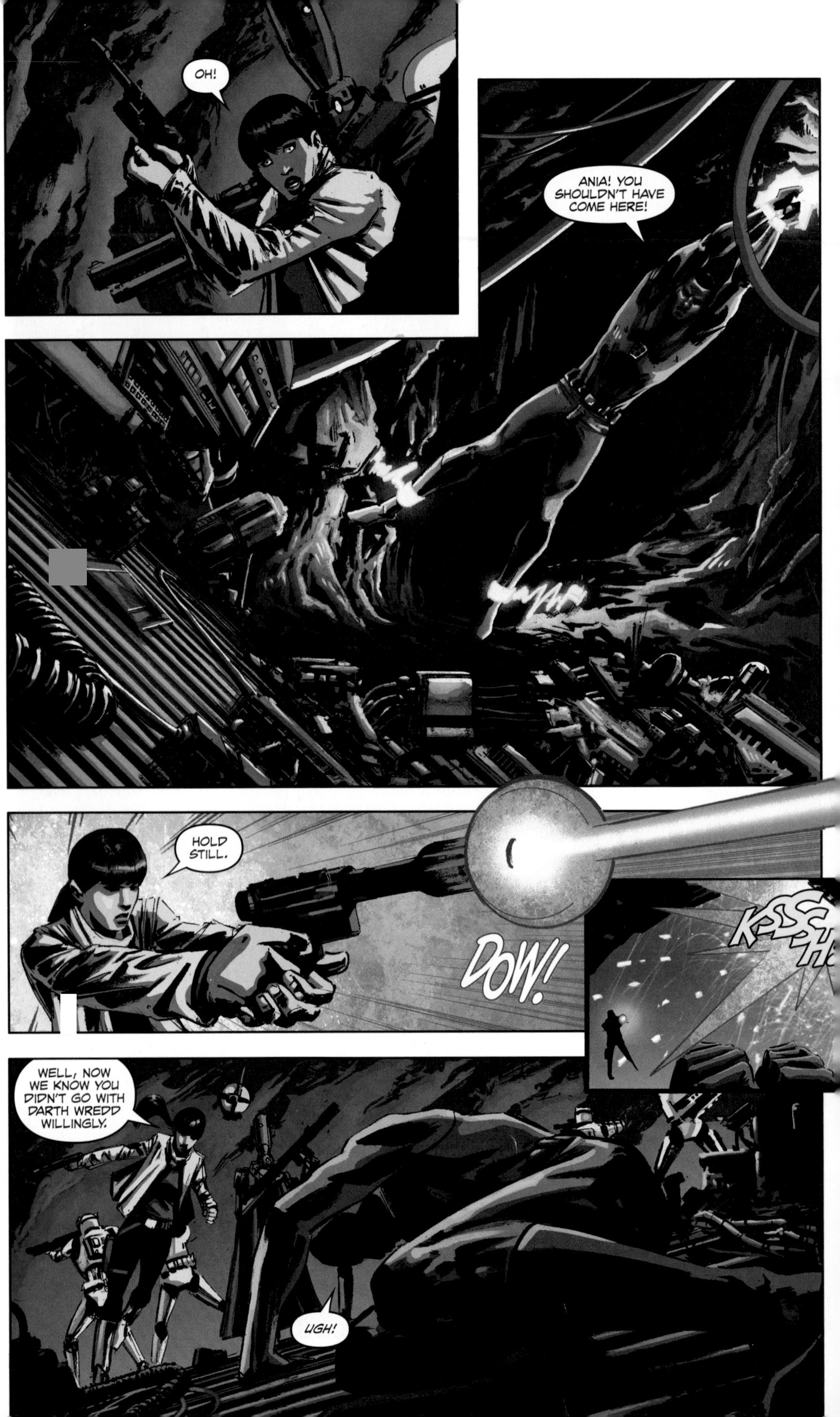
OH!
ANIA! YOU SHOULDN'T HAVE COME HERE!
HOLD STILL.
DOW!
KSSH
WELL, NOW WE KNOW YOU DIDN'T GO WITH DARTH WREDD WILLINGLY.
UGH!

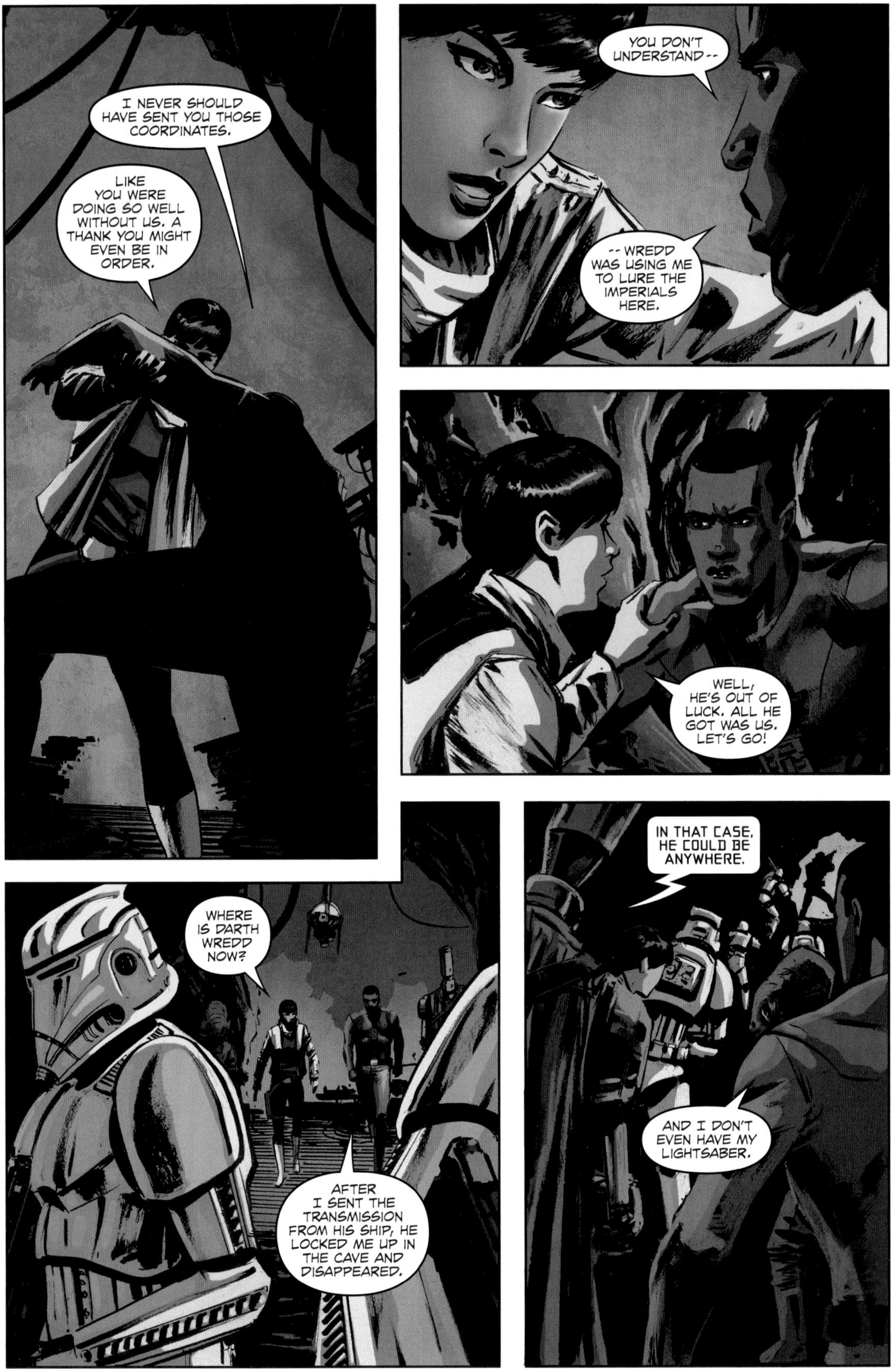
I NEVER SHOULD HAVE SENT YOU THOSE COORDINATES.
LIKE YOU WERE DOING SO WELL WITHOUT US. A THANK YOU MIGHT EVEN BE IN ORDER.
YOU DON'T UNDERSTAND--
--WREDD WAS USING ME TO LURE THE IMPERIALS HERE.
WELL, HE'S OUT OF LUCK. ALL HE GOT WAS US. LET'S GO!
WHERE IS DARTH WREDD NOW?
AFTER I SENT THE TRANSMISSION FROM HIS SHIP, HE LOCKED ME UP IN THE CAVE AND DISAPPEARED.
IN THAT CASE, HE COULD BE ANYWHERE.
AND I DON'T EVEN HAVE MY LIGHTSABER.

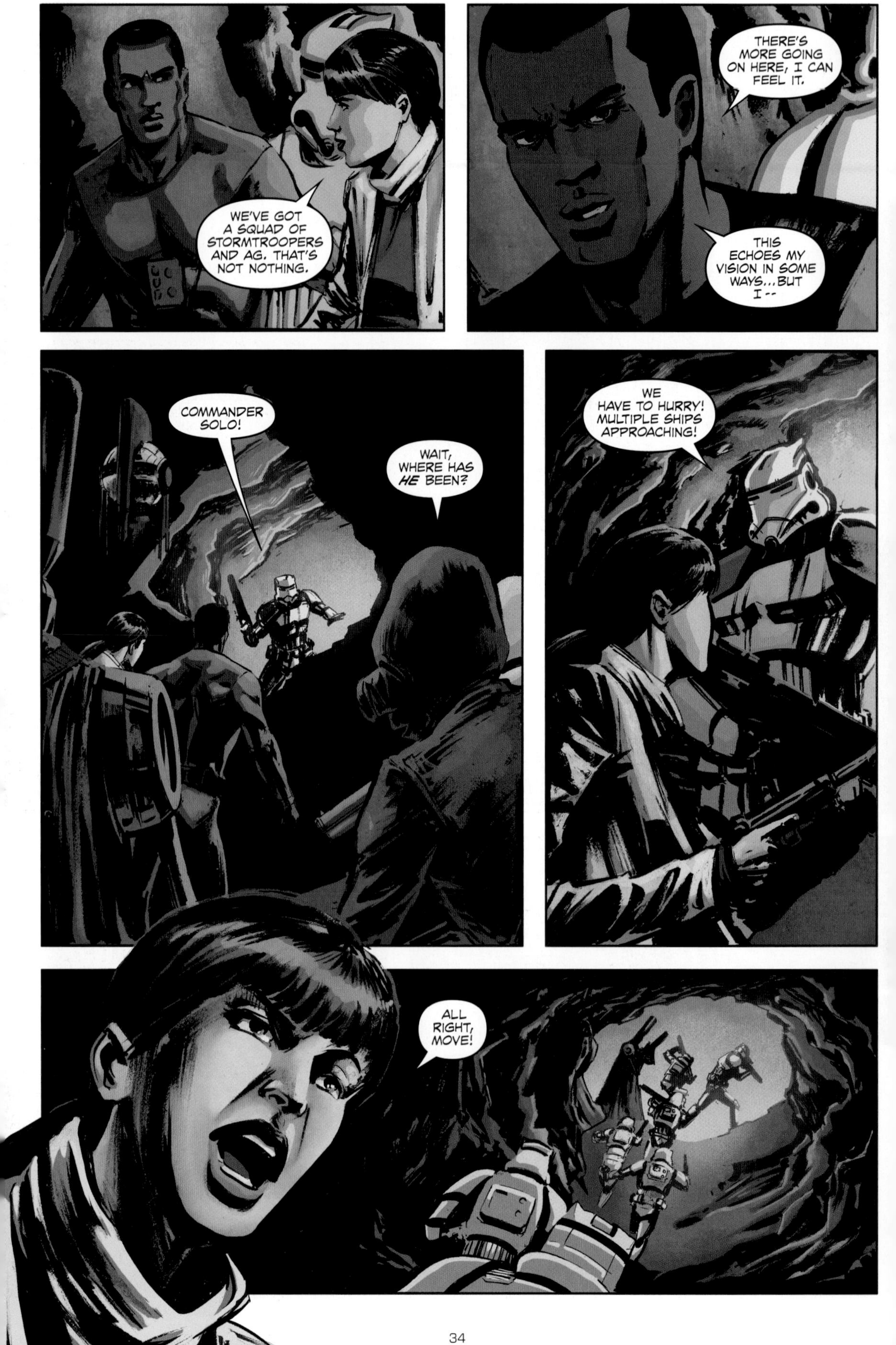
WE'VE GOT A SQUAD OF STORMTROOPERS AND AG. THAT'S NOT NOTHING.
THERE'S MORE GOING ON HERE, I CAN FEEL IT.
THIS ECHOES MY VISION IN SOME WAYS... BUT I --
COMMANDER SOLO!
WAIT, WHERE HAS *HE* BEEN?
WE HAVE TO HURRY! MULTIPLE SHIPS APPROACHING!
ALL RIGHT, MOVE!

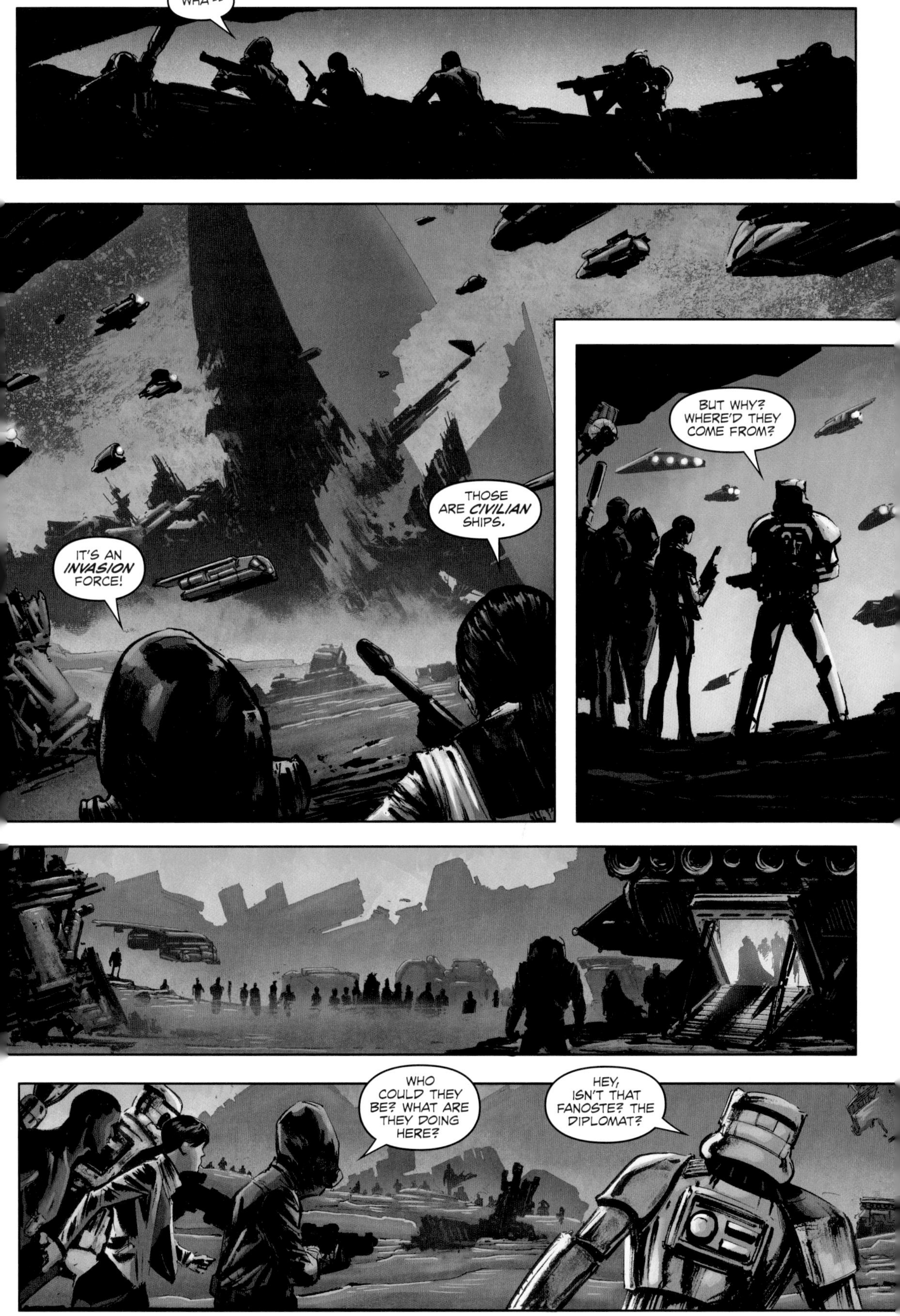
WHA --
IT'S AN INVASION FORCE!
THOSE ARE CIVILIAN SHIPS.
BUT WHY? WHERE'D THEY COME FROM?
WHO COULD THEY BE? WHAT ARE THEY DOING HERE?
HEY, ISN'T THAT FANOSTE? THE DIPLOMAT?

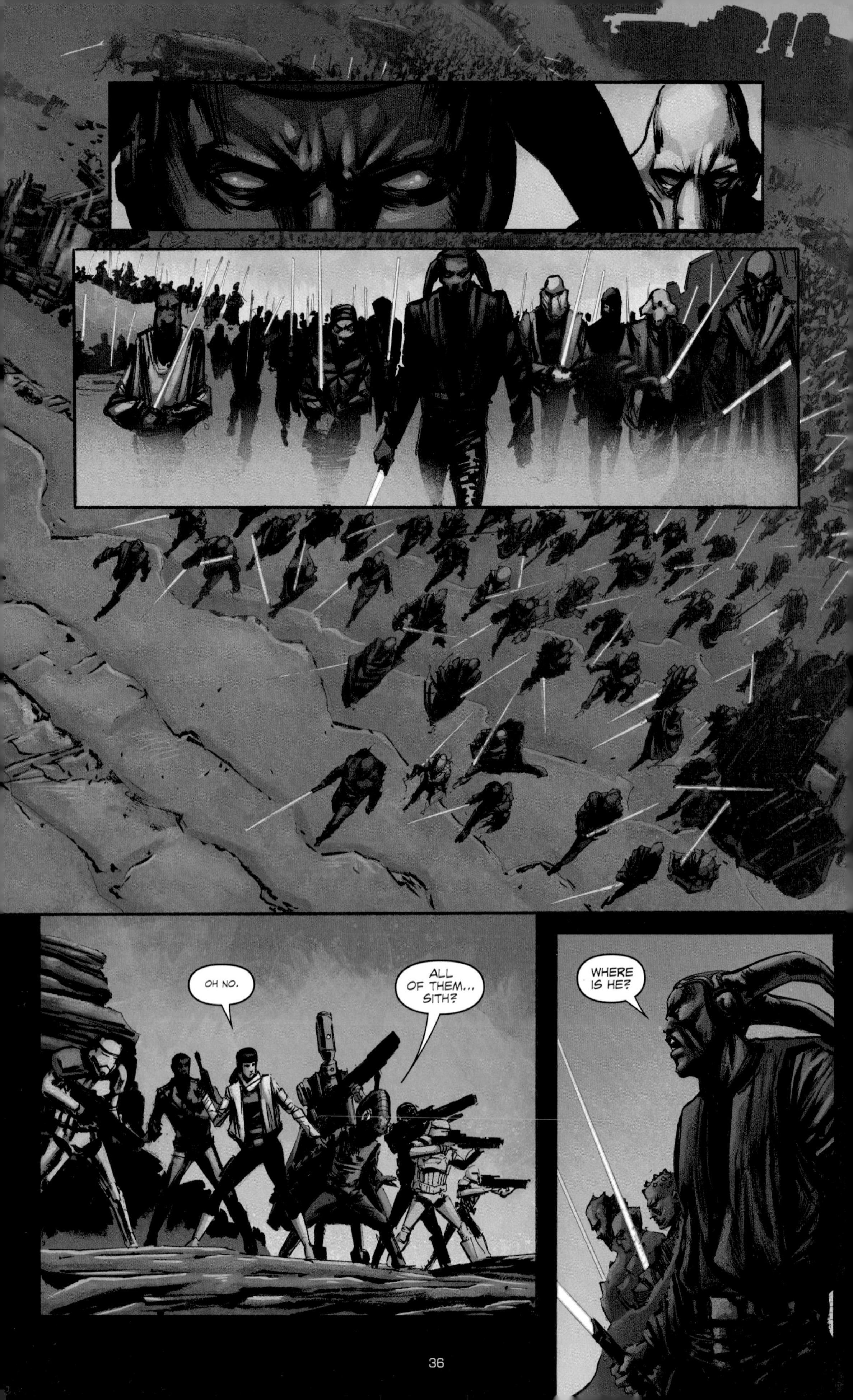
OH NO.
ALL OF THEM... SITH?
WHERE IS HE?

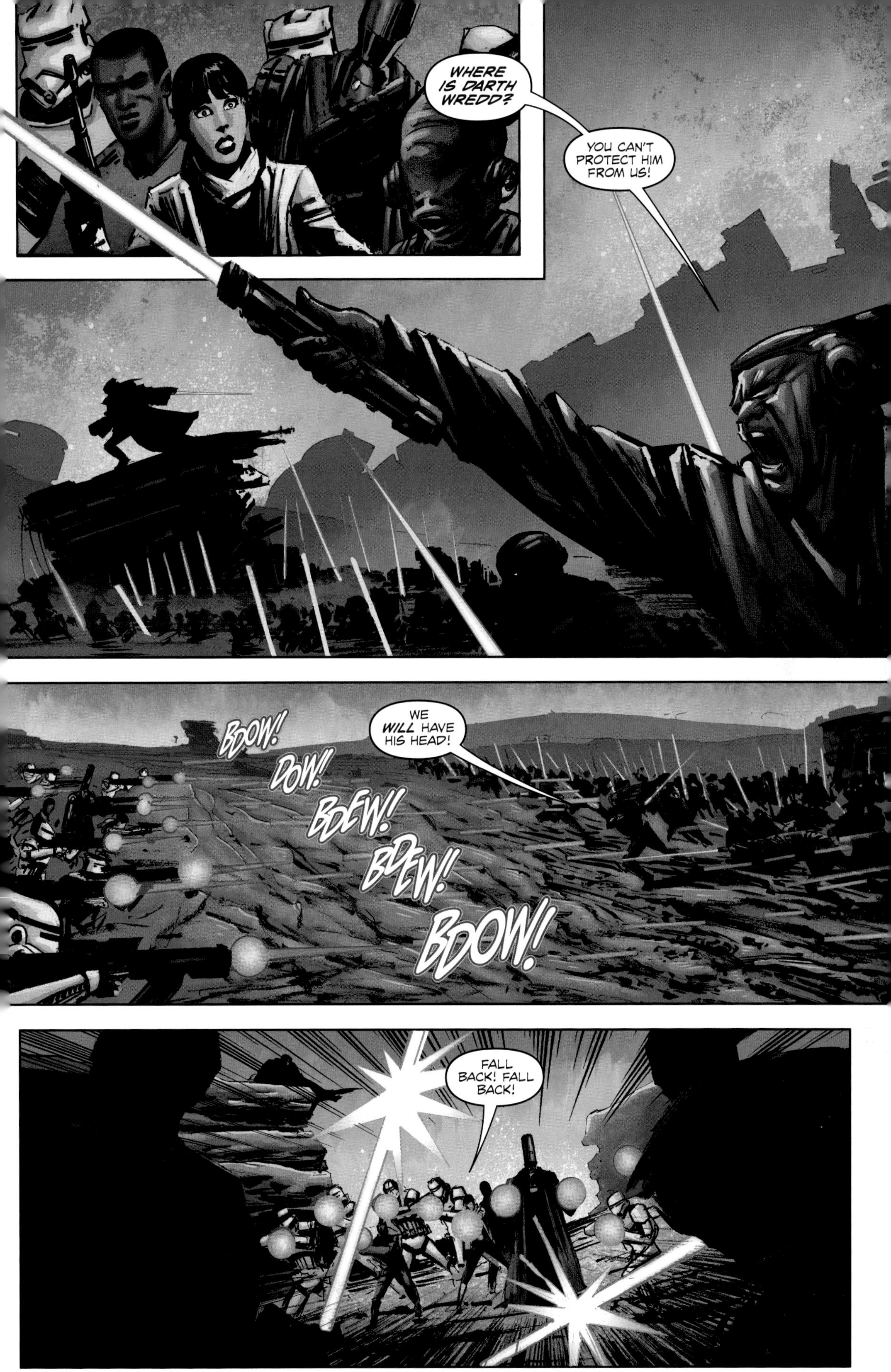
WHERE IS DARTH WREDD?
YOU CAN'T PROTECT HIM FROM US!
BDOW!
DOW!
BDEW!
BDEW!
BDOW!
WE WILL HAVE HIS HEAD!
FALL BACK! FALL BACK!

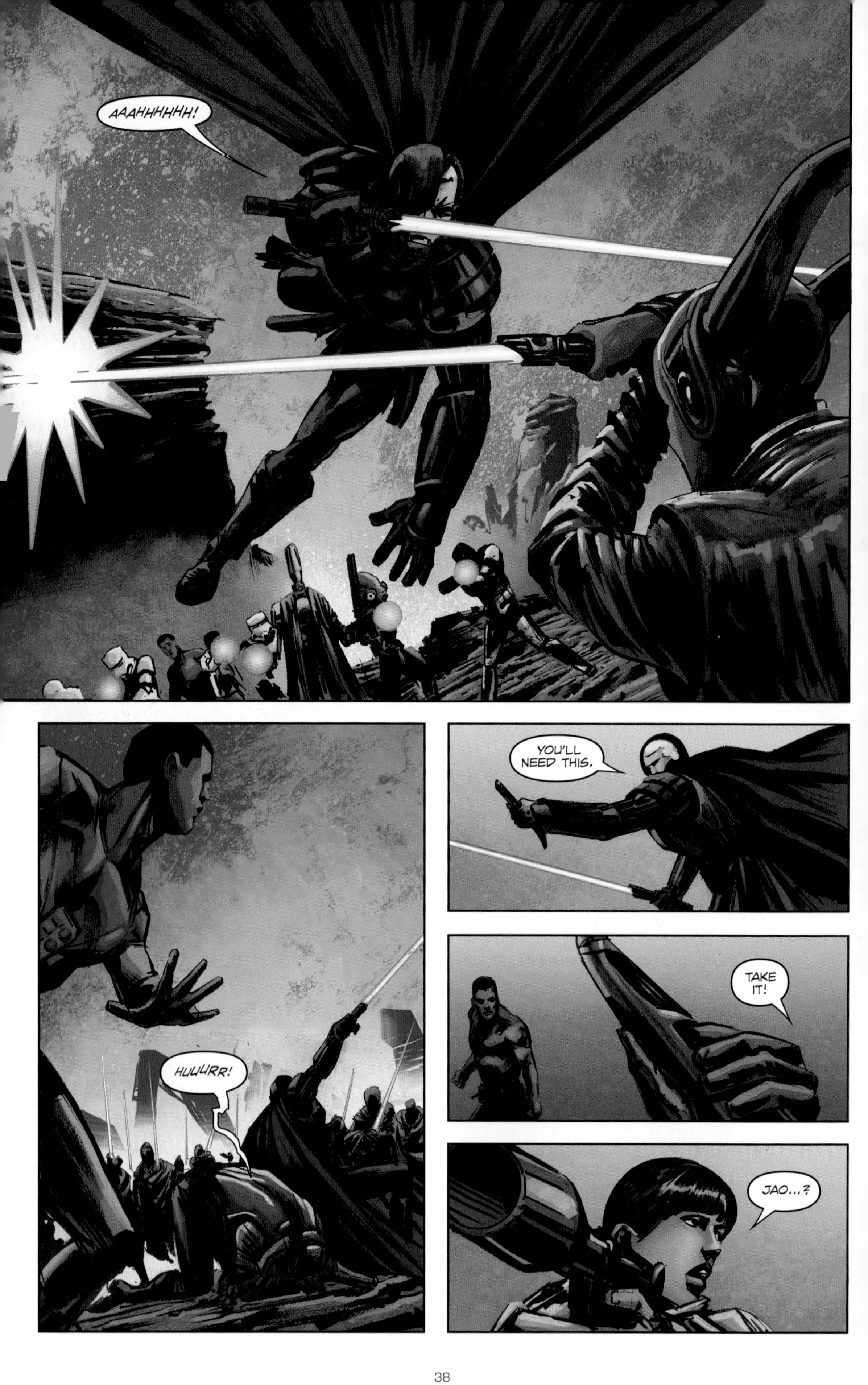
AAAHHHHHHH!
HUUURR!
YOU'LL NEED THIS.
TAKE IT!
JAO...?

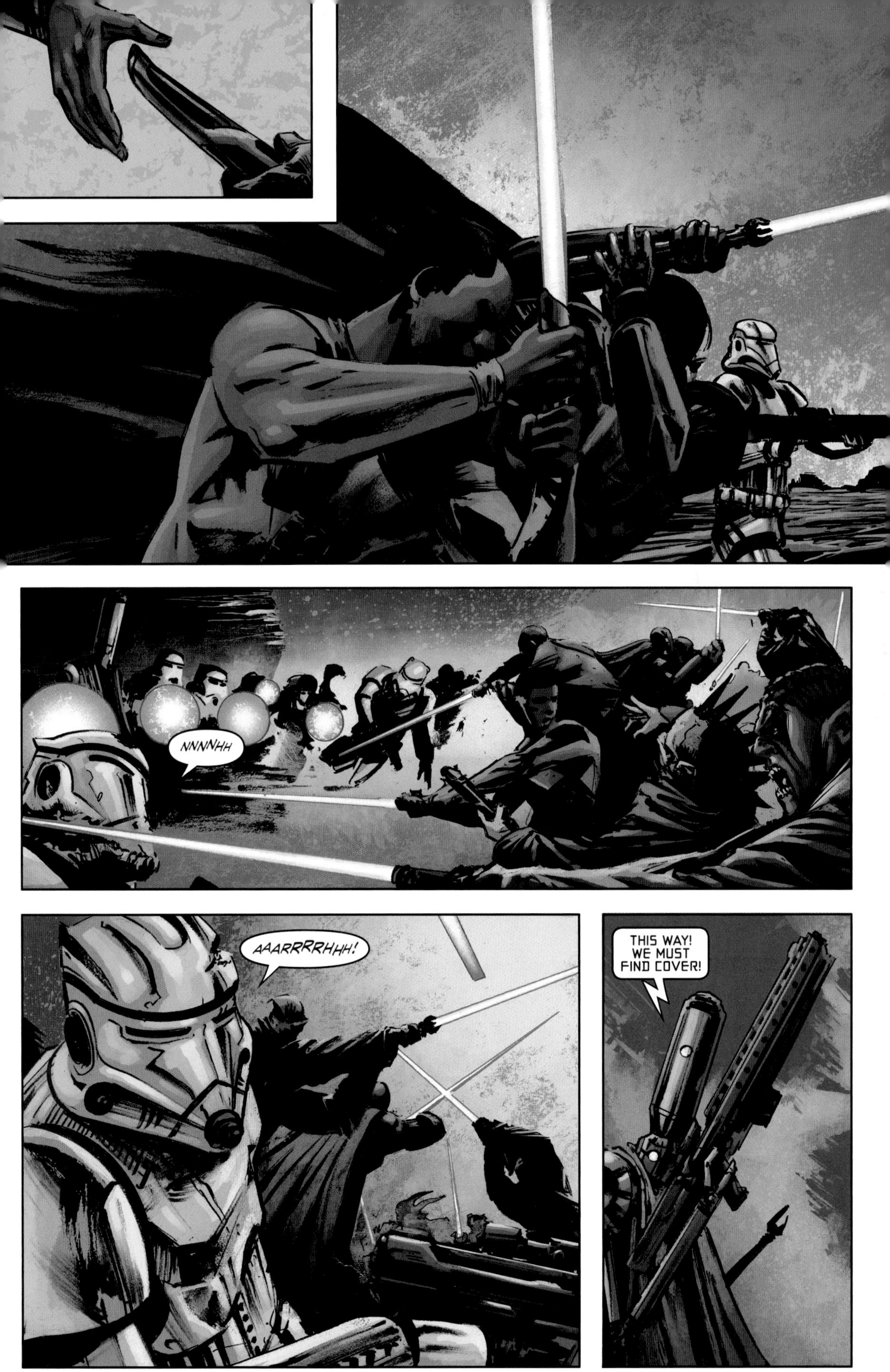
NNNNHH
AAARRRRHHH!
THIS WAY! WE MUST FIND COVER!

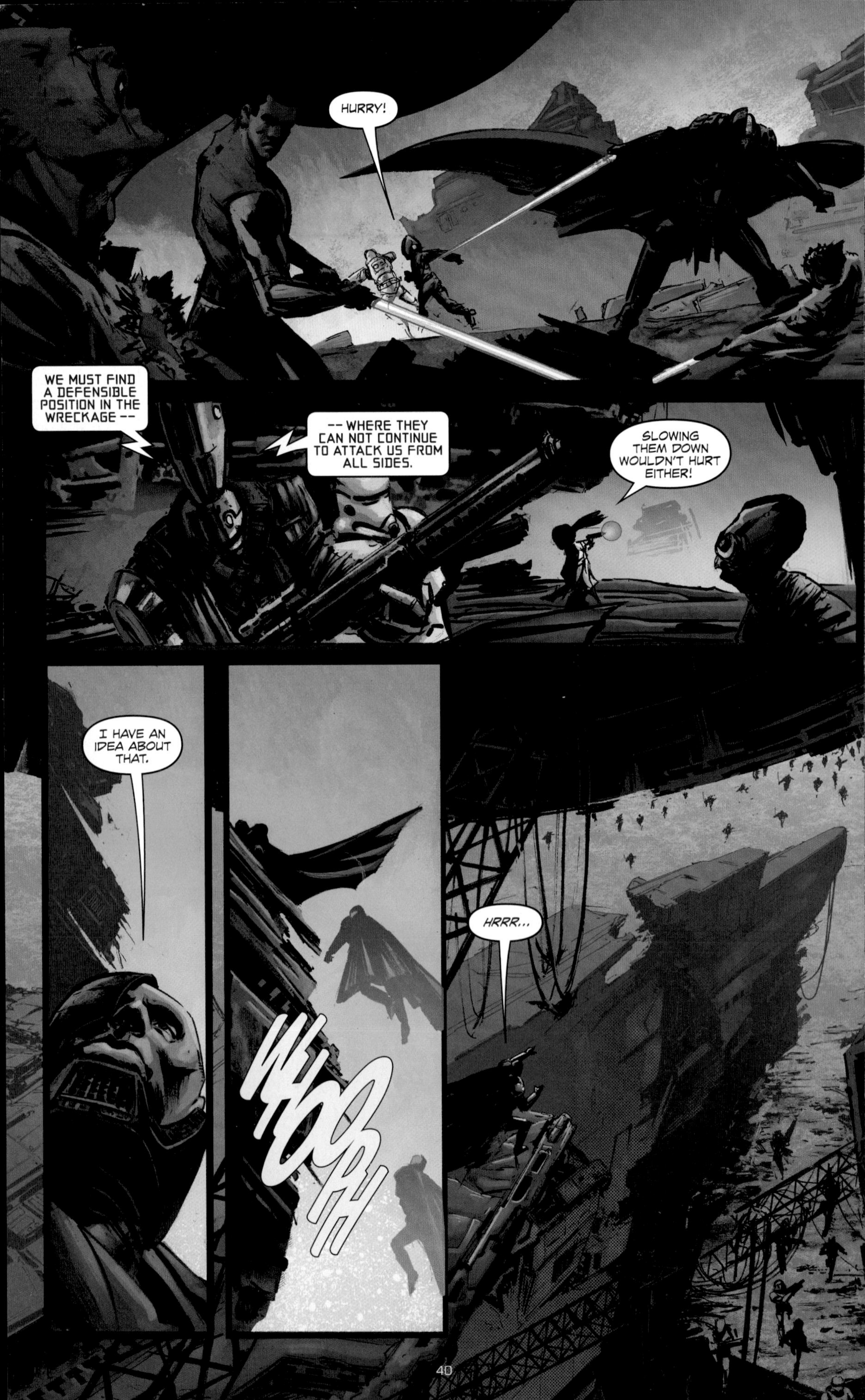
HURRY!
WE MUST FIND A DEFENSIBLE POSITION IN THE WRECKAGE --
-- WHERE THEY CAN NOT CONTINUE TO ATTACK US FROM ALL SIDES.
SLOWING THEM DOWN WOULDN'T HURT EITHER!
I HAVE AN IDEA ABOUT THAT.
WHOOSH
HRRR...

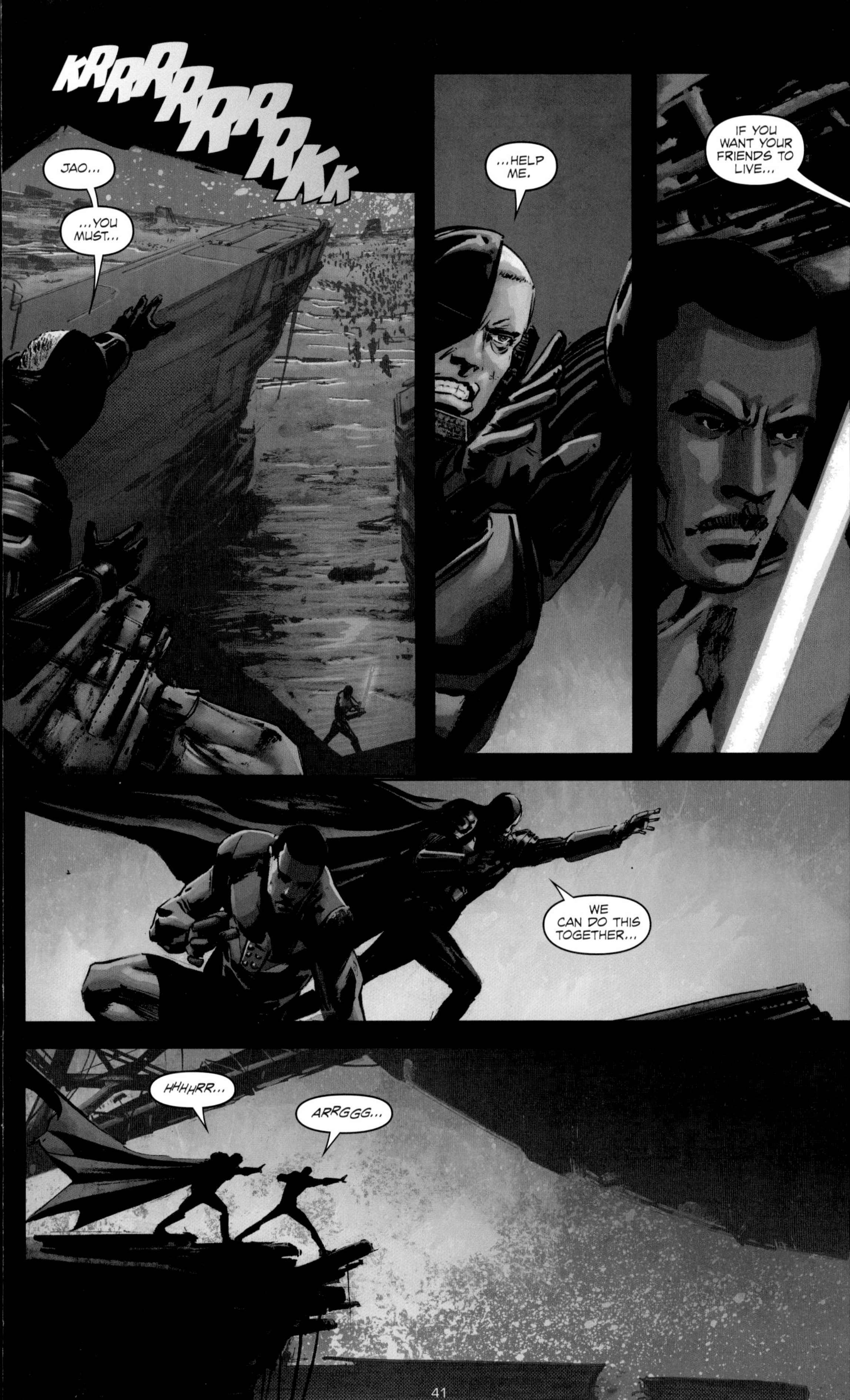
KRRRRRRRRKK
JAO...
...YOU MUST...
...HELP ME.
IF YOU WANT YOUR FRIENDS TO LIVE...
WE CAN DO THIS TOGETHER...
HHHHRR...
ARRGGG...

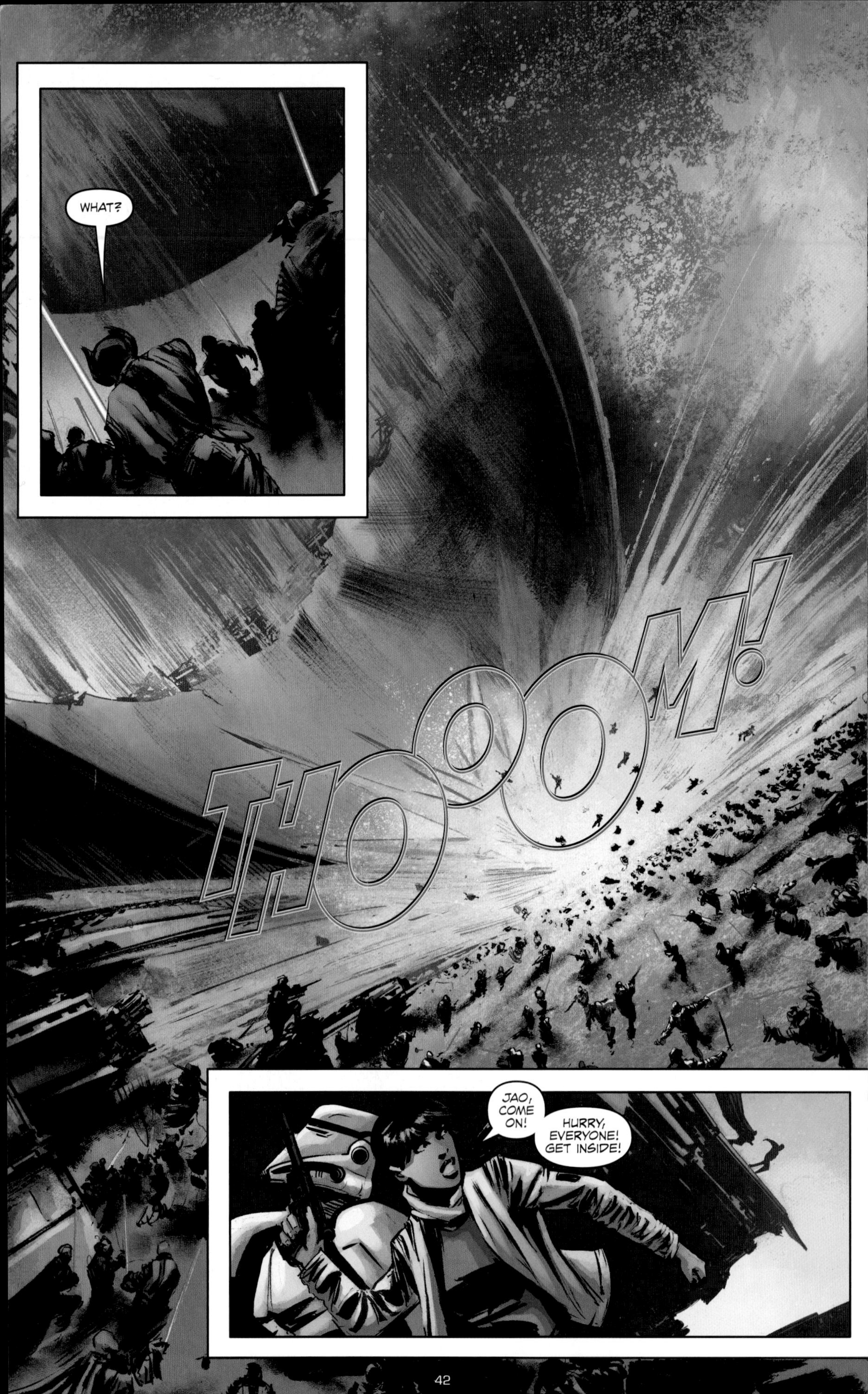
WHAT?
THOOOM!
JAO, COME ON!
HURRY, EVERYONE! GET INSIDE!

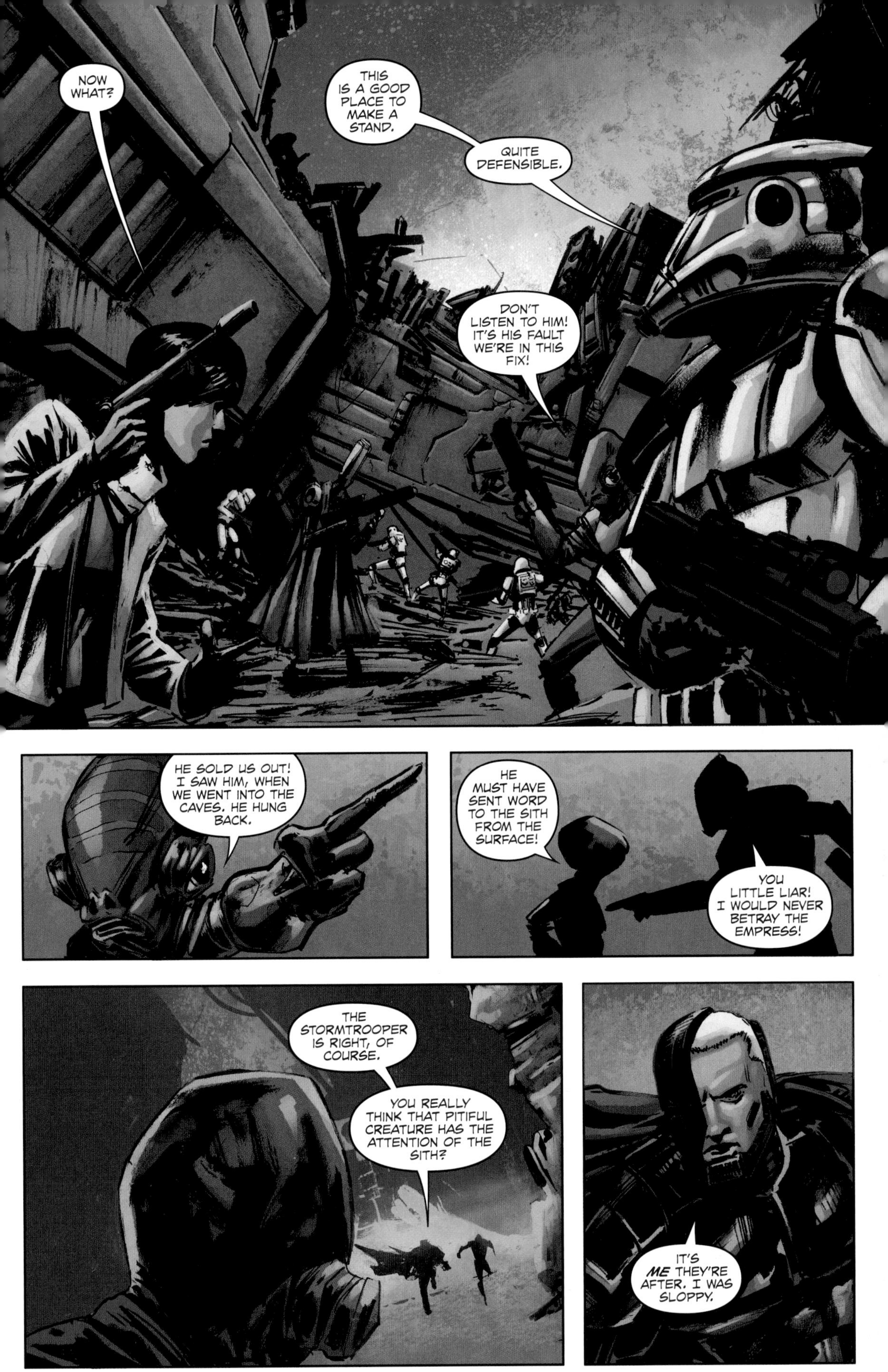

NOW WHAT?
THIS IS A GOOD PLACE TO MAKE A STAND.
QUITE DEFENSIBLE.
DON'T LISTEN TO HIM! IT'S HIS FAULT WE'RE IN THIS FIX!
HE SOLD US OUT! I SAW HIM, WHEN WE WENT INTO THE CAVES. HE HUNG BACK.
HE MUST HAVE SENT WORD TO THE SITH FROM THE SURFACE!
YOU LITTLE LIAR! I WOULD NEVER BETRAY THE EMPRESS!
THE STORMTROOPER IS RIGHT, OF COURSE.
YOU REALLY THINK THAT PITIFUL CREATURE HAS THE ATTENTION OF THE SITH?
IT'S ME THEY'RE AFTER. I WAS SLOPPY.

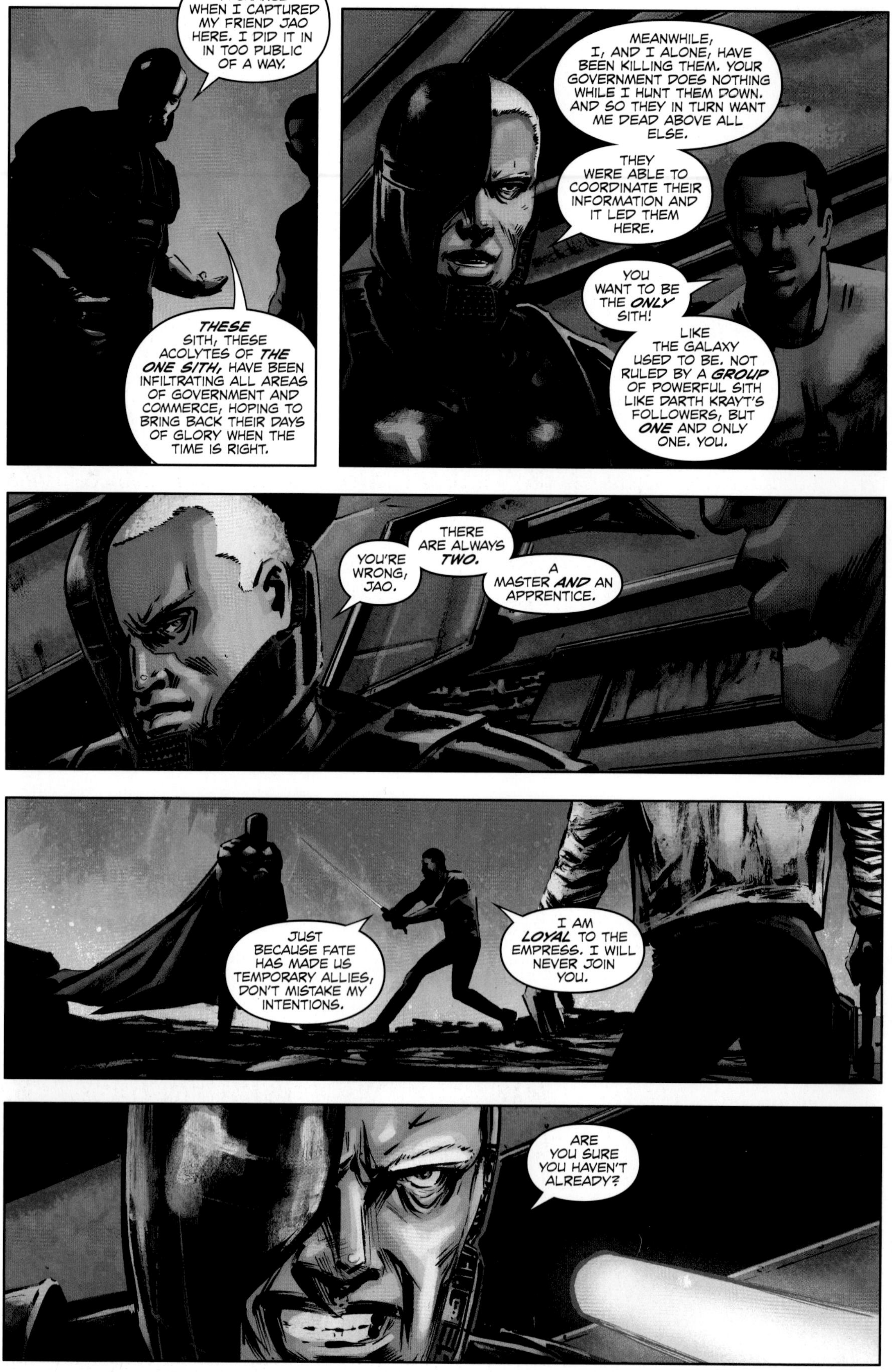

I TOOK A CHANCE WHEN I CAPTURED MY FRIEND JAO HERE. I DID IT IN IN TOO PUBLIC OF A WAY.
THESE SITH, THESE ACOLYTES OF THE ONE SITH, HAVE BEEN INFILTRATING ALL AREAS OF GOVERNMENT AND COMMERCE, HOPING TO BRING BACK THEIR DAYS OF GLORY WHEN THE TIME IS RIGHT.
MEANWHILE, I, AND I ALONE, HAVE BEEN KILLING THEM. YOUR GOVERNMENT DOES NOTHING WHILE I HUNT THEM DOWN. AND SO THEY IN TURN WANT ME DEAD ABOVE ALL ELSE.
THEY WERE ABLE TO COORDINATE THEIR INFORMATION AND IT LED THEM HERE.
YOU WANT TO BE THE ONLY SITH!
LIKE THE GALAXY USED TO BE. NOT RULED BY A GROUP OF POWERFUL SITH LIKE DARTH KRAYT'S FOLLOWERS, BUT ONE AND ONLY ONE. YOU.
YOU'RE WRONG, JAO.
THERE ARE ALWAYS TWO.
A MASTER AND AN APPRENTICE.
I AM LOYAL TO THE EMPRESS. I WILL NEVER JOIN YOU.
JUST BECAUSE FATE HAS MADE US TEMPORARY ALLIES, DON'T MISTAKE MY INTENTIONS.
ARE YOU SURE YOU HAVEN'T ALREADY?

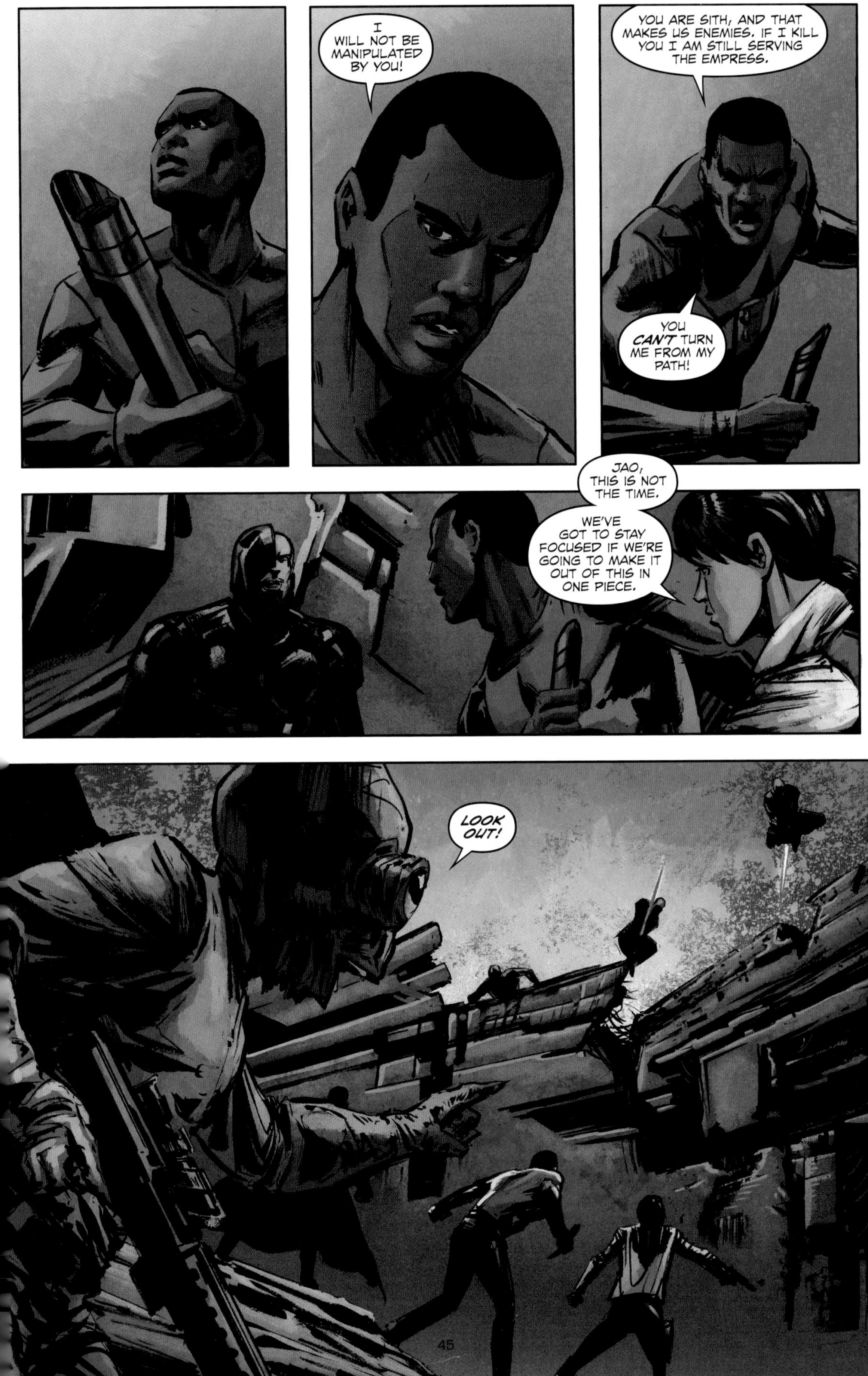
I WILL NOT BE MANIPULATED BY YOU!
YOU ARE SITH, AND THAT MAKES US ENEMIES. IF I KILL YOU I AM STILL SERVING THE EMPRESS.
YOU CAN'T TURN ME FROM MY PATH!
JAO, THIS IS NOT THE TIME.
WE'VE GOT TO STAY FOCUSED IF WE'RE GOING TO MAKE IT OUT OF THIS IN ONE PIECE.
LOOK OUT!

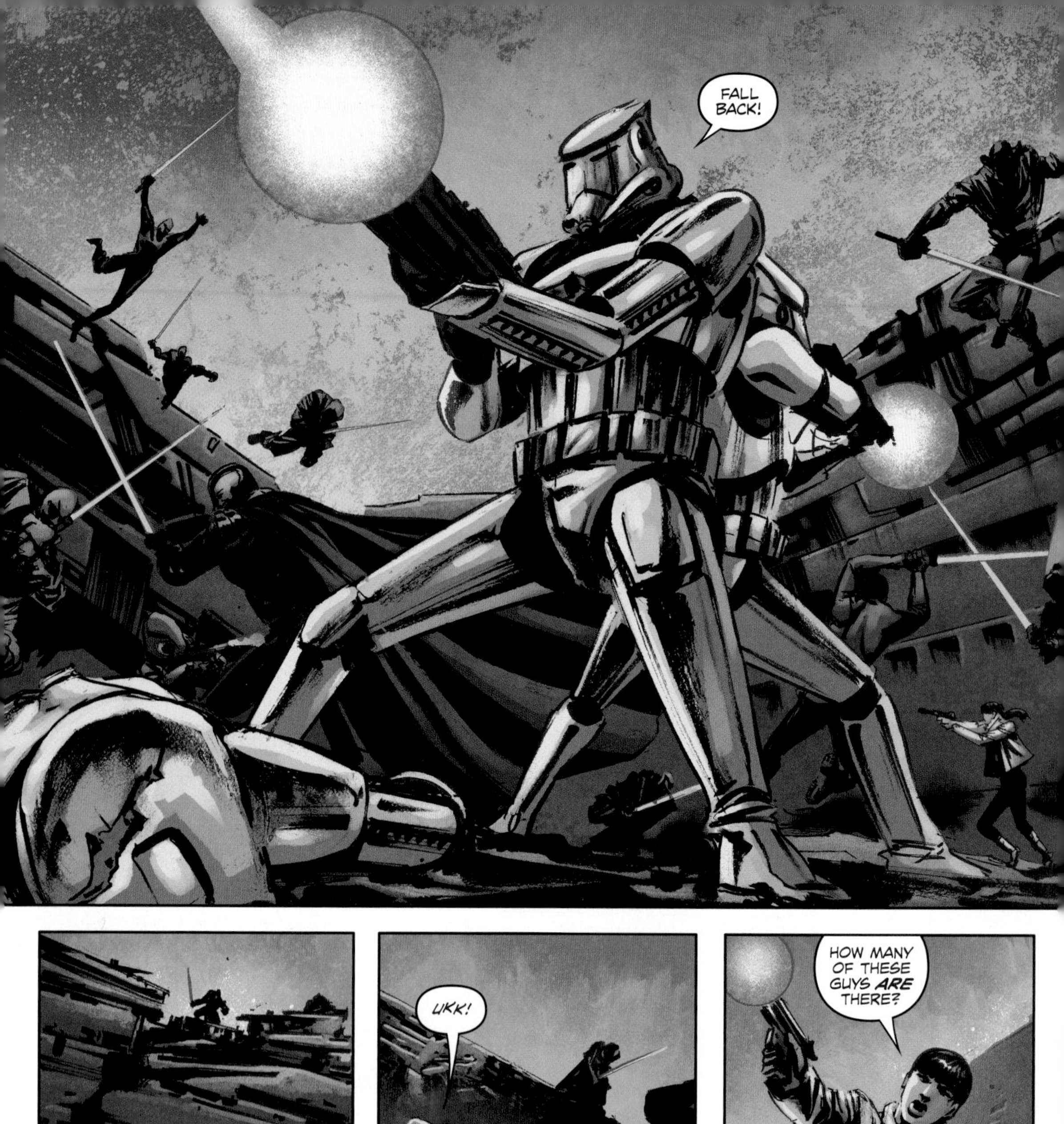
FALL BACK!

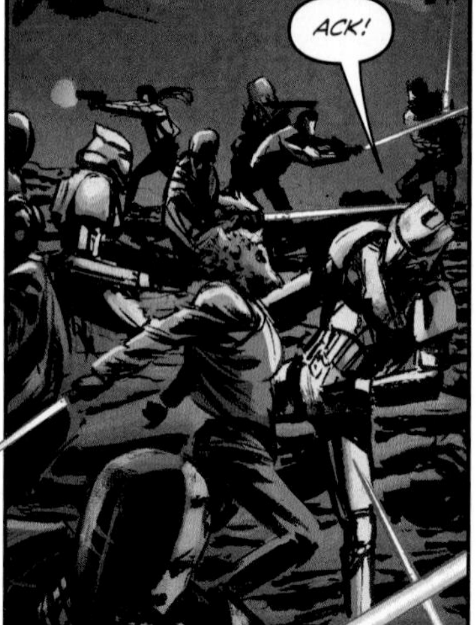
ACK!

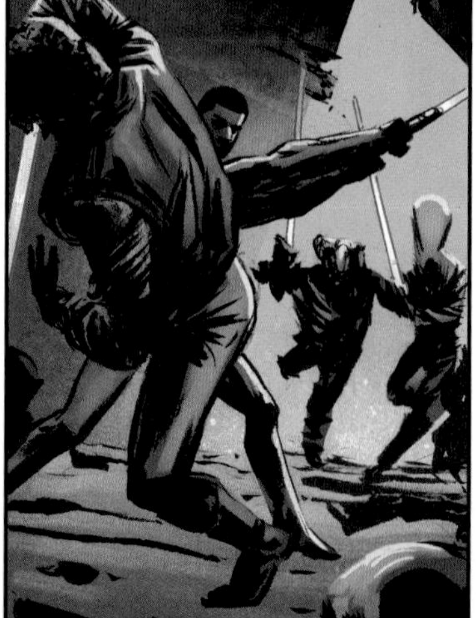
UKK!

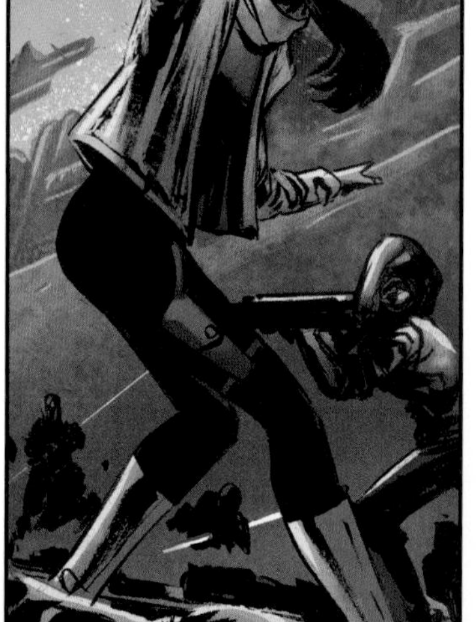
HOW MANY OF THESE GUYS *ARE* THERE?

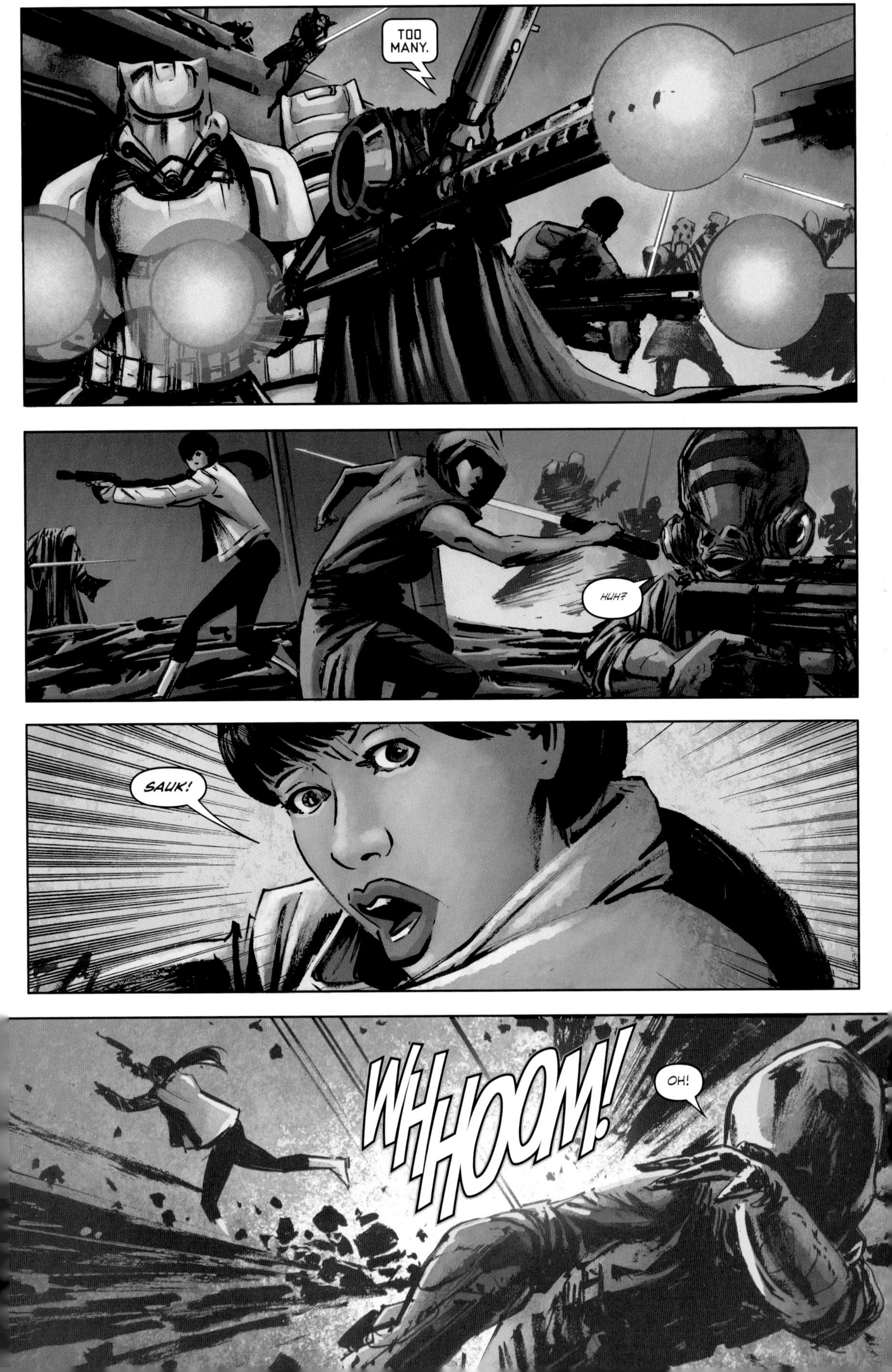
TOO MANY.
HUH?
SAUK!
WHHOOM!
OH!

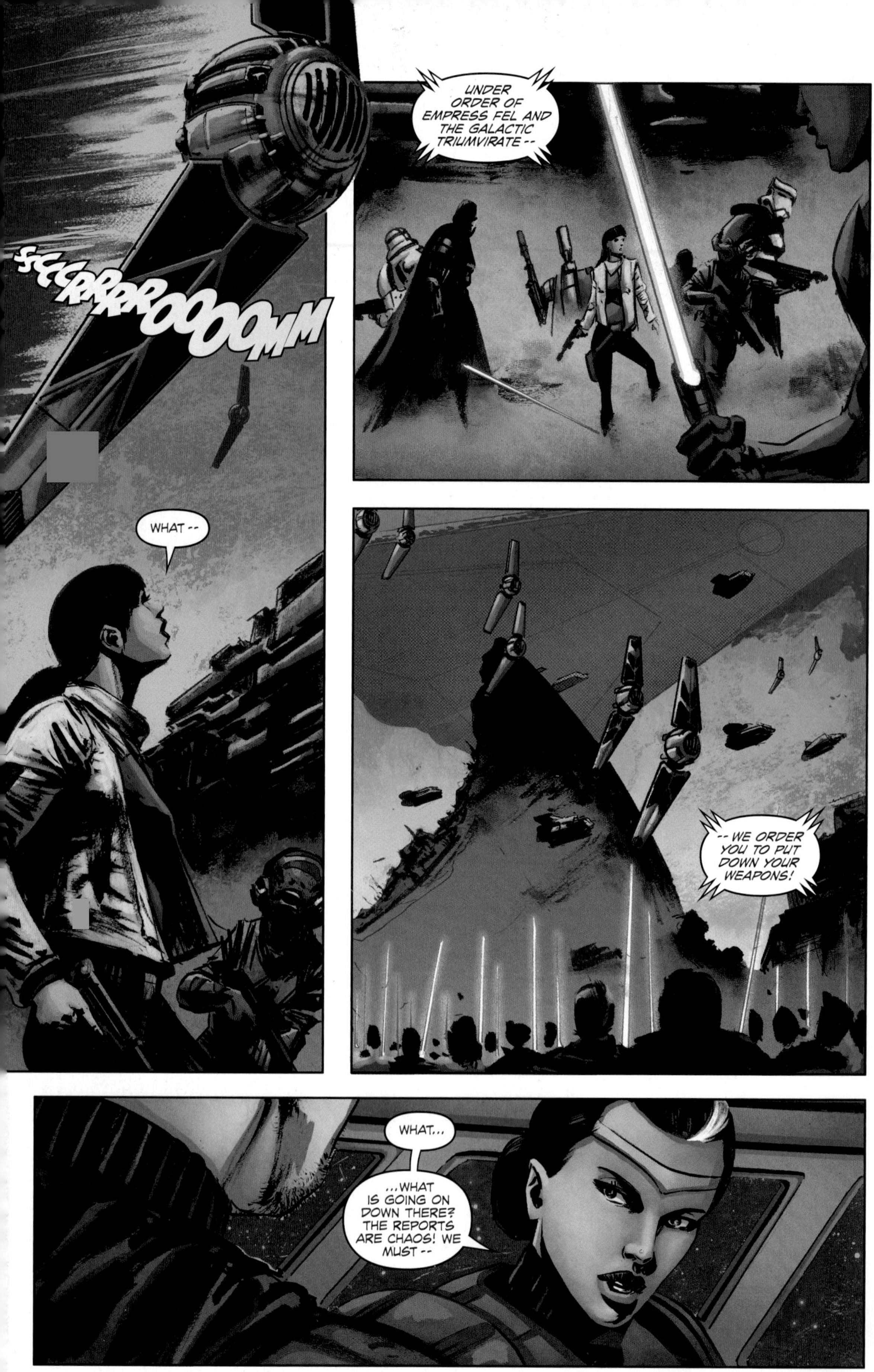
SCCRRRROOOOOMM
UNDER ORDER OF EMPRESS FEL AND THE GALACTIC TRIUMVIRATE --
WHAT --
-- WE ORDER YOU TO PUT DOWN YOUR WEAPONS!
WHAT...
...WHAT IS GOING ON DOWN THERE? THE REPORTS ARE CHAOS! WE MUST --

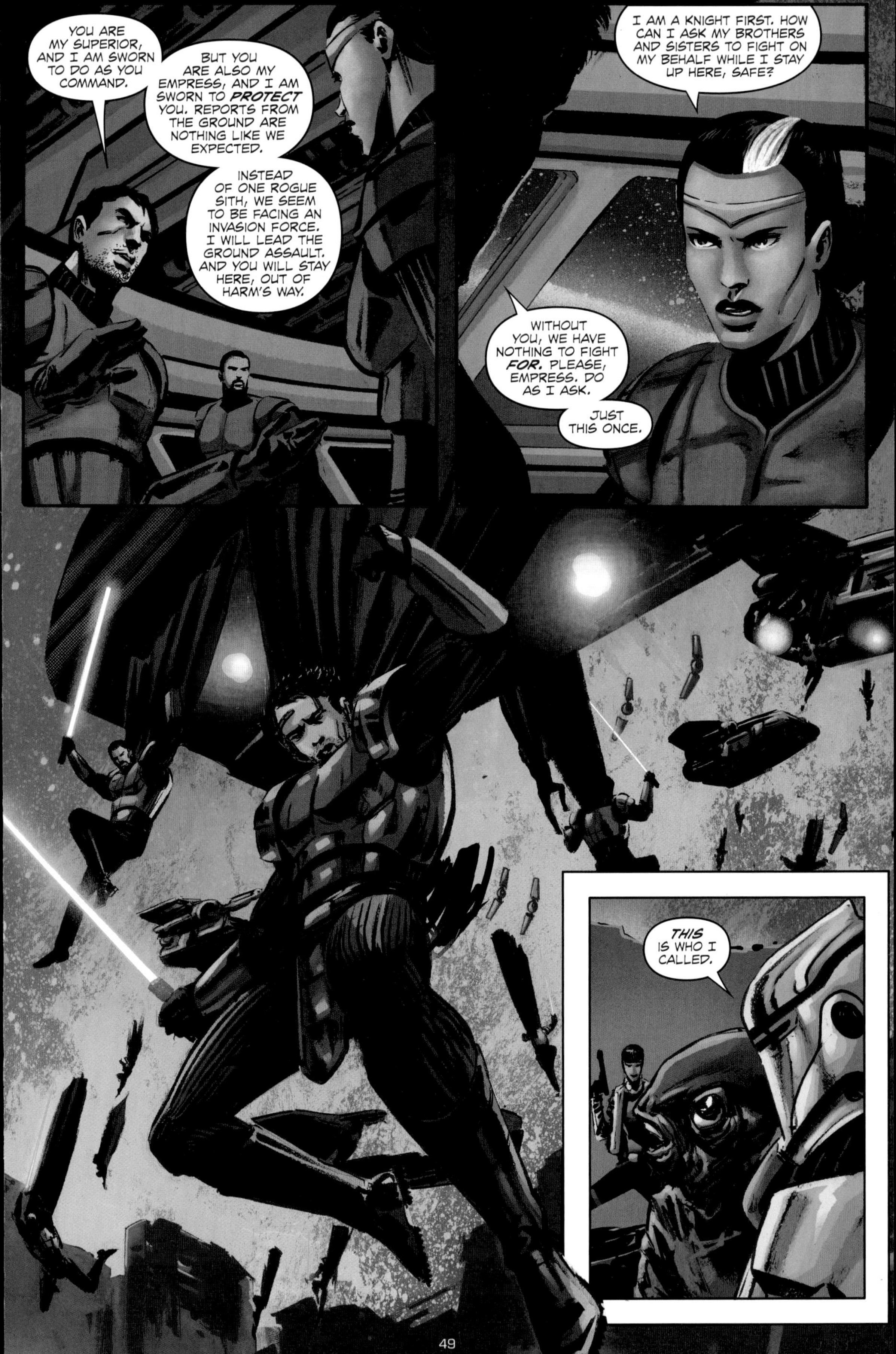
YOU ARE MY SUPERIOR, AND I AM SWORN TO DO AS YOU COMMAND.
BUT YOU ARE ALSO MY EMPRESS, AND I AM SWORN TO *PROTECT* YOU. REPORTS FROM THE GROUND ARE NOTHING LIKE WE EXPECTED.
INSTEAD OF ONE ROGUE SITH, WE SEEM TO BE FACING AN INVASION FORCE. I WILL LEAD THE GROUND ASSAULT. AND YOU WILL STAY HERE, OUT OF HARM'S WAY.
I AM A KNIGHT FIRST. HOW CAN I ASK MY BROTHERS AND SISTERS TO FIGHT ON MY BEHALF WHILE I STAY UP HERE, SAFE?
WITHOUT YOU, WE HAVE NOTHING TO FIGHT *FOR.* PLEASE, EMPRESS. DO AS I ASK.
JUST THIS ONCE.
THIS IS WHO I CALLED.

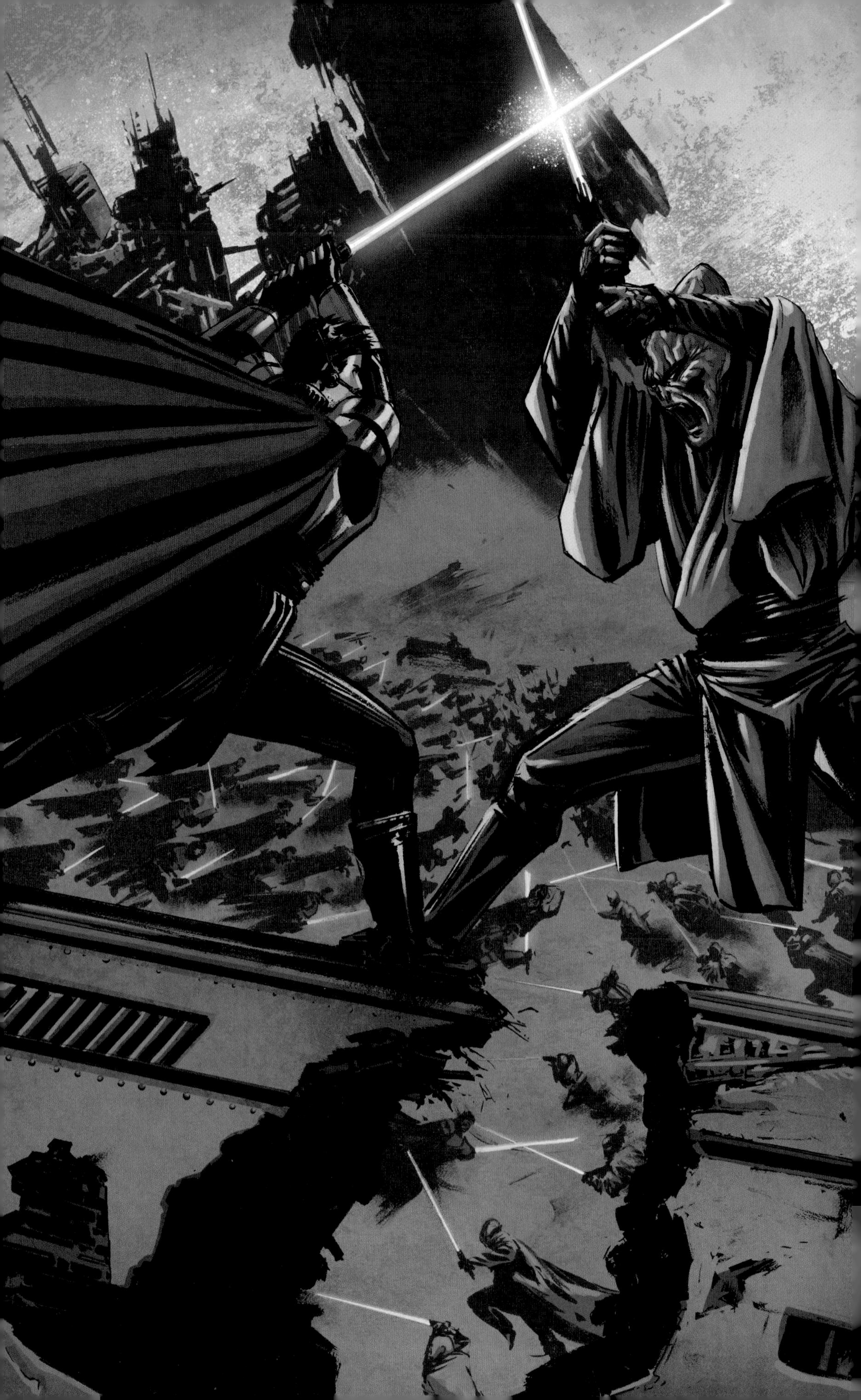

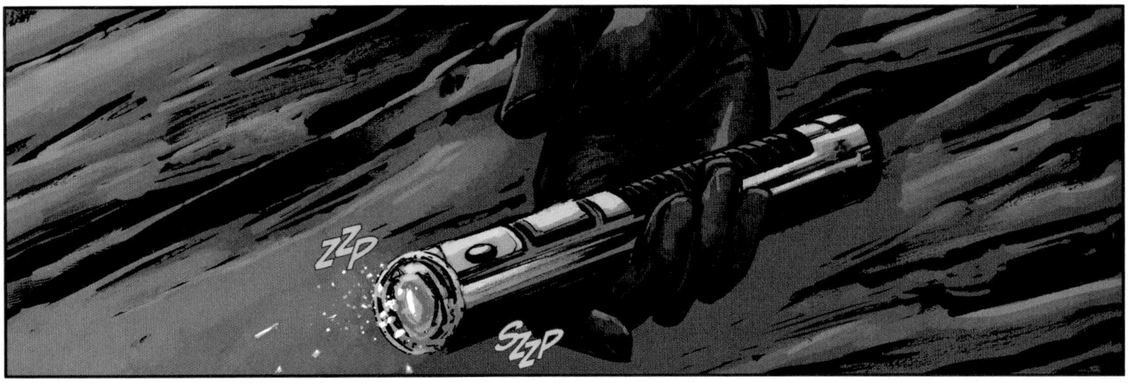
ZZP
SZZP
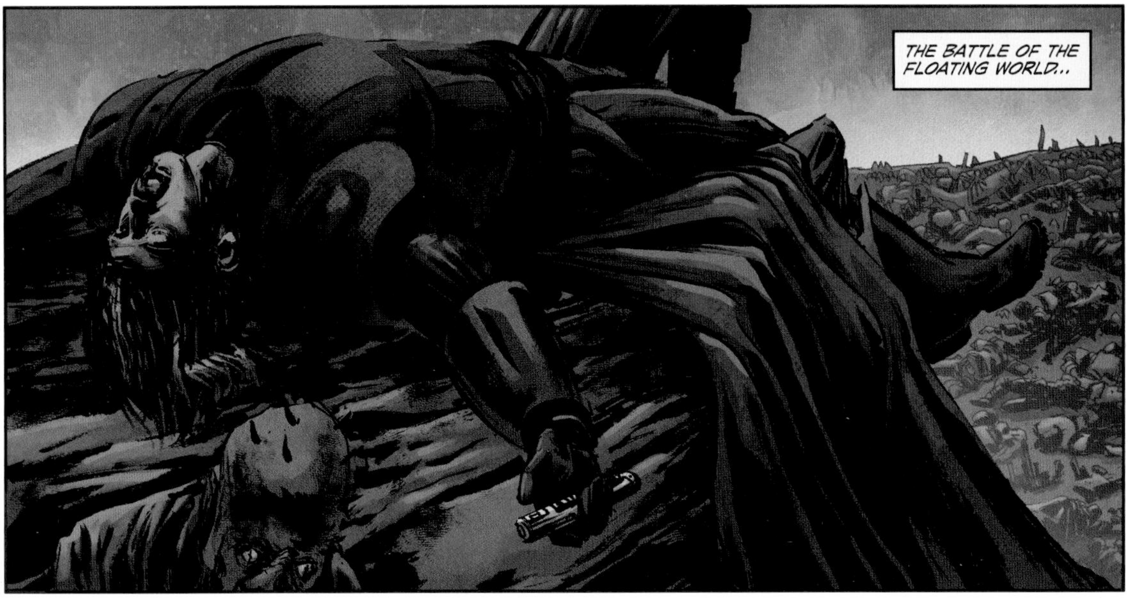
THE BATTLE OF THE FLOATING WORLD...
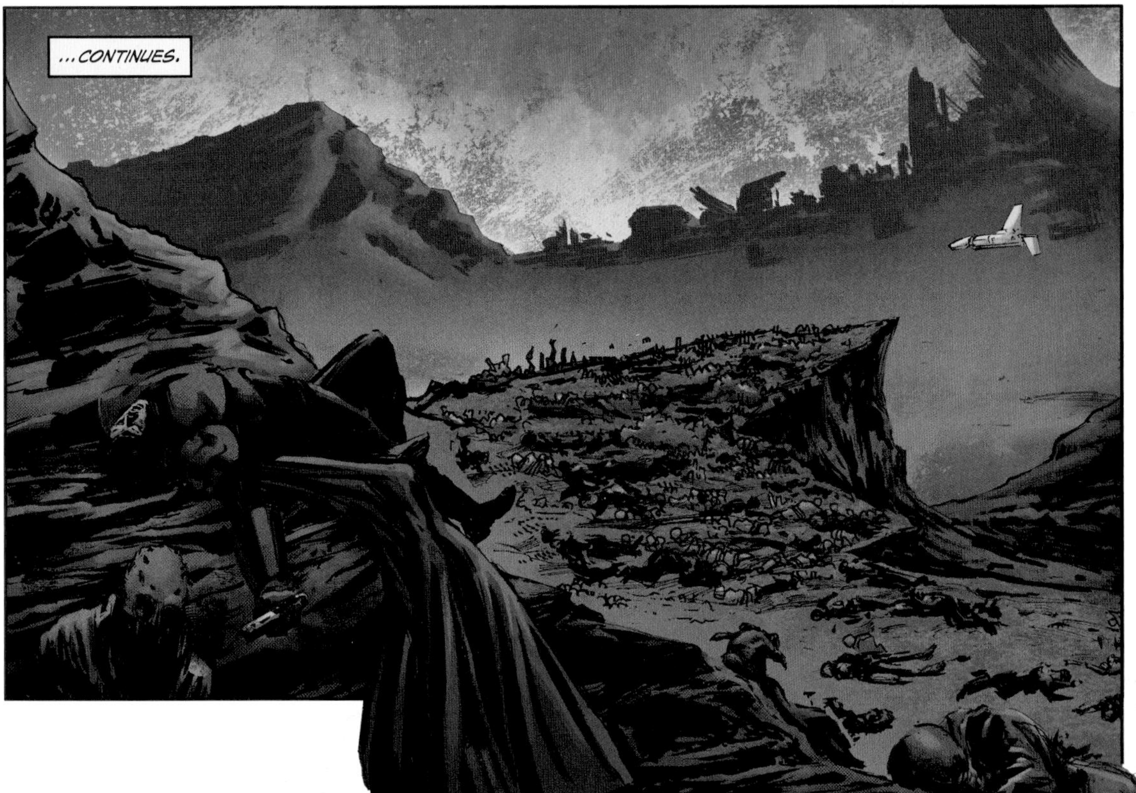
...CONTINUES.

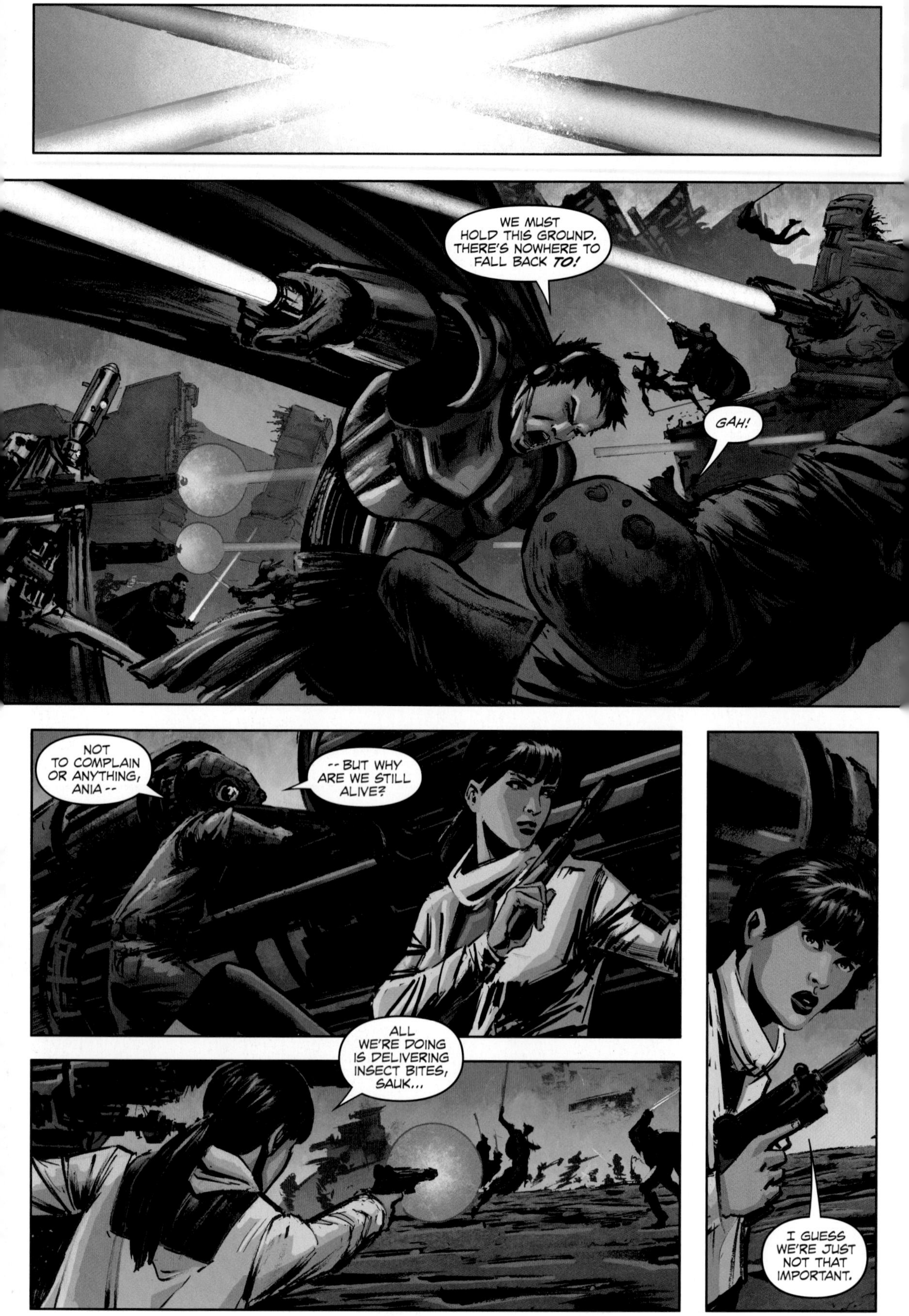
WE MUST HOLD THIS GROUND. THERE'S NOWHERE TO FALL BACK TO!
GAH!
NOT TO COMPLAIN OR ANYTHING, ANIA --
-- BUT WHY ARE WE STILL ALIVE?
ALL WE'RE DOING IS DELIVERING INSECT BITES, SAUK...
I GUESS WE'RE JUST NOT THAT IMPORTANT.

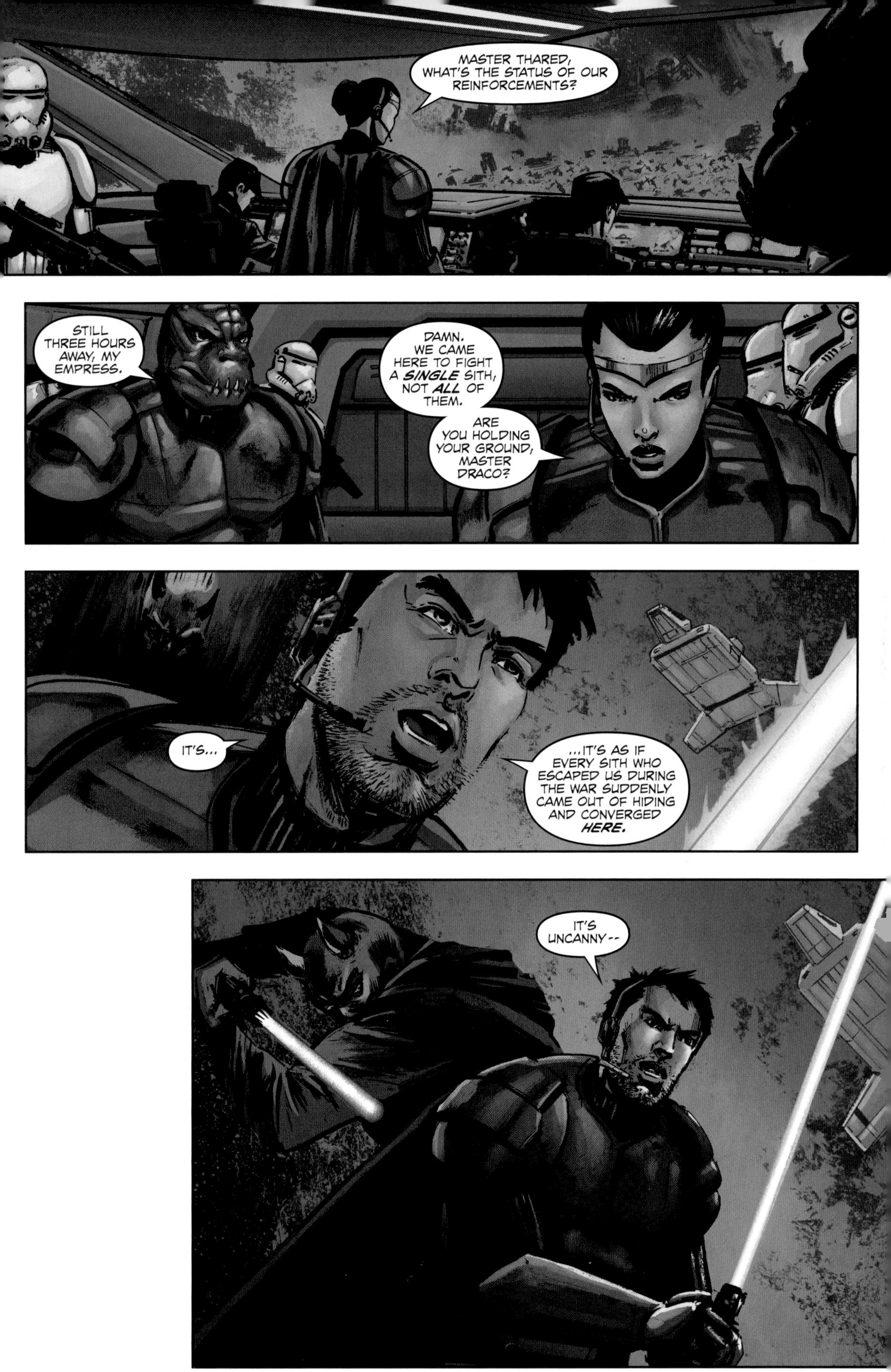
MASTER THARED, WHAT'S THE STATUS OF OUR REINFORCEMENTS?
STILL THREE HOURS AWAY, MY EMPRESS.
DAMN. WE CAME HERE TO FIGHT A ***SINGLE*** SITH, NOT ***ALL*** OF THEM.
ARE YOU HOLDING YOUR GROUND, MASTER DRACO?
IT'S...
...IT'S AS IF EVERY SITH WHO ESCAPED US DURING THE WAR SUDDENLY CAME OUT OF HIDING AND CONVERGED ***HERE.***
IT'S UNCANNY--

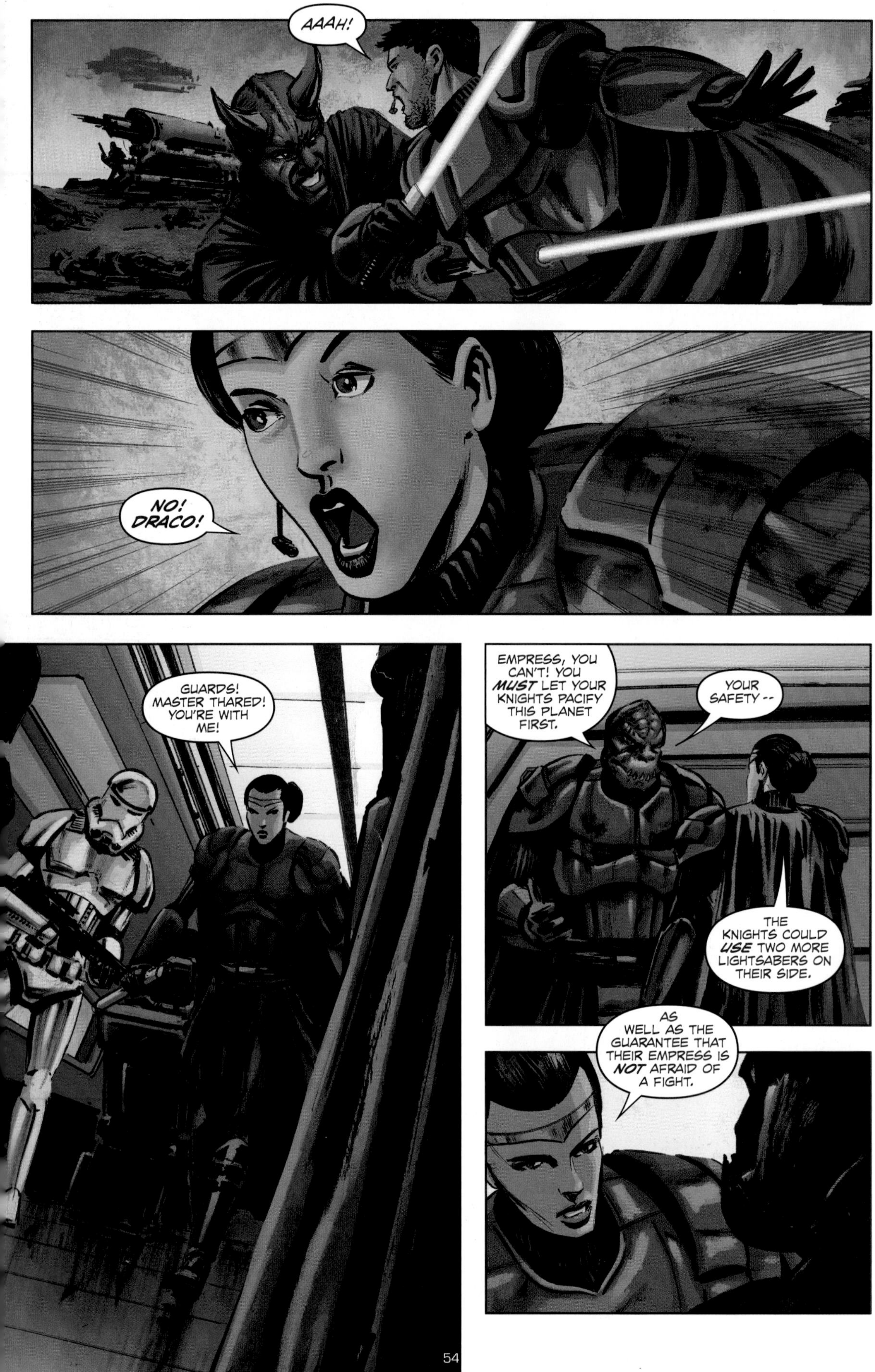
AAAH!
NO! DRACO!
GUARDS! MASTER THARED! YOU'RE WITH ME!
EMPRESS, YOU CAN'T! YOU MUST LET YOUR KNIGHTS PACIFY THIS PLANET FIRST.
YOUR SAFETY --
THE KNIGHTS COULD USE TWO MORE LIGHTSABERS ON THEIR SIDE.
AS WELL AS THE GUARANTEE THAT THEIR EMPRESS IS NOT AFRAID OF A FIGHT.

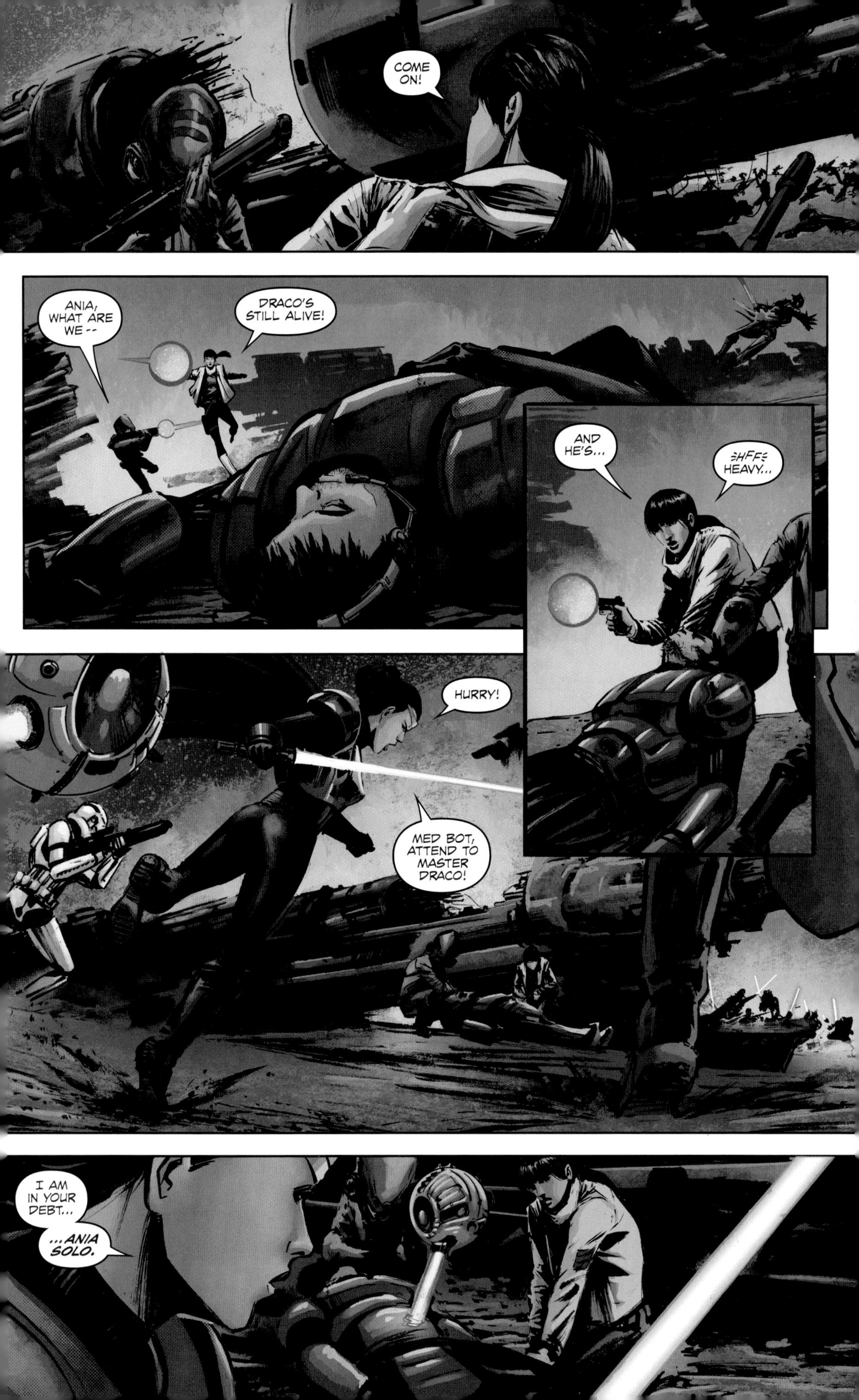
COME ON!
ANIA, WHAT ARE WE --
DRACO'S STILL ALIVE!
AND HE'S...
HFF HEAVY...
HURRY!
MED BOT, ATTEND TO MASTER DRACO!
I AM IN YOUR DEBT...
...ANIA SOLO.

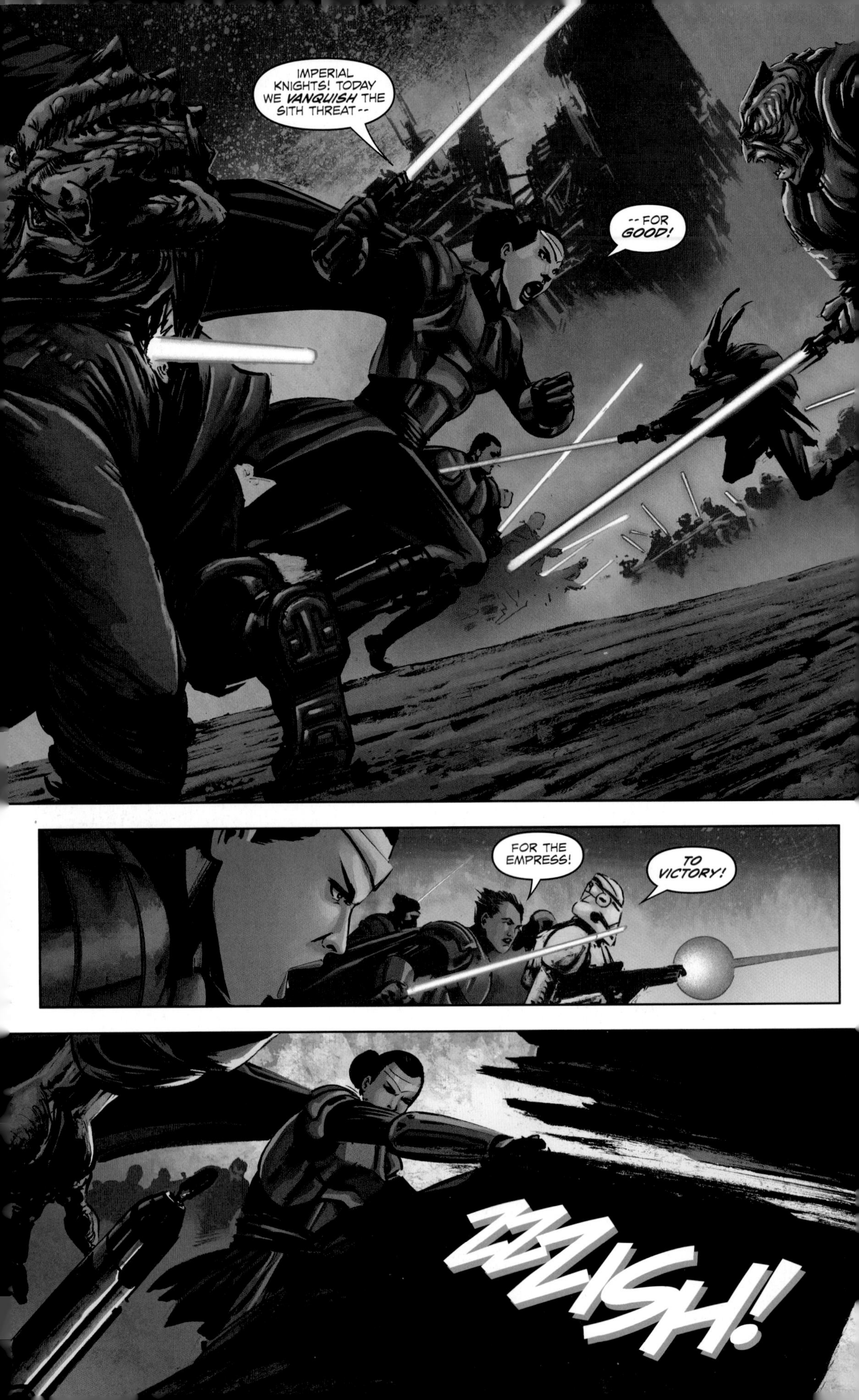
IMPERIAL KNIGHTS! TODAY WE VANQUISH THE SITH THREAT--
--FOR GOOD!
FOR THE EMPRESS!
TO VICTORY!
ZZZISH!

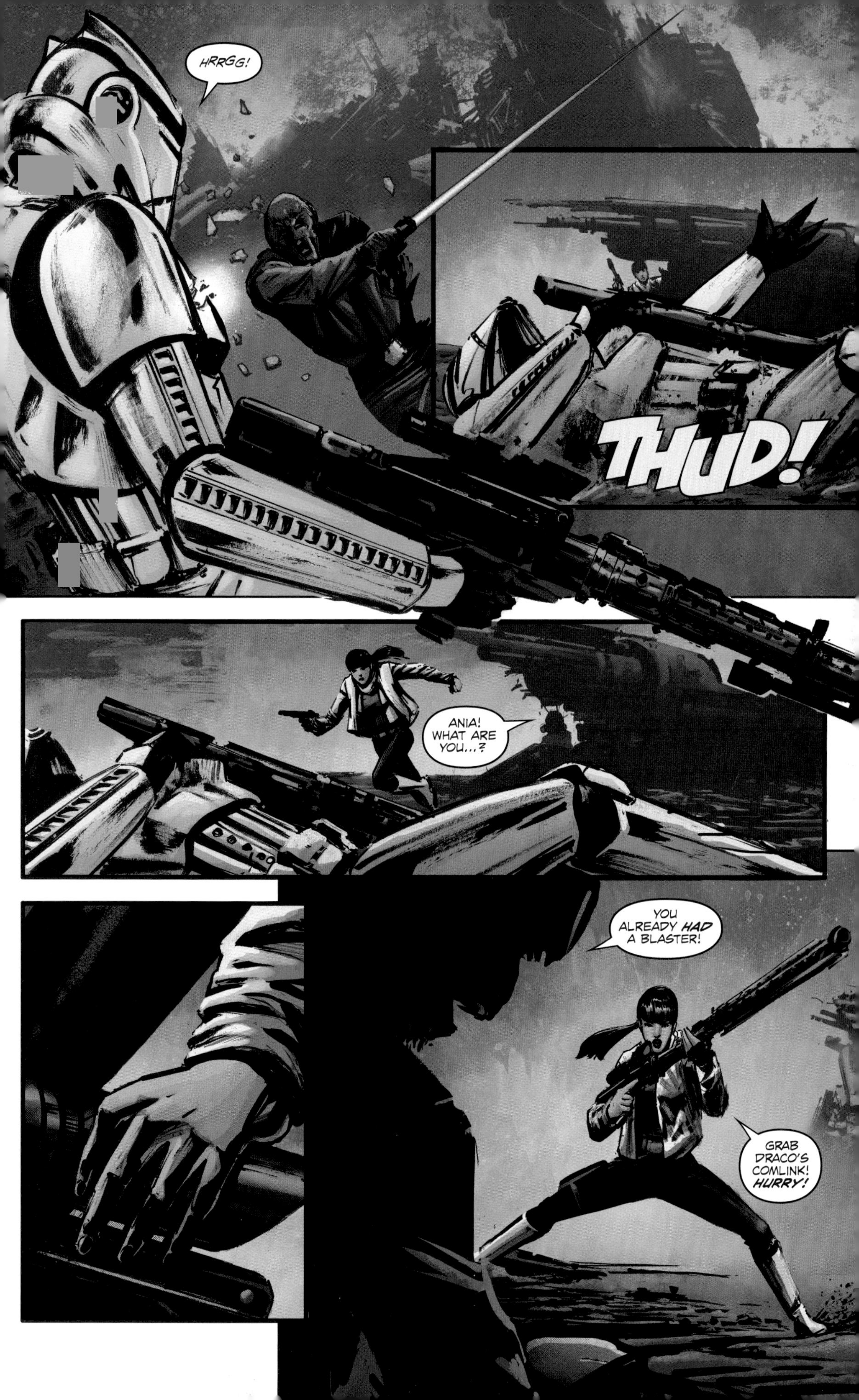
HRRGG!
THUD!
ANIA! WHAT ARE YOU...?
YOU ALREADY HAD A BLASTER!
GRAB DRACO'S COMLINK! HURRY!

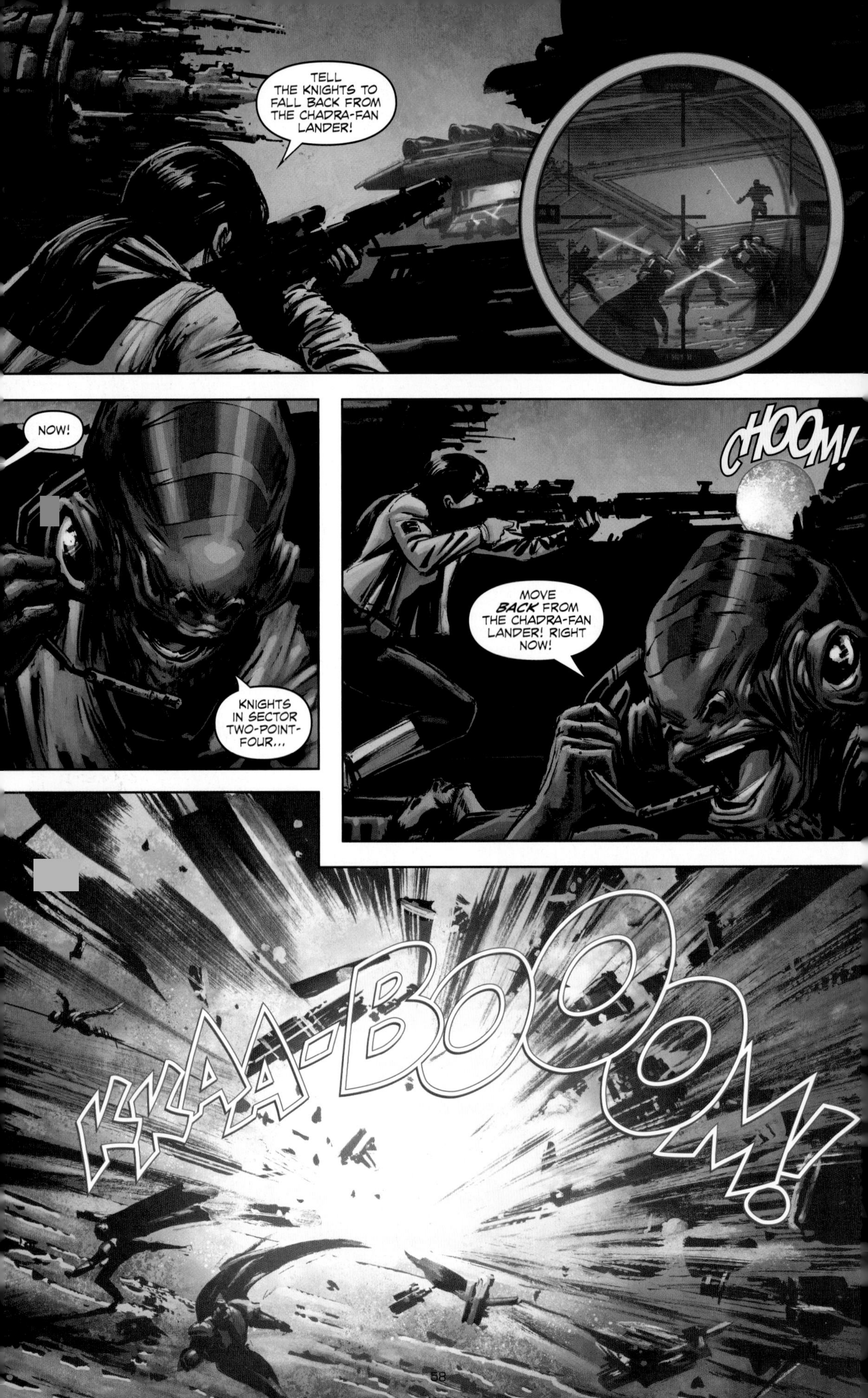
TELL THE KNIGHTS TO FALL BACK FROM THE CHADRA-FAN LANDER!
NOW!
KNIGHTS IN SECTOR TWO-POINT-FOUR...
CHOOM!
MOVE **BACK** FROM THE CHADRA-FAN LANDER! RIGHT NOW!
KLAA-BOOOOM!

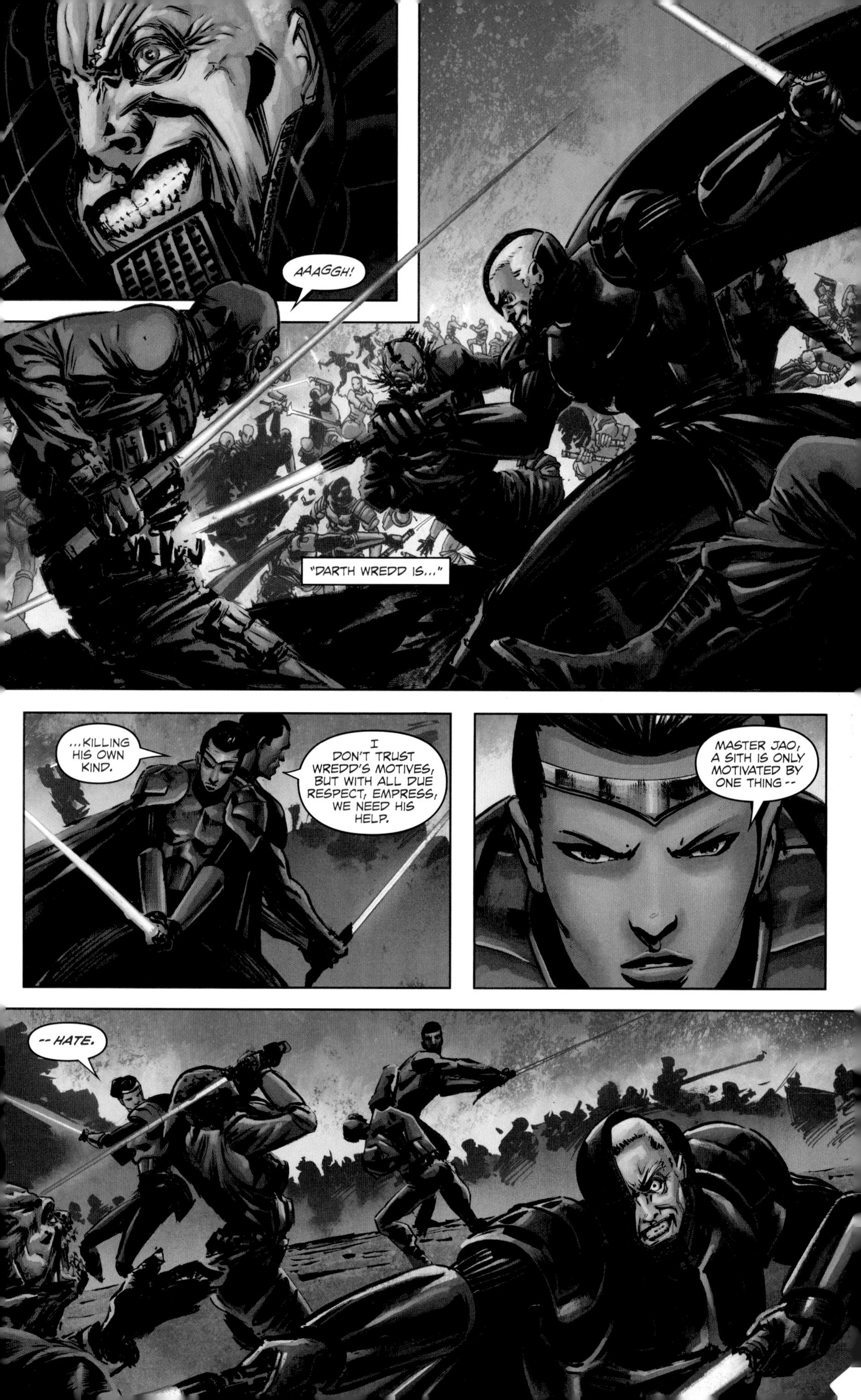
AAAGGH!
"DARTH WREDD IS..."
...KILLING HIS OWN KIND.
I DON'T TRUST WREDD'S MOTIVES, BUT WITH ALL DUE RESPECT, EMPRESS, WE NEED HIS HELP.
MASTER JAO, A SITH IS ONLY MOTIVATED BY ONE THING --
-- HATE.

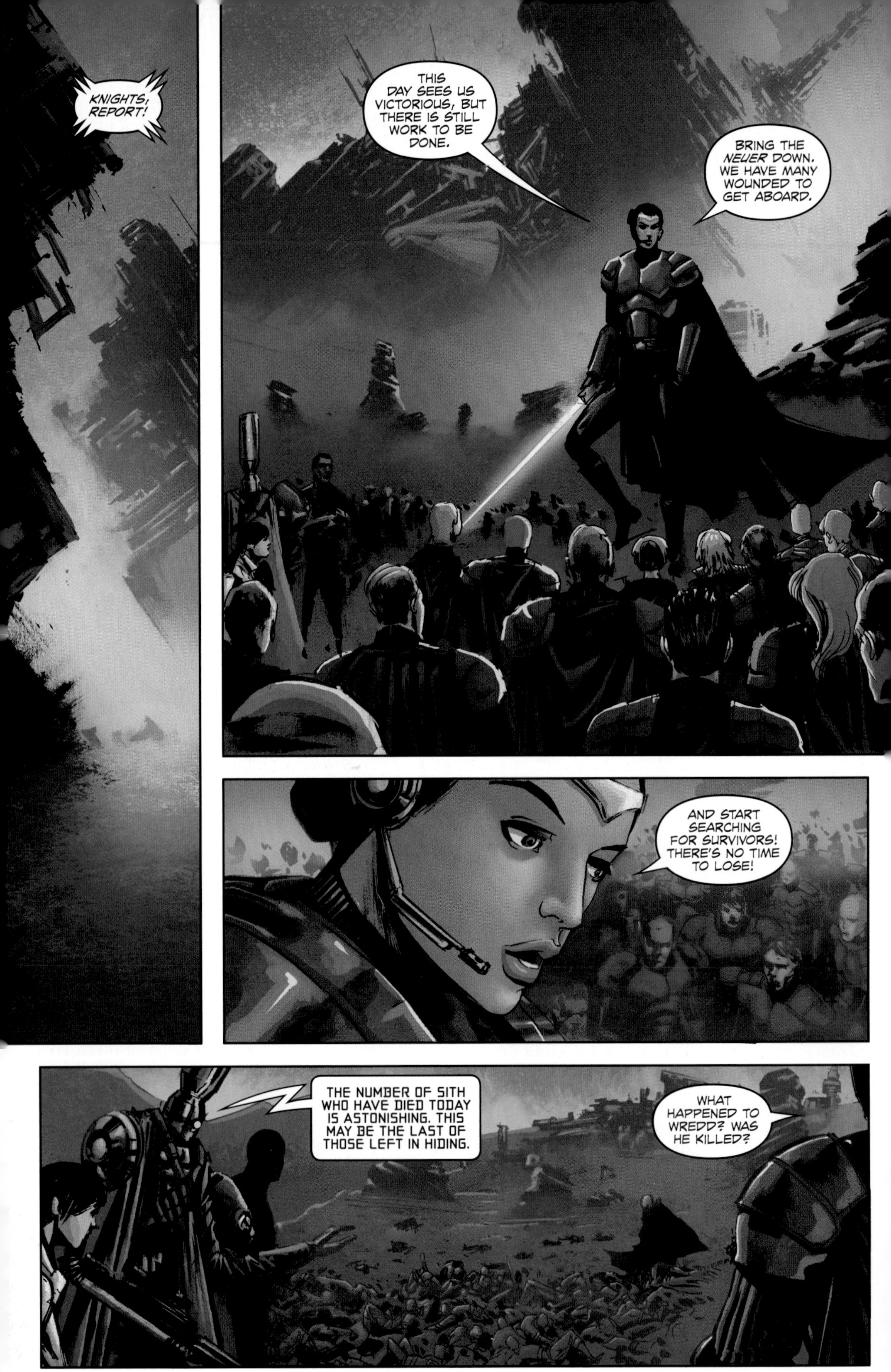

KNIGHTS, REPORT!
THIS DAY SEES US VICTORIOUS, BUT THERE IS STILL WORK TO BE DONE.
BRING THE *NEUER* DOWN. WE HAVE MANY WOUNDED TO GET ABOARD.
AND START SEARCHING FOR SURVIVORS! THERE'S NO TIME TO LOSE!
THE NUMBER OF SITH WHO HAVE DIED TODAY IS ASTONISHING. THIS MAY BE THE LAST OF THOSE LEFT IN HIDING.
WHAT HAPPENED TO WREDD? WAS HE KILLED?

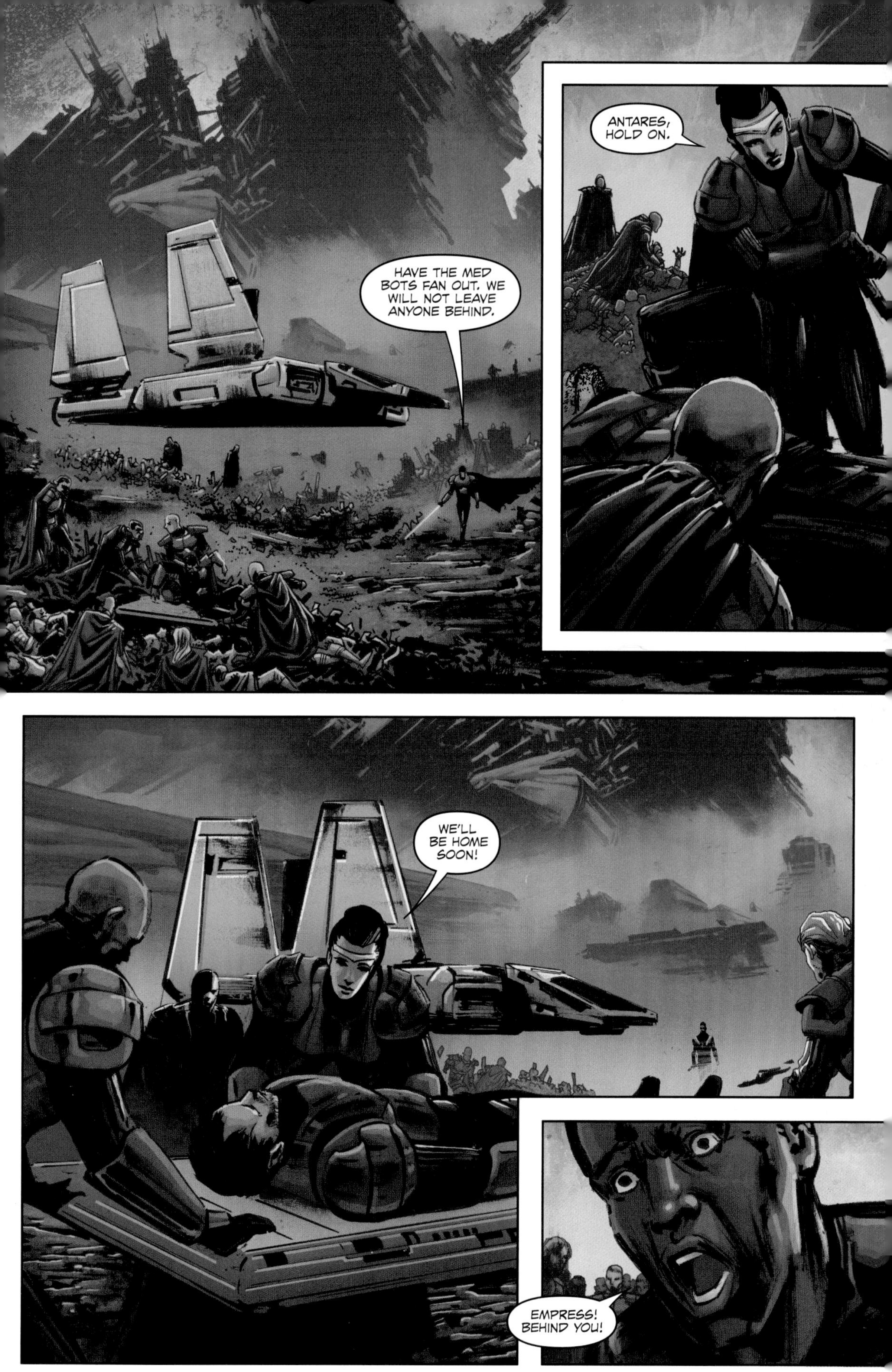
HAVE THE MED BOTS FAN OUT. WE WILL NOT LEAVE ANYONE BEHIND.
ANTARES, HOLD ON.
WE'LL BE HOME SOON!
EMPRESS! BEHIND YOU!

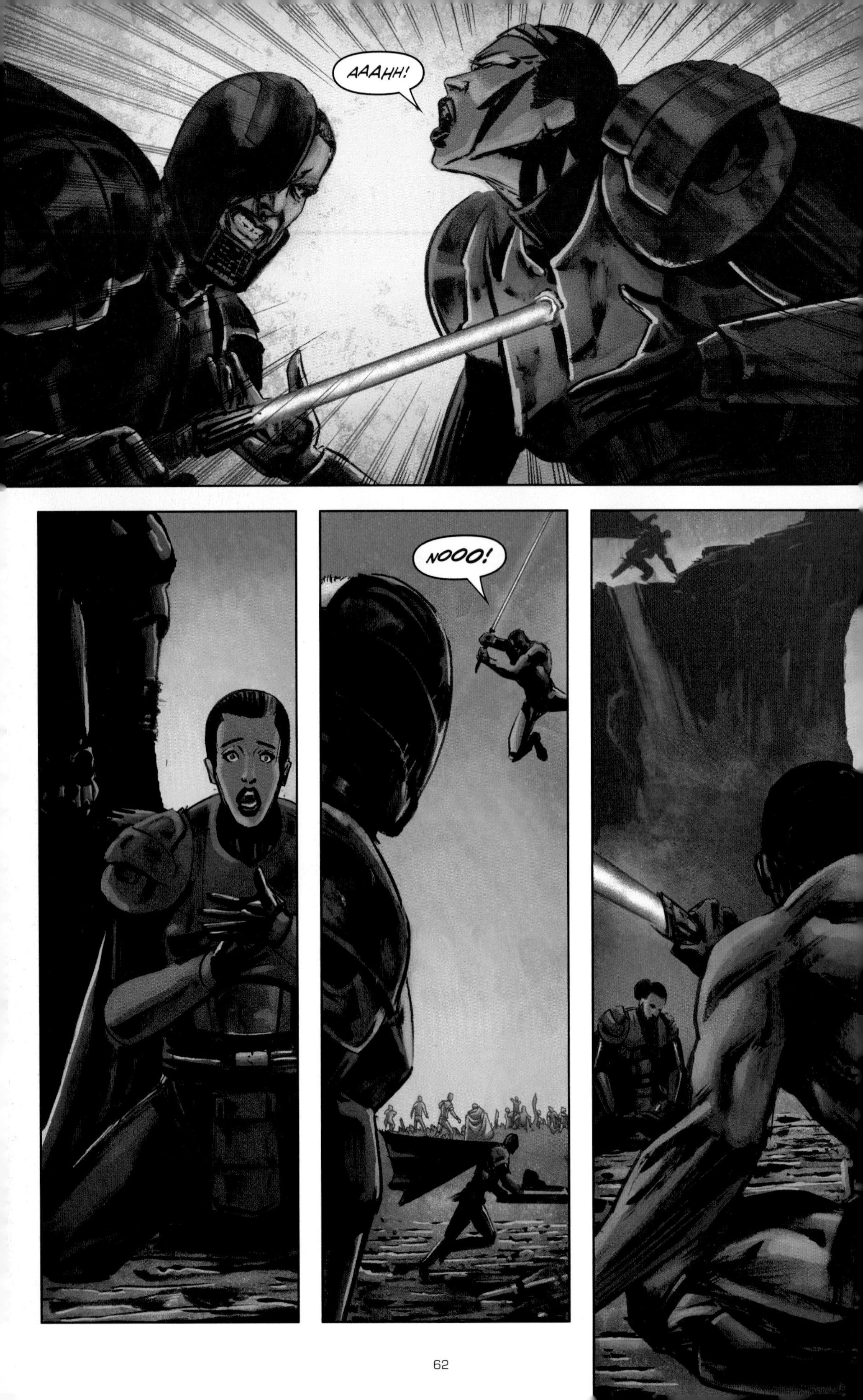
AAAHH!
NOOO!

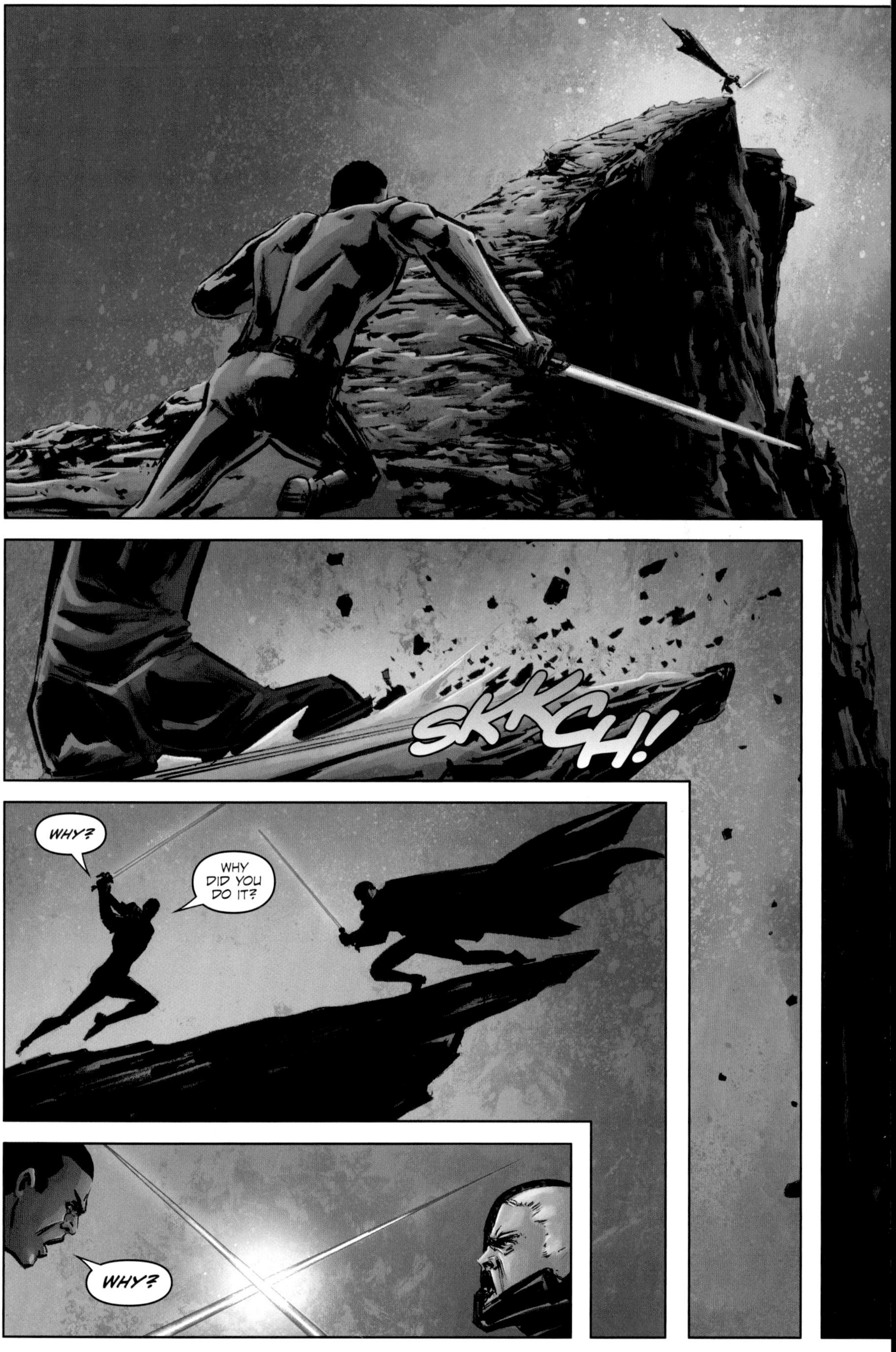
SKKCH!
WHY?
WHY DID YOU DO IT?
WHY?

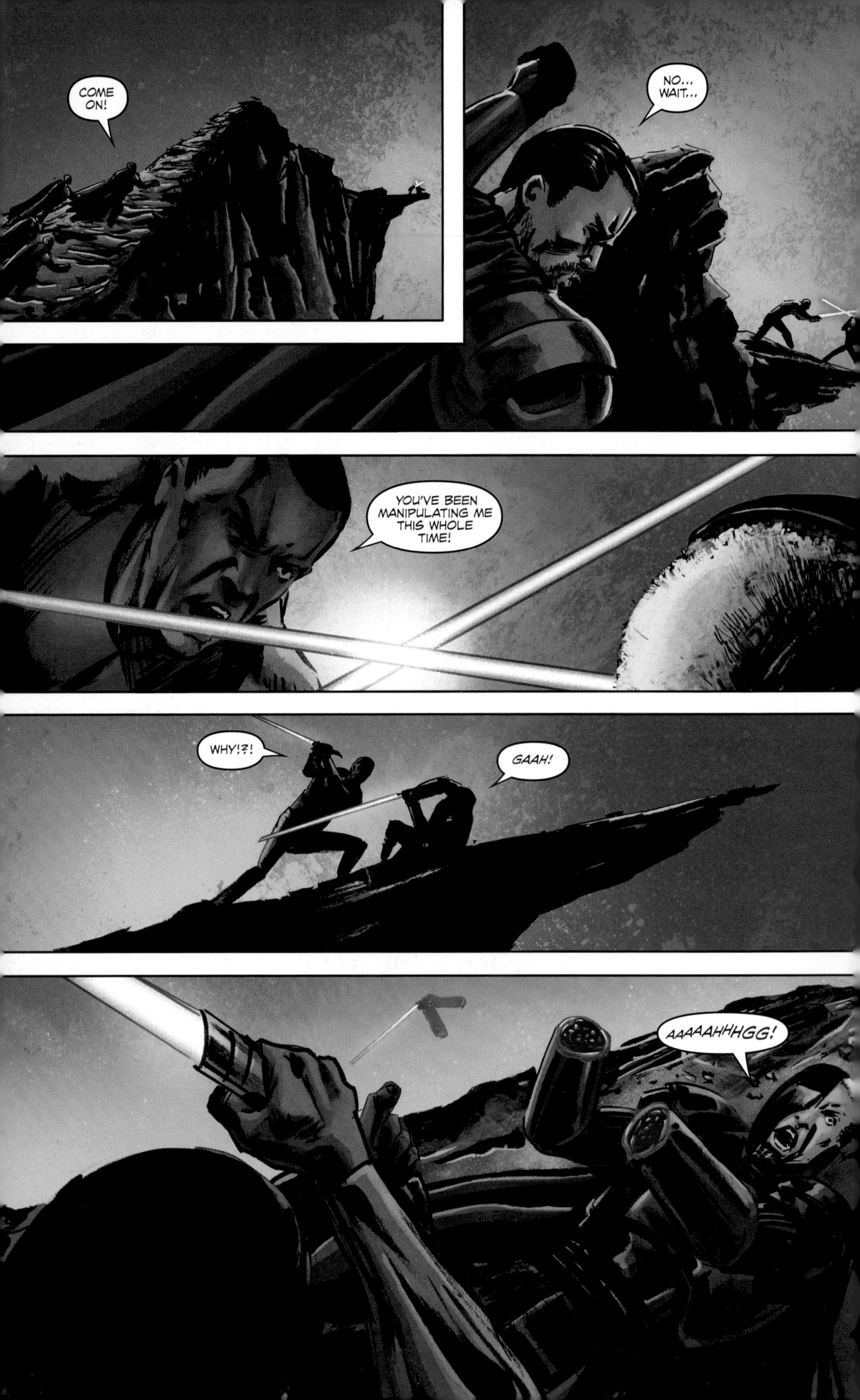
COME ON!
NO... WAIT...
YOU'VE BEEN MANIPULATING ME THIS WHOLE TIME!
WHY!?!
GAAH!
AAAAAHHHGG!

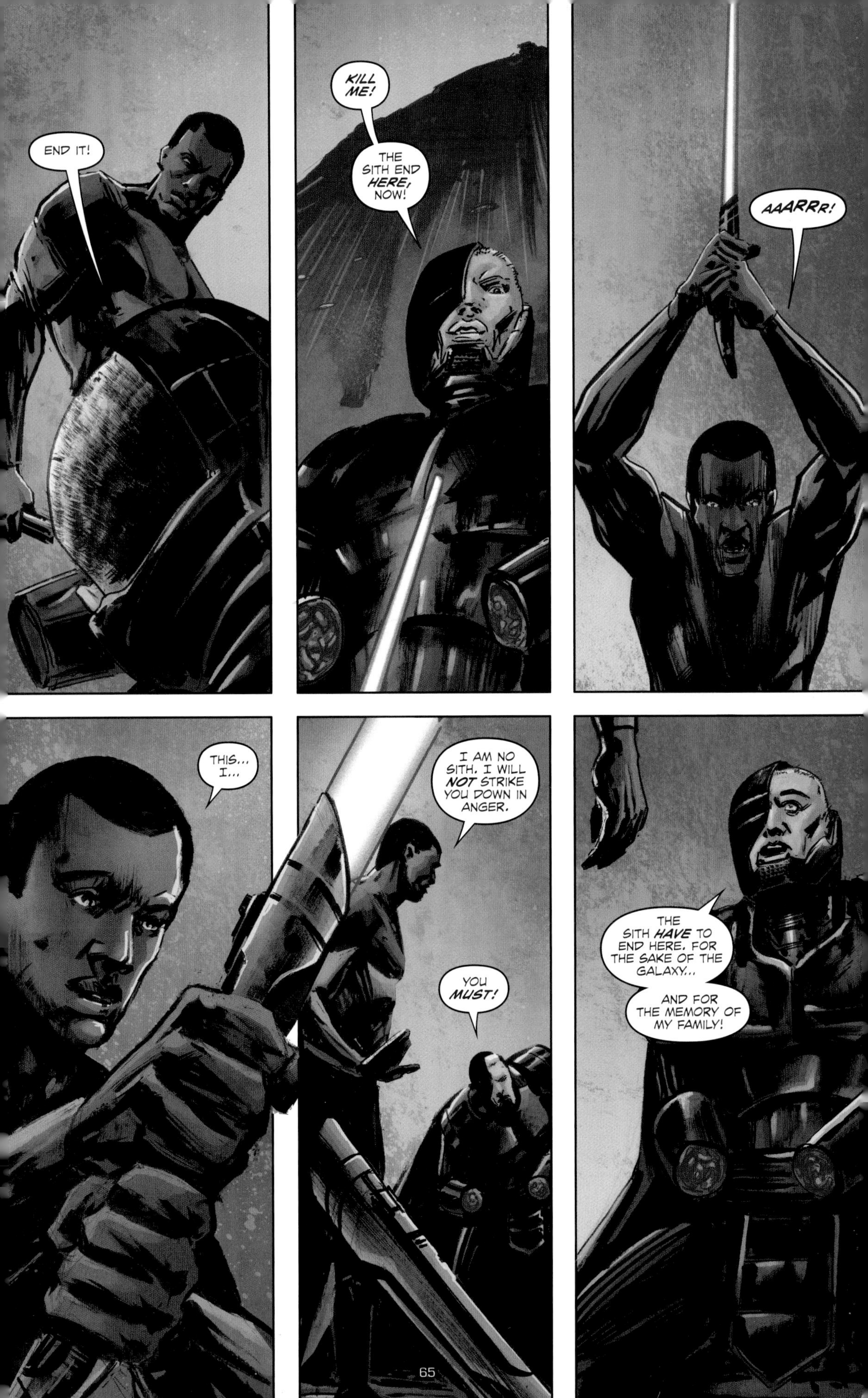
END IT!
KILL ME!
THE SITH END HERE, NOW!
AAARRr!
THIS... I...
I AM NO SITH. I WILL NOT STRIKE YOU DOWN IN ANGER.
YOU MUST!
THE SITH HAVE TO END HERE. FOR THE SAKE OF THE GALAXY...
AND FOR THE MEMORY OF MY FAMILY!

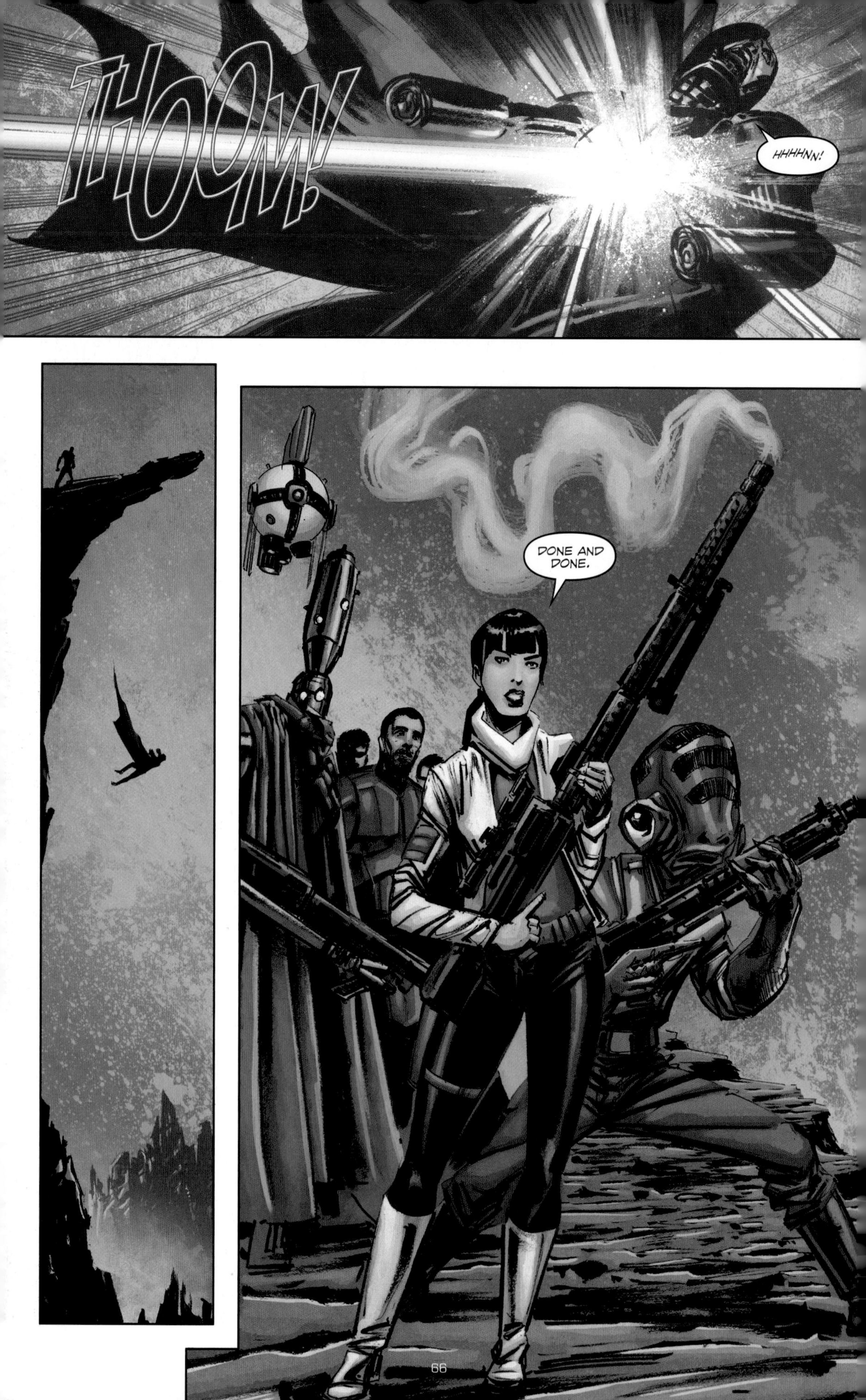
THOOM!
HHHHNN!
DONE AND DONE.

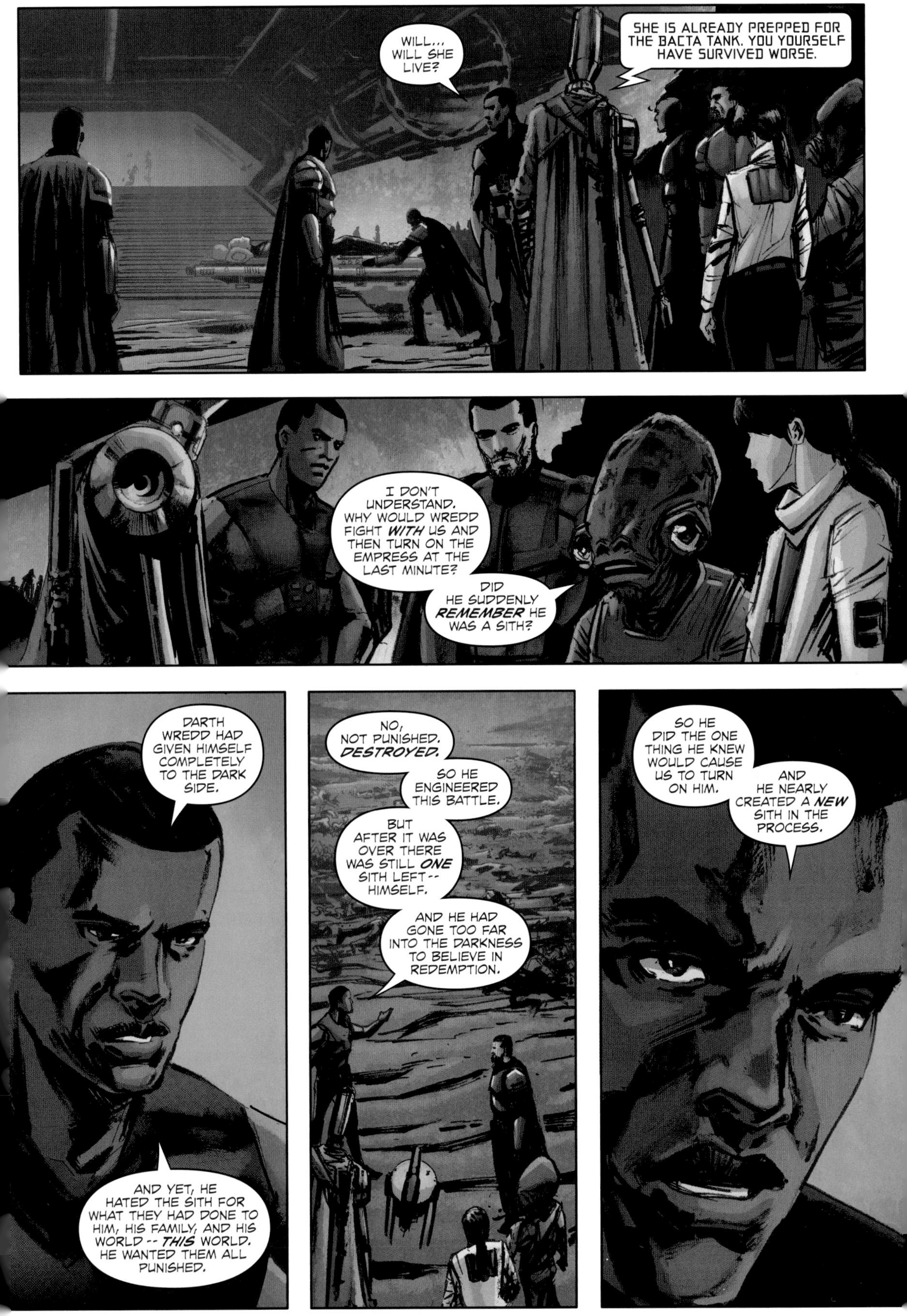
WILL... WILL SHE LIVE?
SHE IS ALREADY PREPPED FOR THE BACTA TANK. YOU YOURSELF HAVE SURVIVED WORSE.
I DON'T UNDERSTAND. WHY WOULD WREDD FIGHT *WITH* US AND THEN TURN ON THE EMPRESS AT THE LAST MINUTE?
DID HE SUDDENLY *REMEMBER* HE WAS A SITH?
DARTH WREDD HAD GIVEN HIMSELF COMPLETELY TO THE DARK SIDE.
AND YET, HE HATED THE SITH FOR WHAT THEY HAD DONE TO HIM, HIS FAMILY, AND HIS WORLD -- *THIS* WORLD. HE WANTED THEM ALL PUNISHED.
NO, NOT PUNISHED. *DESTROYED.*
SO HE ENGINEERED THIS BATTLE.
BUT AFTER IT WAS OVER THERE WAS STILL *ONE* SITH LEFT -- HIMSELF.
AND HE HAD GONE TOO FAR INTO THE DARKNESS TO BELIEVE IN REDEMPTION.
SO HE DID THE ONE THING HE KNEW WOULD CAUSE US TO TURN ON HIM.
AND HE NEARLY CREATED A *NEW* SITH IN THE PROCESS.

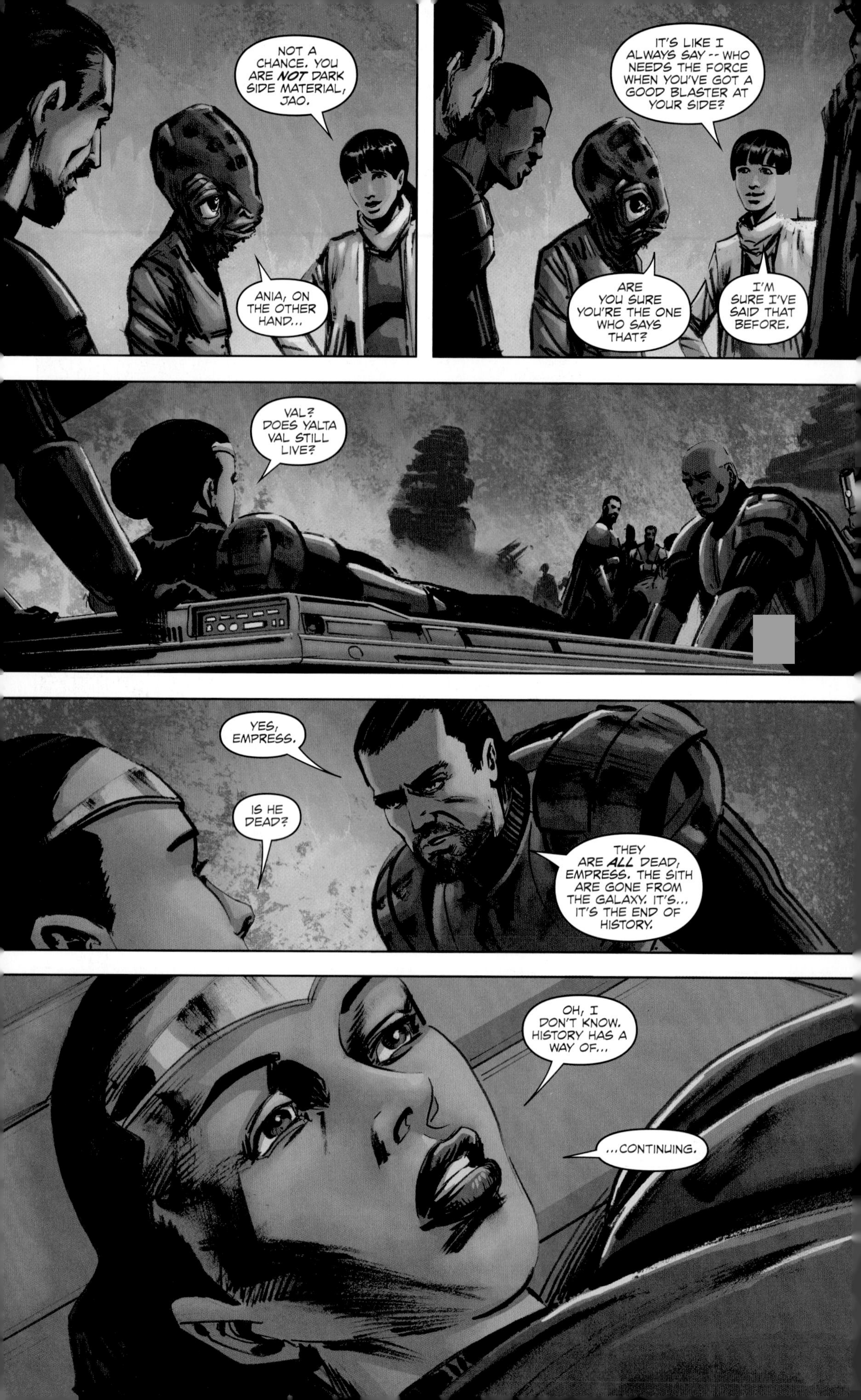
NOT A CHANCE. YOU ARE *NOT* DARK SIDE MATERIAL, JAO.
ANIA, ON THE OTHER HAND...
IT'S LIKE I ALWAYS SAY -- WHO NEEDS THE FORCE WHEN YOU'VE GOT A GOOD BLASTER AT YOUR SIDE?
ARE YOU SURE YOU'RE THE ONE WHO SAYS THAT?
I'M SURE I'VE SAID THAT BEFORE.
VAL? DOES YALTA VAL STILL LIVE?
YES, EMPRESS.
IS HE DEAD?
THEY ARE *ALL* DEAD, EMPRESS. THE SITH ARE GONE FROM THE GALAXY. IT'S... IT'S THE END OF HISTORY.
OH, I DON'T KNOW. HISTORY HAS A WAY OF...
...CONTINUING.

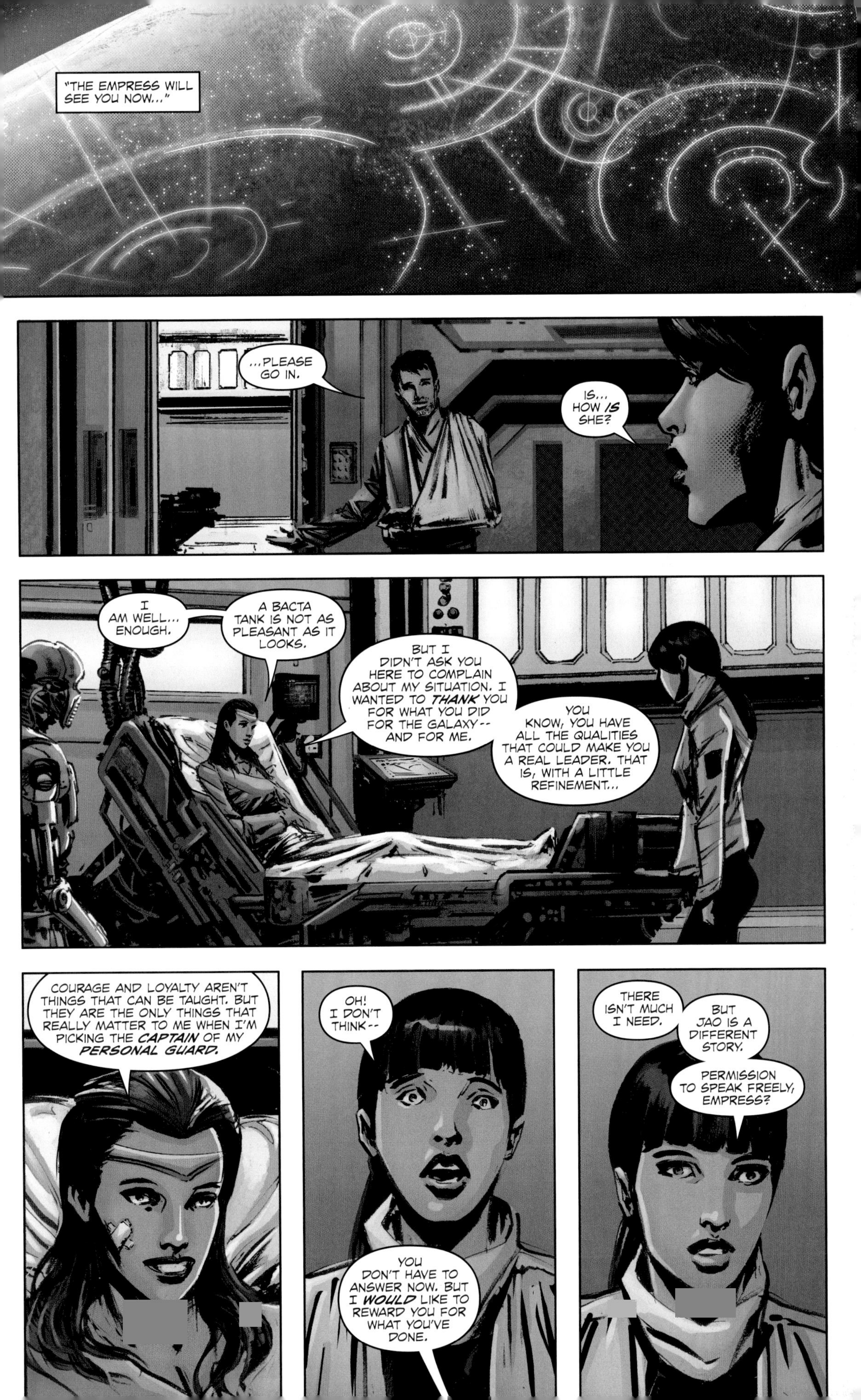
"THE EMPRESS WILL SEE YOU NOW..."
...PLEASE GO IN.
IS... HOW *IS* SHE?
I AM WELL... ENOUGH.
A BACTA TANK IS NOT AS PLEASANT AS IT LOOKS.
BUT I DIDN'T ASK YOU HERE TO COMPLAIN ABOUT MY SITUATION. I WANTED TO *THANK* YOU FOR WHAT YOU DID FOR THE GALAXY--AND FOR ME.
YOU KNOW, YOU HAVE ALL THE QUALITIES THAT COULD MAKE YOU A REAL LEADER. THAT IS, WITH A LITTLE REFINEMENT...
COURAGE AND LOYALTY AREN'T THINGS THAT CAN BE TAUGHT. BUT THEY ARE THE ONLY THINGS THAT REALLY MATTER TO ME WHEN I'M PICKING THE *CAPTAIN* OF MY *PERSONAL GUARD.*
OH! I DON'T THINK--
YOU DON'T HAVE TO ANSWER NOW. BUT I *WOULD* LIKE TO REWARD YOU FOR WHAT YOU'VE DONE.
THERE ISN'T MUCH I NEED.
BUT JAO IS A DIFFERENT STORY.
PERMISSION TO SPEAK FREELY, EMPRESS?

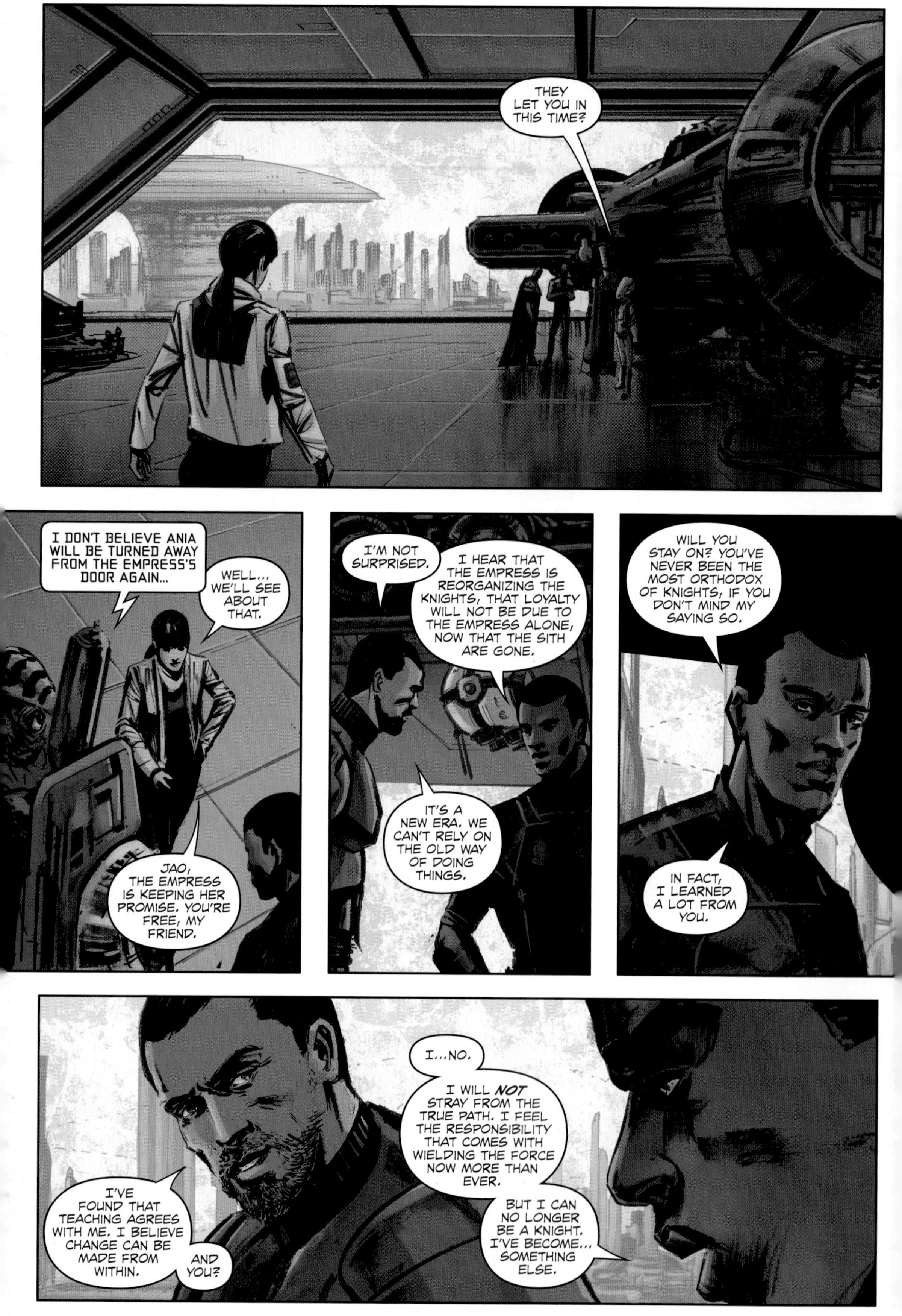
THEY LET YOU IN THIS TIME?
I DON'T BELIEVE ANIA WILL BE TURNED AWAY FROM THE EMPRESS'S DOOR AGAIN...
WELL... WE'LL SEE ABOUT THAT.
JAO, THE EMPRESS IS KEEPING HER PROMISE. YOU'RE FREE, MY FRIEND.
I'M NOT SURPRISED.
I HEAR THAT THE EMPRESS IS REORGANIZING THE KNIGHTS, THAT LOYALTY WILL NOT BE DUE TO THE EMPRESS ALONE, NOW THAT THE SITH ARE GONE.
IT'S A NEW ERA. WE CAN'T RELY ON THE OLD WAY OF DOING THINGS.
WILL YOU STAY ON? YOU'VE NEVER BEEN THE MOST ORTHODOX OF KNIGHTS, IF YOU DON'T MIND MY SAYING SO.
IN FACT, I LEARNED A LOT FROM YOU.
I'VE FOUND THAT TEACHING AGREES WITH ME. I BELIEVE CHANGE CAN BE MADE FROM WITHIN.
AND YOU?
I...NO.
I WILL NOT STRAY FROM THE TRUE PATH. I FEEL THE RESPONSIBILITY THAT COMES WITH WIELDING THE FORCE NOW MORE THAN EVER.
BUT I CAN NO LONGER BE A KNIGHT. I'VE BECOME... SOMETHING ELSE.

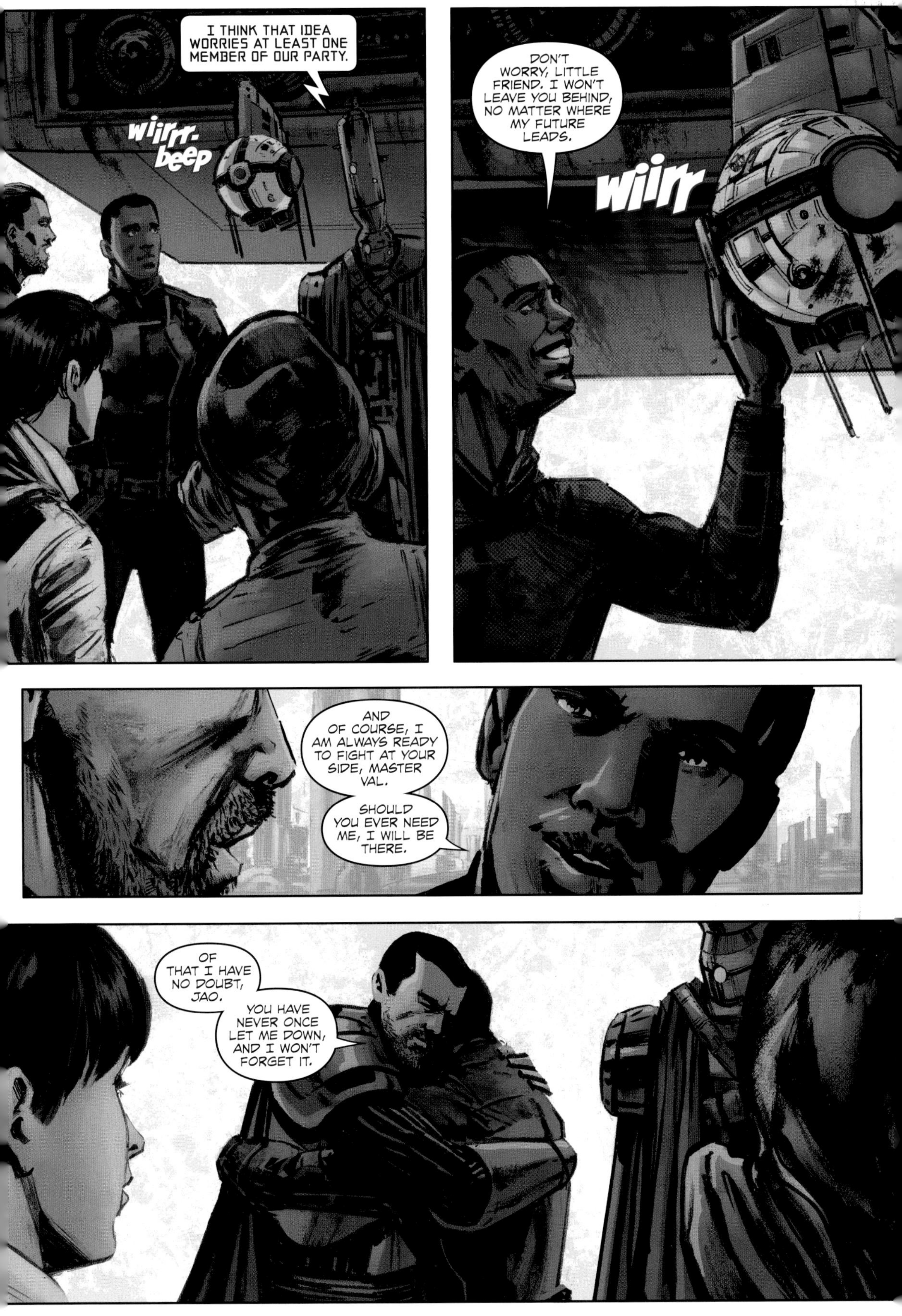
I THINK THAT IDEA WORRIES AT LEAST ONE MEMBER OF OUR PARTY.
wiirrr-beep
DON'T WORRY, LITTLE FRIEND. I WON'T LEAVE YOU BEHIND, NO MATTER WHERE MY FUTURE LEADS.
wiirr
AND OF COURSE, I AM ALWAYS READY TO FIGHT AT YOUR SIDE, MASTER VAL.
SHOULD YOU EVER NEED ME, I WILL BE THERE.
OF THAT I HAVE NO DOUBT, JAO.
YOU HAVE NEVER ONCE LET ME DOWN, AND I WON'T FORGET IT.

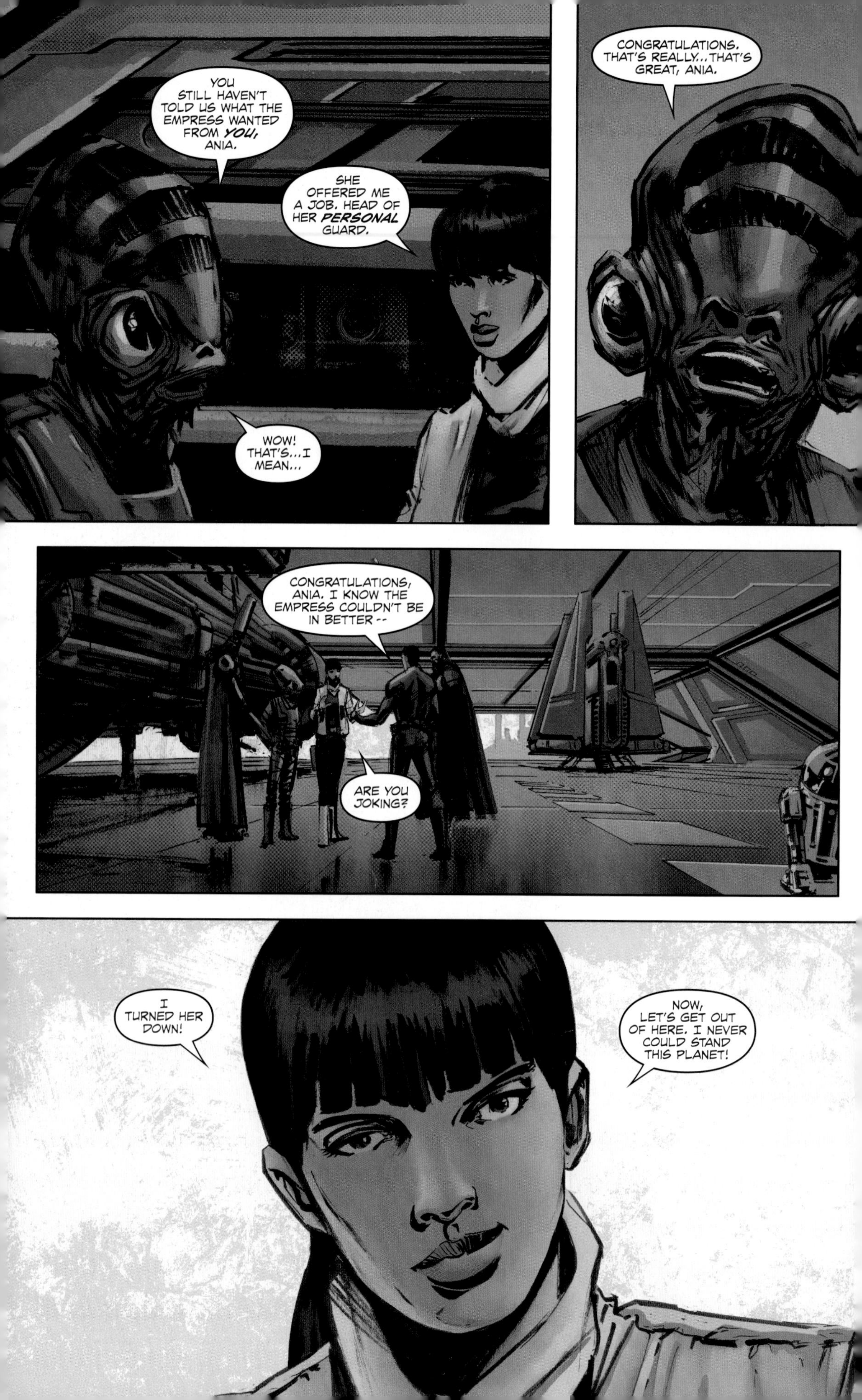
YOU STILL HAVEN'T TOLD US WHAT THE EMPRESS WANTED FROM *YOU,* ANIA.
SHE OFFERED ME A JOB. HEAD OF HER *PERSONAL* GUARD.
WOW! THAT'S... I MEAN...
CONGRATULATIONS. THAT'S REALLY... THAT'S GREAT, ANIA.
CONGRATULATIONS, ANIA. I KNOW THE EMPRESS COULDN'T BE IN BETTER --
ARE YOU JOKING?
I TURNED HER DOWN!
NOW, LET'S GET OUT OF HERE. I NEVER COULD STAND THIS PLANET!

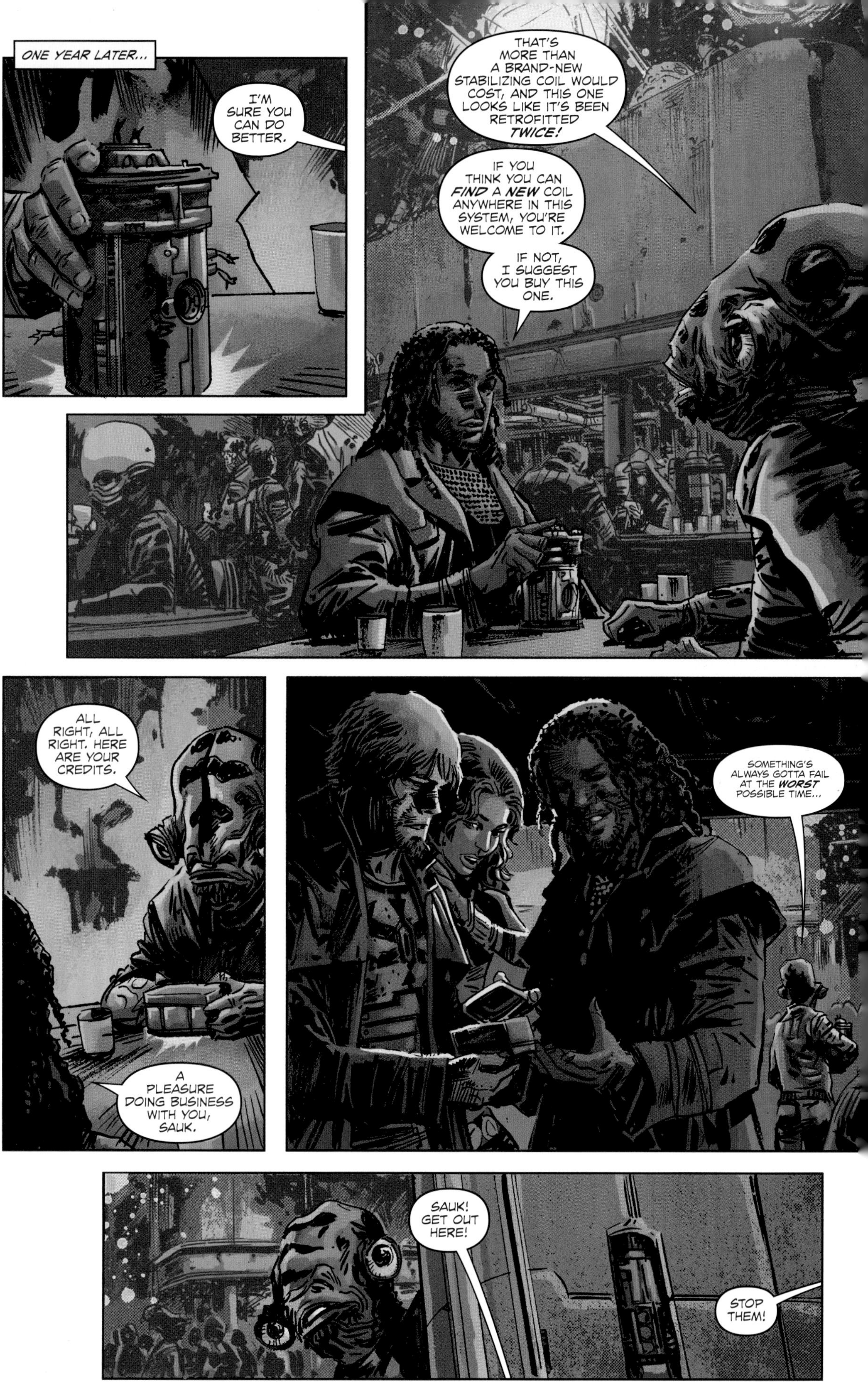
ONE YEAR LATER...
I'M SURE YOU CAN DO BETTER.
THAT'S MORE THAN A BRAND-NEW STABILIZING COIL WOULD COST, AND THIS ONE LOOKS LIKE IT'S BEEN RETROFITTED TWICE!
IF YOU THINK YOU CAN FIND A NEW COIL ANYWHERE IN THIS SYSTEM, YOU'RE WELCOME TO IT.
IF NOT, I SUGGEST YOU BUY THIS ONE.
ALL RIGHT, ALL RIGHT. HERE ARE YOUR CREDITS.
A PLEASURE DOING BUSINESS WITH YOU, SAUK.
SOMETHING'S ALWAYS GOTTA FAIL AT THE WORST POSSIBLE TIME...
SAUK! GET OUT HERE!
STOP THEM!

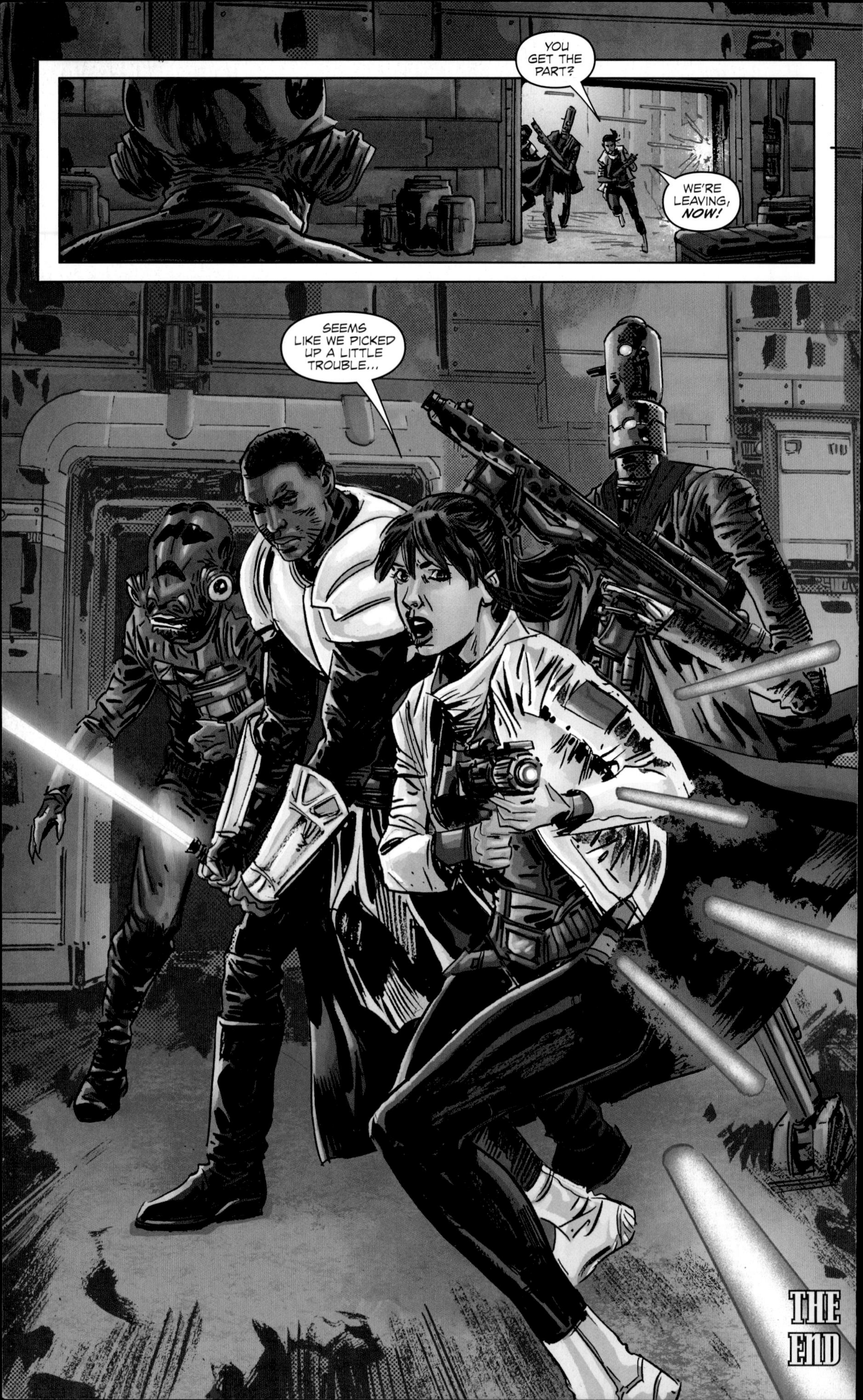
YOU GET THE PART?
WE'RE LEAVING, NOW!
SEEMS LIKE WE PICKED UP A LITTLE TROUBLE...
THE END

LEGACY HANDBOOK

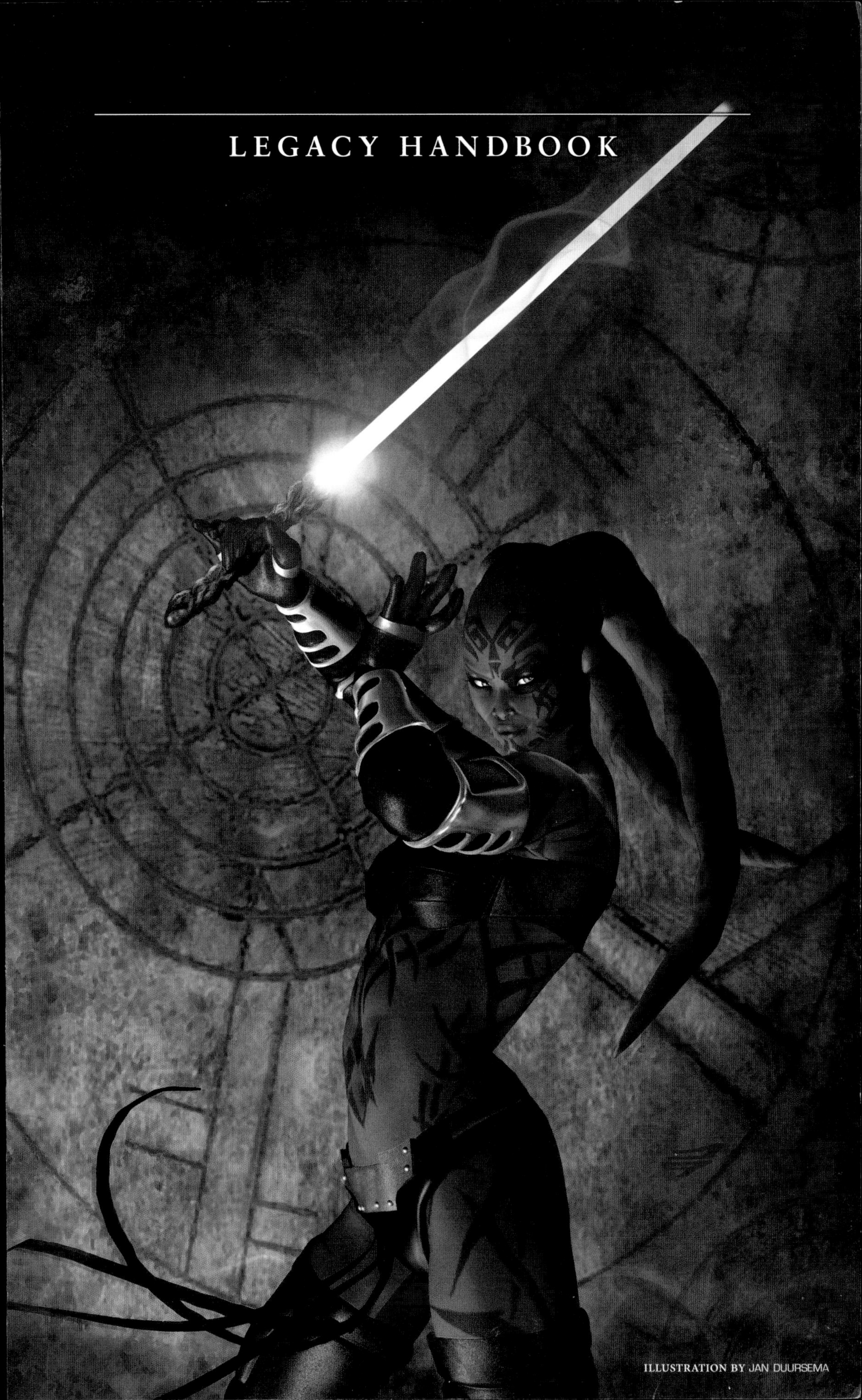

ILLUSTRATION BY JAN DUURSEMA

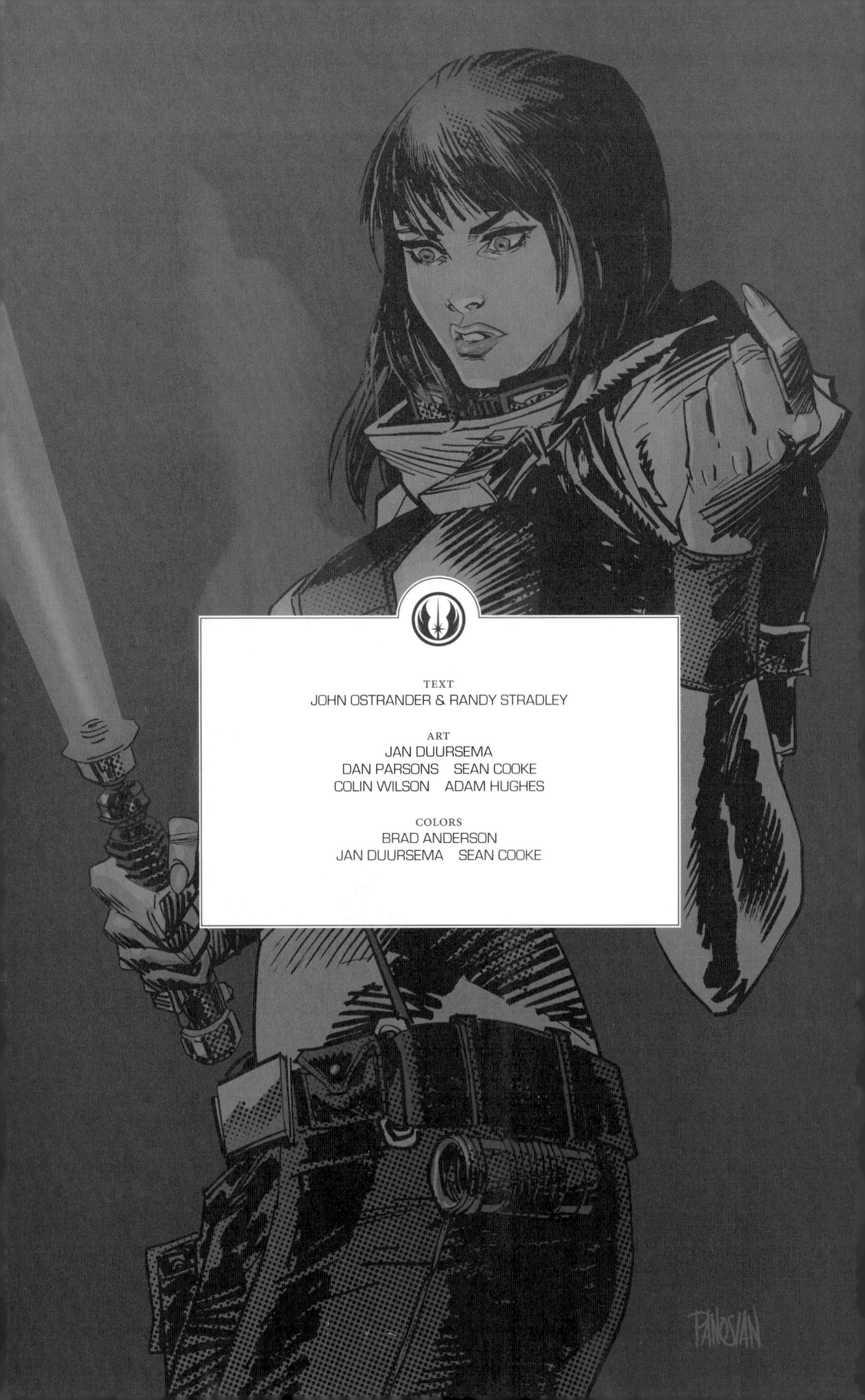
PANOSYAN

TEXT
JOHN OSTRANDER & RANDY STRADLEY

ART
JAN DUURSEMA
DAN PARSONS SEAN COOKE
COLIN WILSON ADAM HUGHES

COLORS
BRAD ANDERSON
JAN DUURSEMA SEAN COOKE

THE STATE OF THE GALAXY

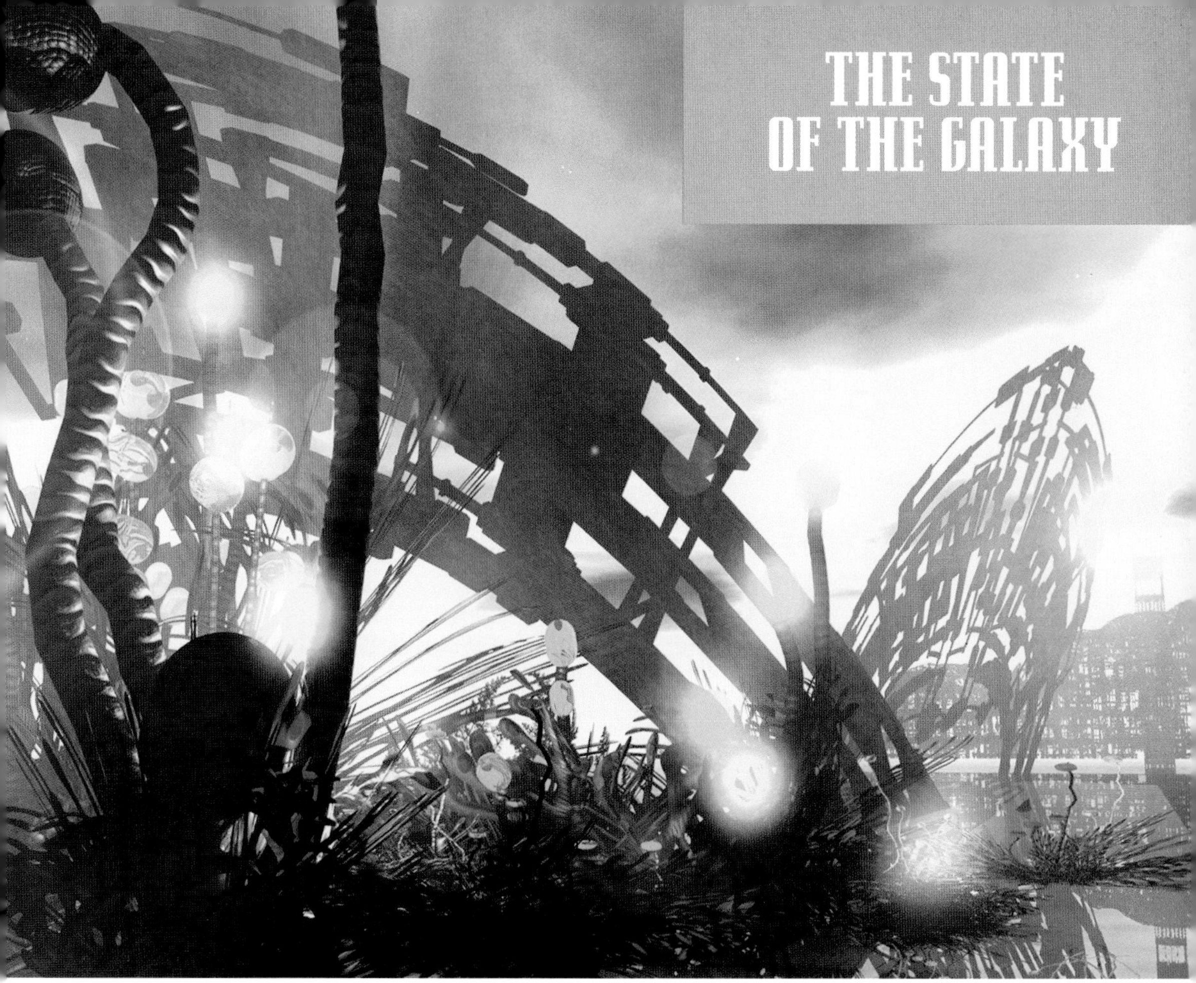

Twenty-five years after Luke Skywalker and the Rebel Alliance freed the galaxy from the tyranny of Emperor Palpatine and Darth Vader, a new threat emerged: alien invaders called Yuuzhan Vong. The Yuuzhan Vong conquered many worlds—including the galactic capital Coruscant—and transformed those planets to accommodate their own native flora. Hundreds of systems were devastated before the Yuuzhan Vong were finally defeated by the combined forces of the New Republic and the remnants of Palpatine's Empire.

In subsequent years, the Imperial Remnant grew into a larger, more benevolent Empire, and the New Republic was transformed into the Galactic Alliance, still allied with the resurgent Jedi Order. But, unknown to all, a new Sith Order was secretly rising on the planet Korriban.

When the Jedi proposed using now-friendly Yuuzhan Vong scientists known as Shapers to return some of the devastated worlds to their previous fertile states, the Sith saw their opportunity. Sabotaging the Vong's transformation processes, the Sith used the disastrous results to incite war between the Empire and the Galactic Alliance. Emperor Roan Fel tried to end the war, but his own Moffs were secretly allied with the Sith and thwarted his efforts.

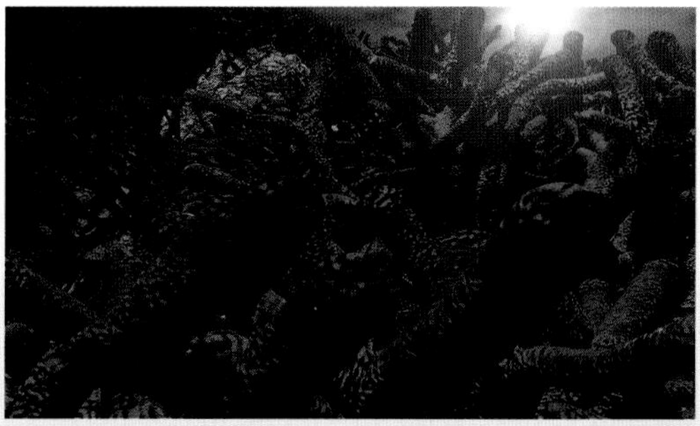

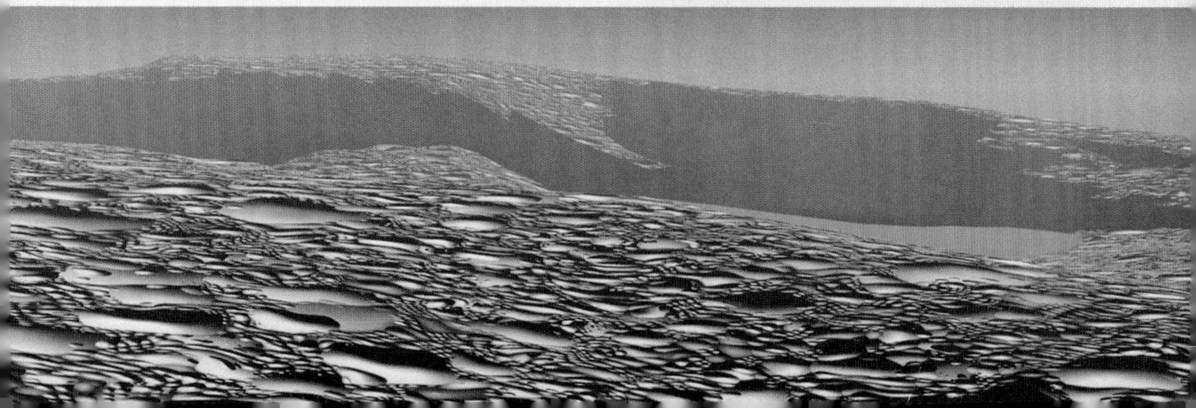

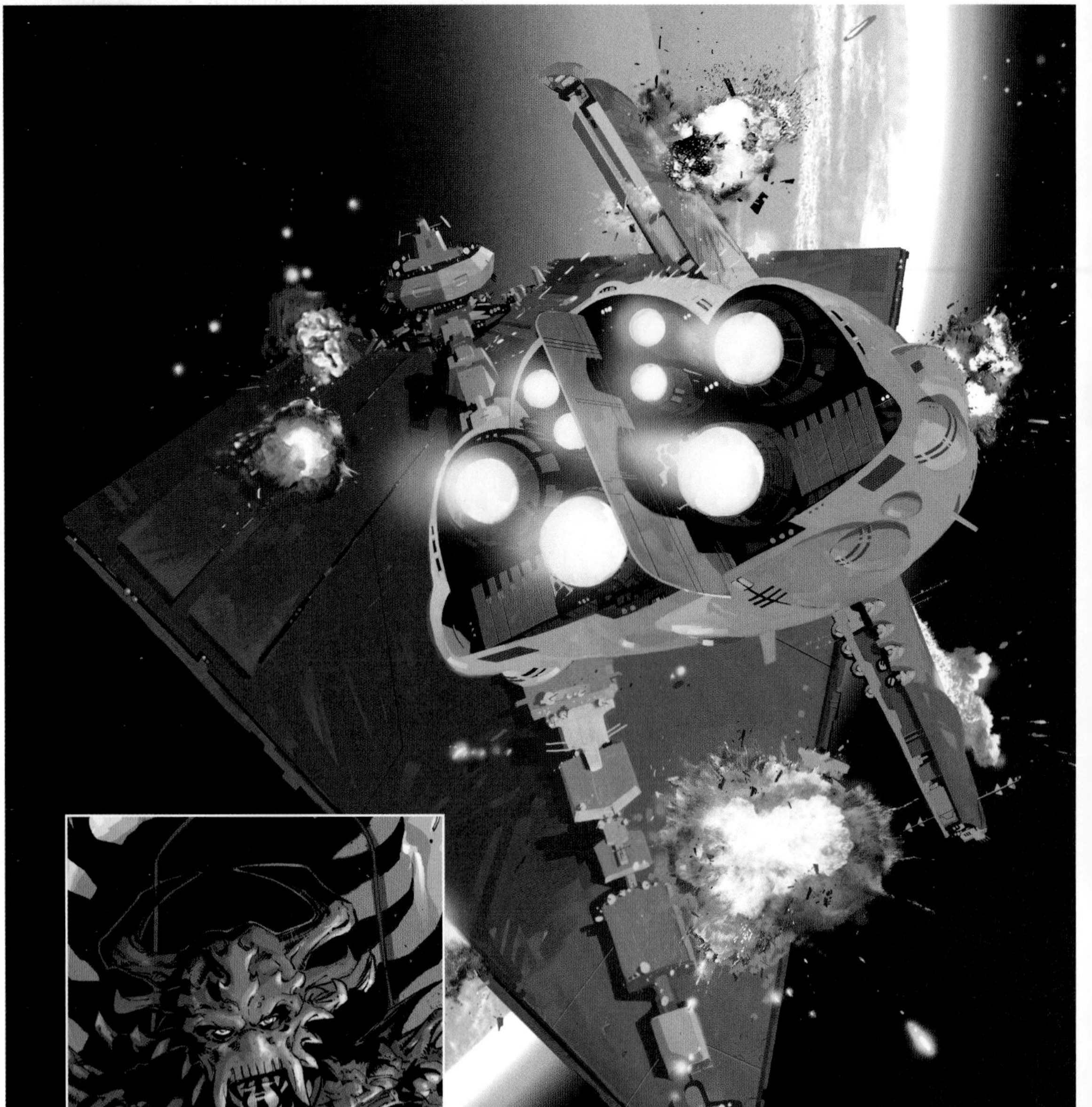

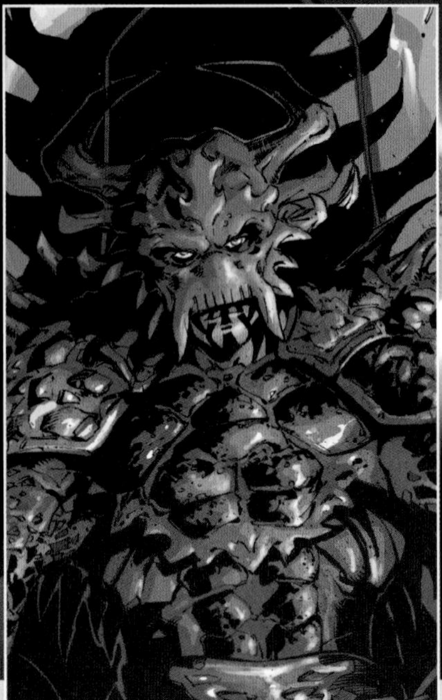

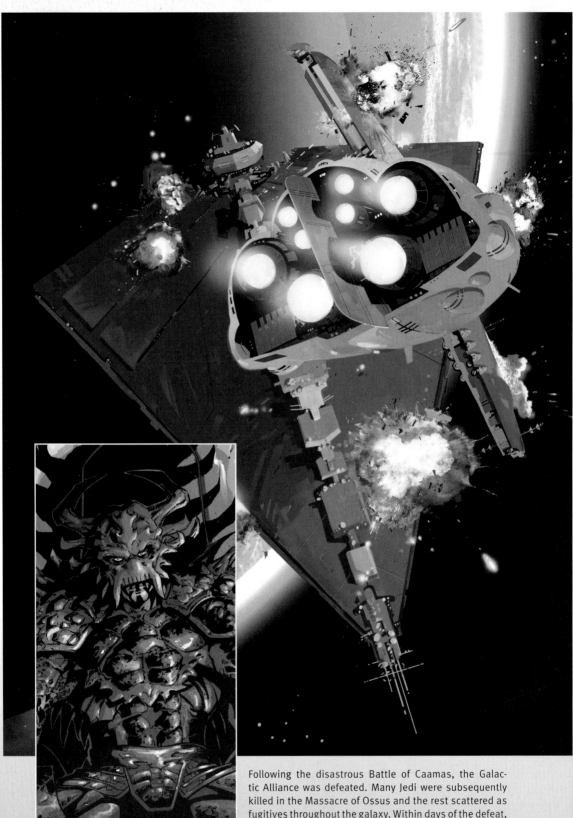

Following the disastrous Battle of Caamas, the Galactic Alliance was defeated. Many Jedi were subsequently killed in the Massacre of Ossus and the rest scattered as fugitives throughout the galaxy. Within days of the defeat, the Sith also moved against Emperor Fel. He, however, escaped into exile, and the Moff Council's supposed victory was turned into defeat as the Sith's leader, Darth Krayt, proclaimed himself emperor . . .

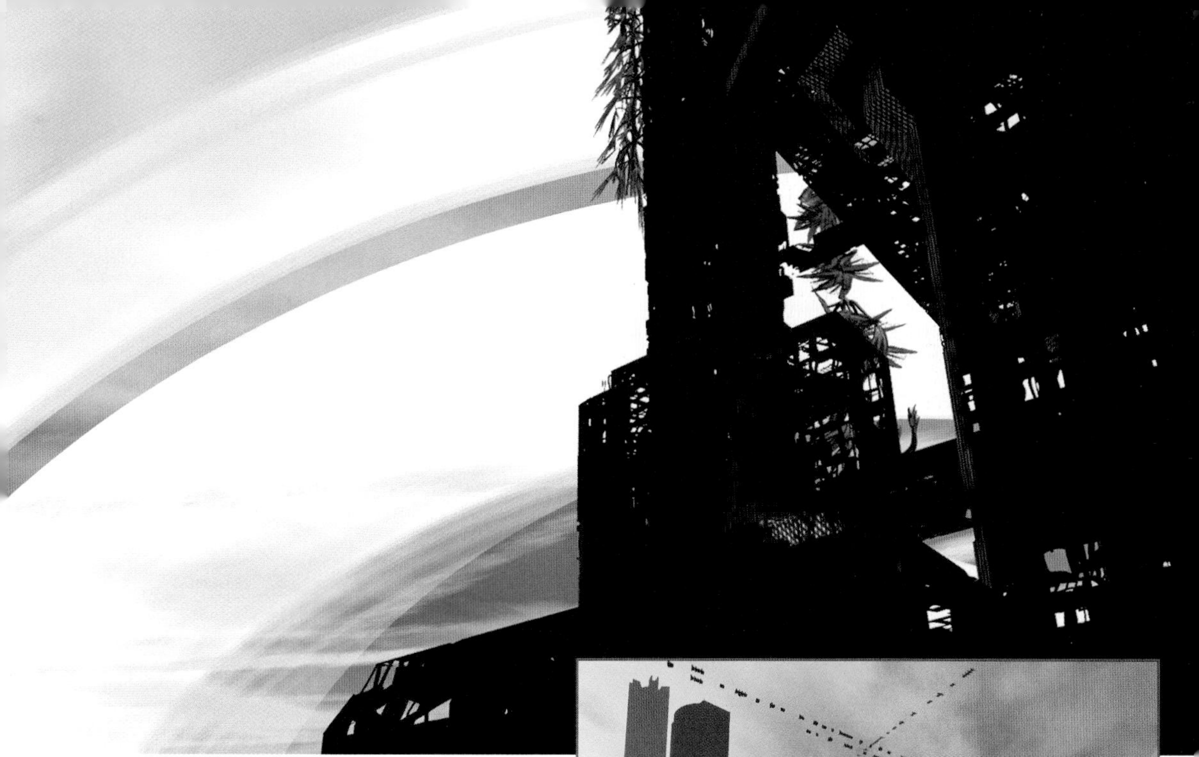

CORUSCANT

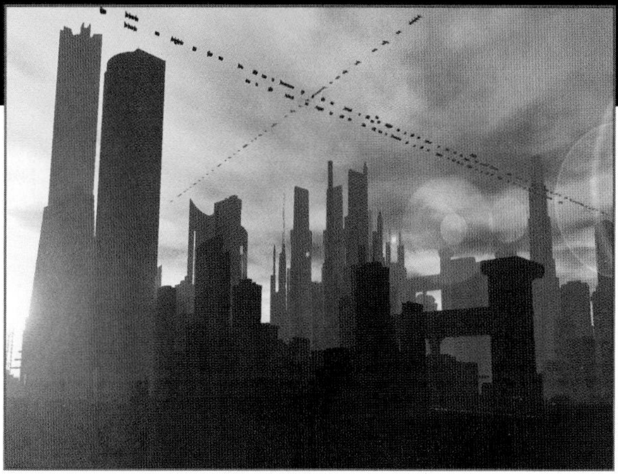

Coruscant was the seat of government for the Old Republic, the Empire, and the New Republic. The Yuuzhan Vong also made it their throne world, moving its orbit closer to the sun and crushing one of its moons to make their "rainbow bridge."

Now under the control of the Sith Empire, the city-planet remains infested with Yuuzhan Vong vegetation, which still uneasily coexists with the planet's durasteel canyons.

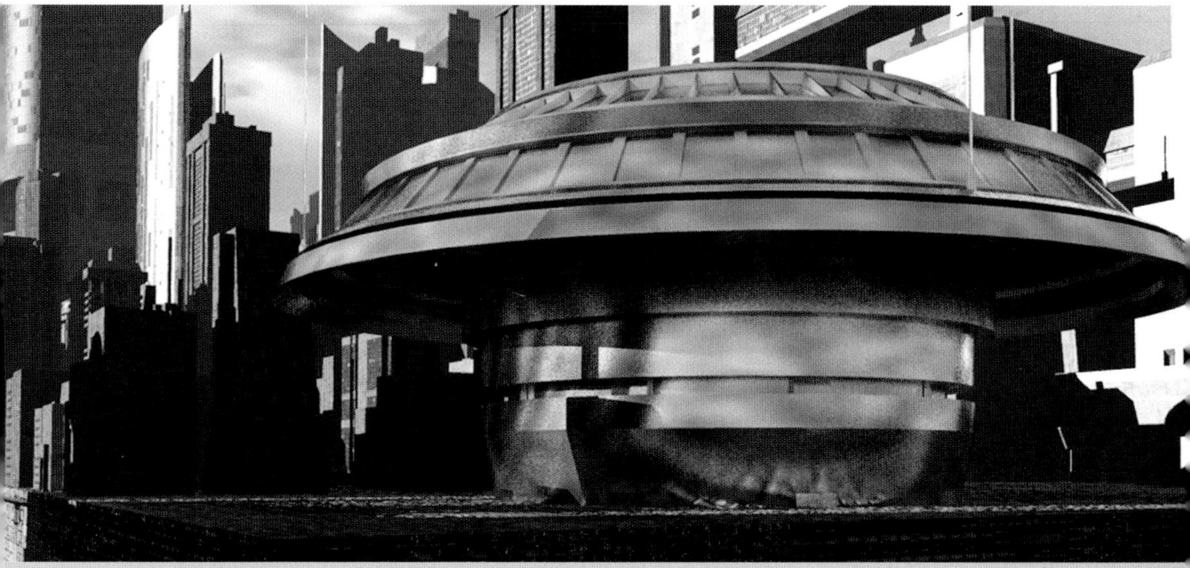

THE SITH EMPIRE

Though outwardly the Empire is little changed, with the Sith in power, the galaxy has become a decidedly less friendly place. The law is inviolate, justice is swift, and retribution is cruel. It is not unusual to see a Sith Lord on the bridge of one of the Empire's capital ships or in command of one of its armies. In addition to their overt presence, the Sith also have many spies. Now nearly all aspects of benevolence that were the hallmarks of the Fel Empire have been ground out of the Imperial bureaucracy.

DARTH KRAYT

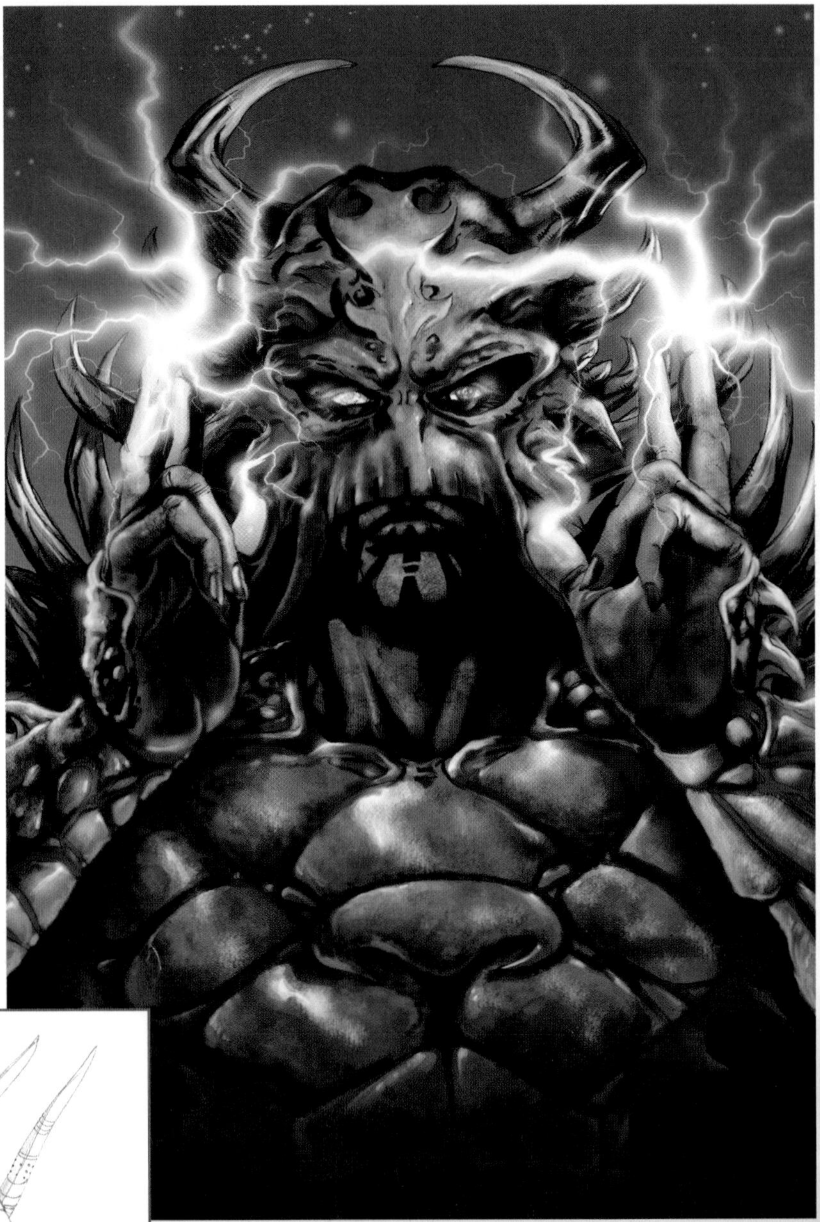

Ancient and deadly, Darth Krayt spent nearly a century secretly building a new Sith Order on Korriban. The Rule of Two is gone, banished by the new Sith leader. Now there is only the One—the Sith Order itself.

Known only to a few is the fact that Krayt was once known as A'Sharad Hett, a Jedi who had survived the Clone Wars and become embittered about the fate of the galaxy. Hett discovered—and learned from—an ancient Sith holocron on the planet Korriban; was captured, tortured, and transformed by the Yuuzhan Vong; and finally emerged as Darth Krayt. A combination of stasis chambers and Sith meditation has allowed him to artificially extend his life, but even Krayt cannot live forever.

Krayt seeks someone who can heal him of the Yuuzhan Vong infection which is slowly overtaking his body. But thus far his efforts to rid himself of the Vong parasites have failed.

Darth Krayt's legion of Sith now outnumber the Jedi. Among his most trusted lieutenants are:

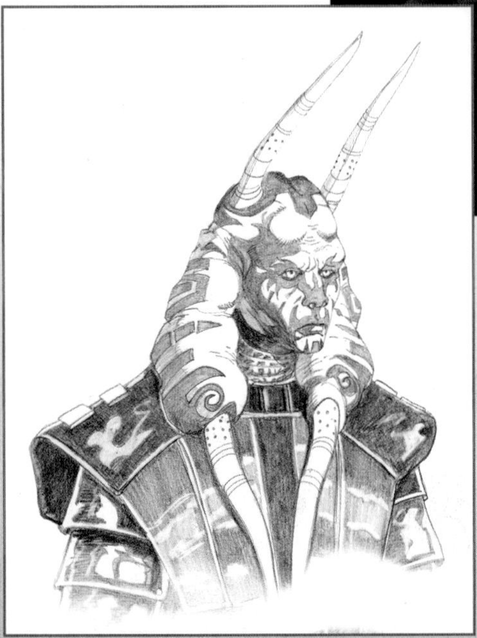

DARTH WYYRLOK

The third Sith Master to hold this name, Wyyrlok is Krayt's second in command, a master of the ritual lore of the Sith and of all the ways of the dark side.

DARTH TALON

One of Krayt's "Hands," she exists solely to execute her Master's will. Talon's tattoos were earned in ritual combat and inscribed by Krayt himself.

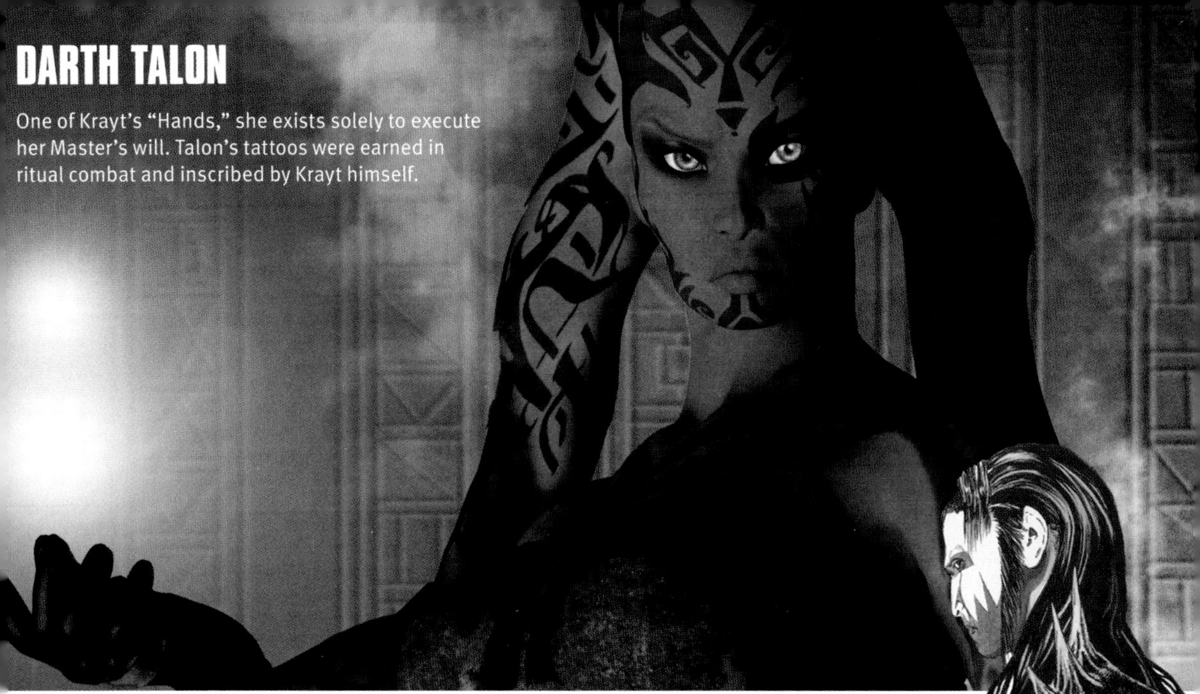

DARTH NIHL

The other of Darth Krayt's Hands, this Nagai warrior was a warlord on his home planet before joining the Sith. He is the top enforcer of Krayt's will out in the galaxy at large, and within the Sith Order itself.

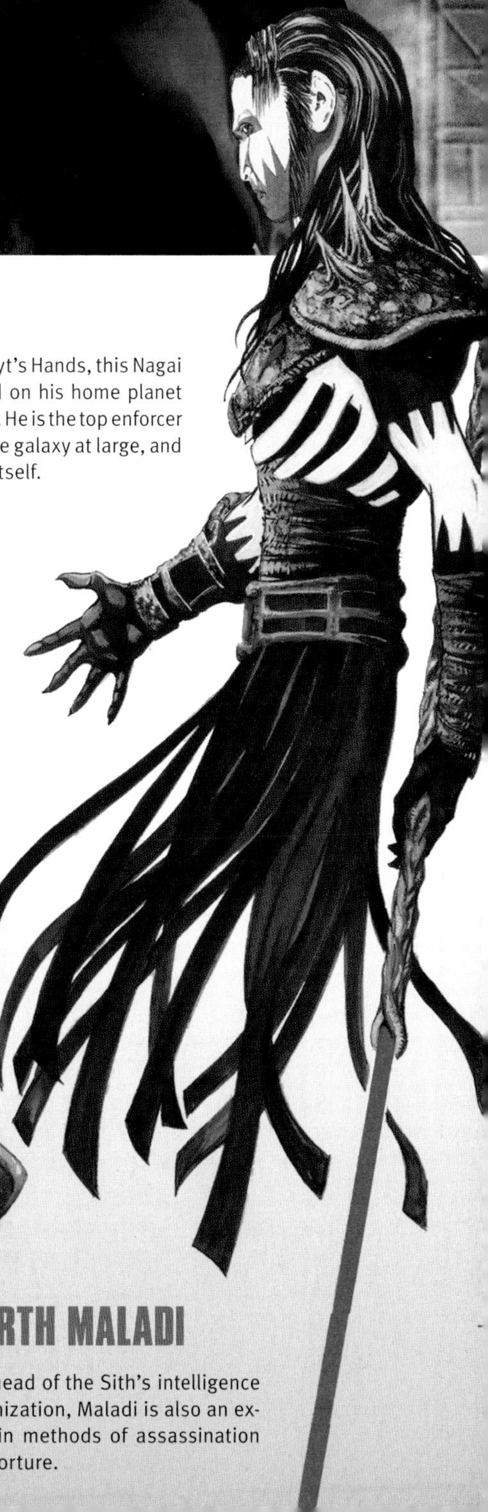

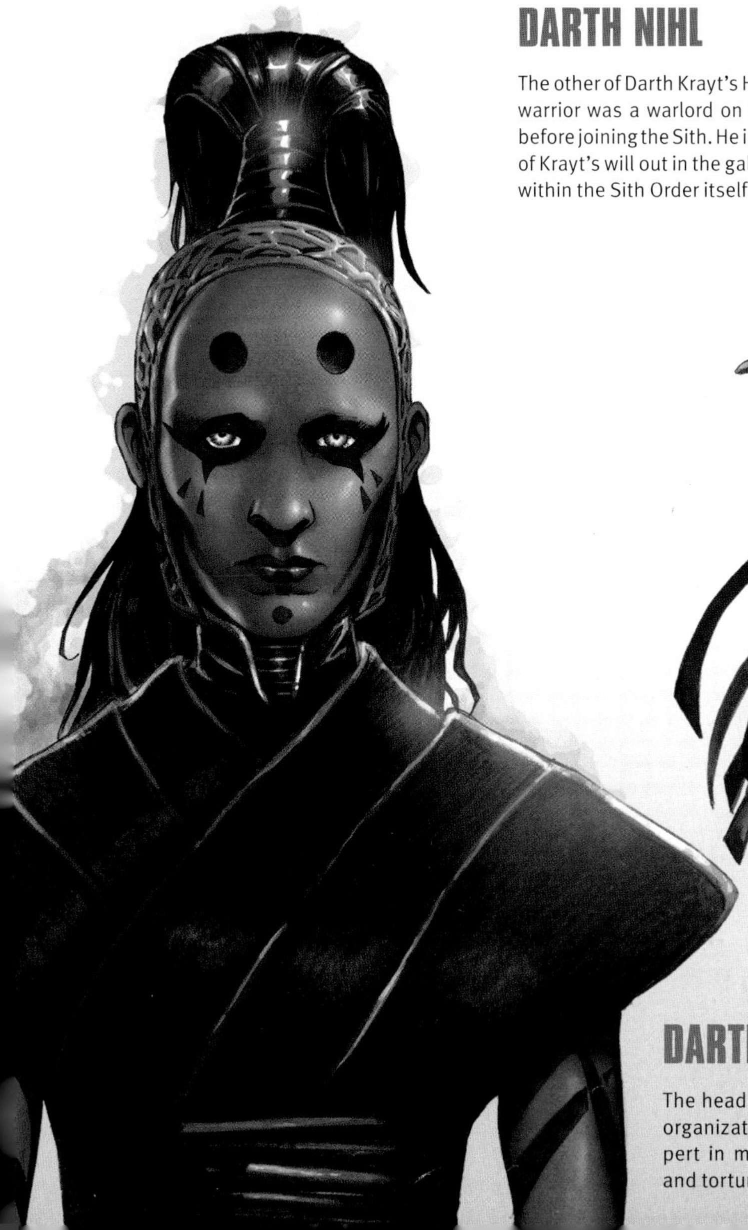

DARTH MALADI

The head of the Sith's intelligence organization, Maladi is also an expert in methods of assassination and torture.

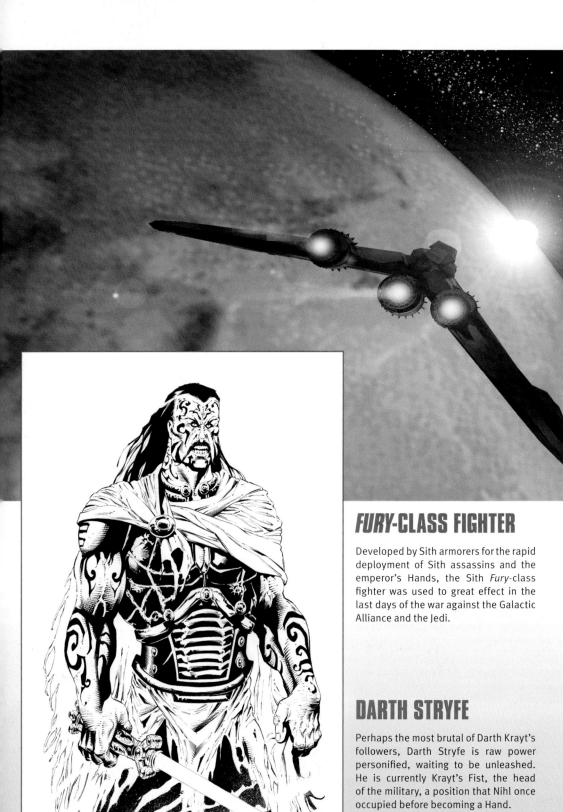

FURY-CLASS FIGHTER

Developed by Sith armorers for the rapid deployment of Sith assassins and the emperor's Hands, the Sith *Fury*-class fighter was used to great effect in the last days of the war against the Galactic Alliance and the Jedi.

DARTH STRYFE

Perhaps the most brutal of Darth Krayt's followers, Darth Stryfe is raw power personified, waiting to be unleashed. He is currently Krayt's Fist, the head of the military, a position that Nihl once occupied before becoming a Hand.

IMPERIAL HIGH MOFF COUNCIL

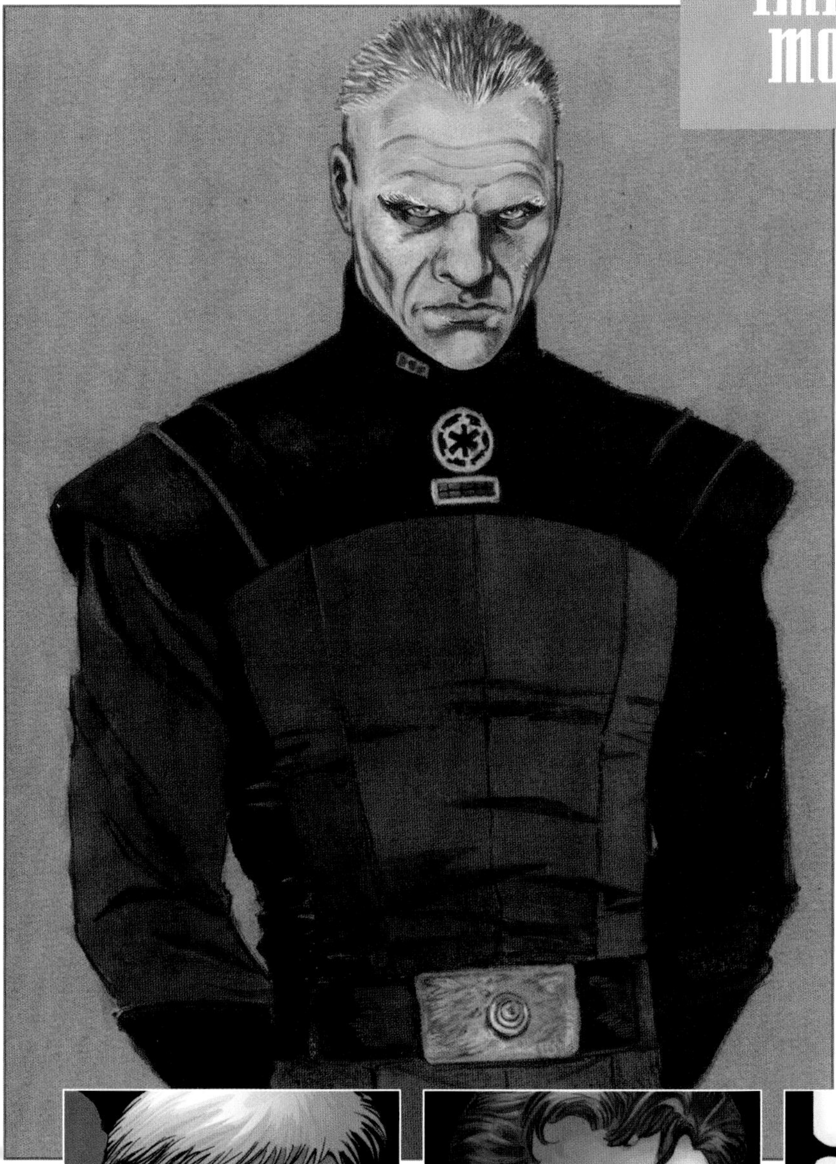

In the Sith Empire, the rule of the emperor is once again absolute. The Imperial High Moffs—the leaders of the various military branches of the Empire—once had a strong voice in Imperial affairs. Now the High Moffs on the Council (as well as the many lesser Moffs) find themselves subservient to the Sith.

Despite appearances, the Council is not a single-minded entity. Some Moffs are hardliners, as xenophobic as their predecessors in Palpatine's day. Some are opportunistic. All have their own agenda.

MOFF MORLISH VEED

Foremost among the Moffs, Morlish Veed was once the Grand Admiral over all of the Empire's fleets. His tactical skills are eclipsed only by his political acumen and his barely concealed ambition toward the Imperial throne—which was thwarted when Krayt assumed power.

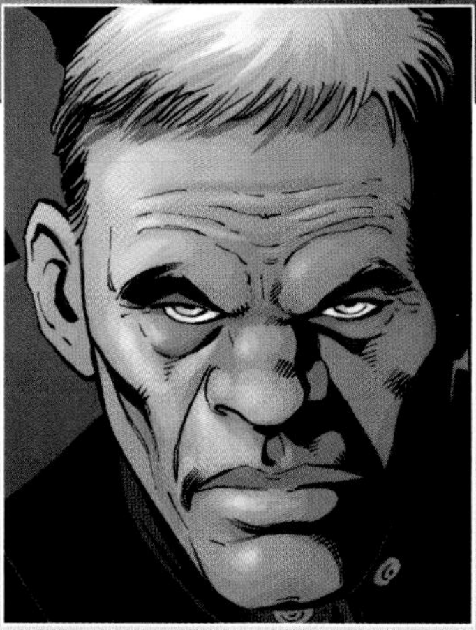

MOFF RULF YAGE

Called the "Hero of Ossus," Yage is in command of the Imperial Navy.

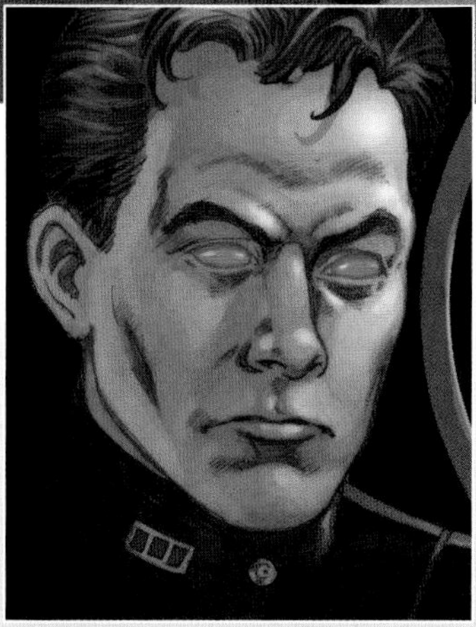

MOFF FEHLAAUR

A Chiss, Fehlaaur serves as the head of the Diplomatic Corps.

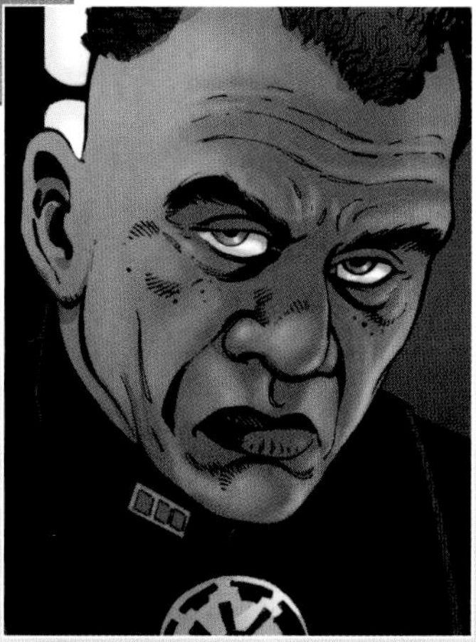

MOFF GEIST

The head of the Imperial Army, Geist's favorite tactics are threats and intimidation.

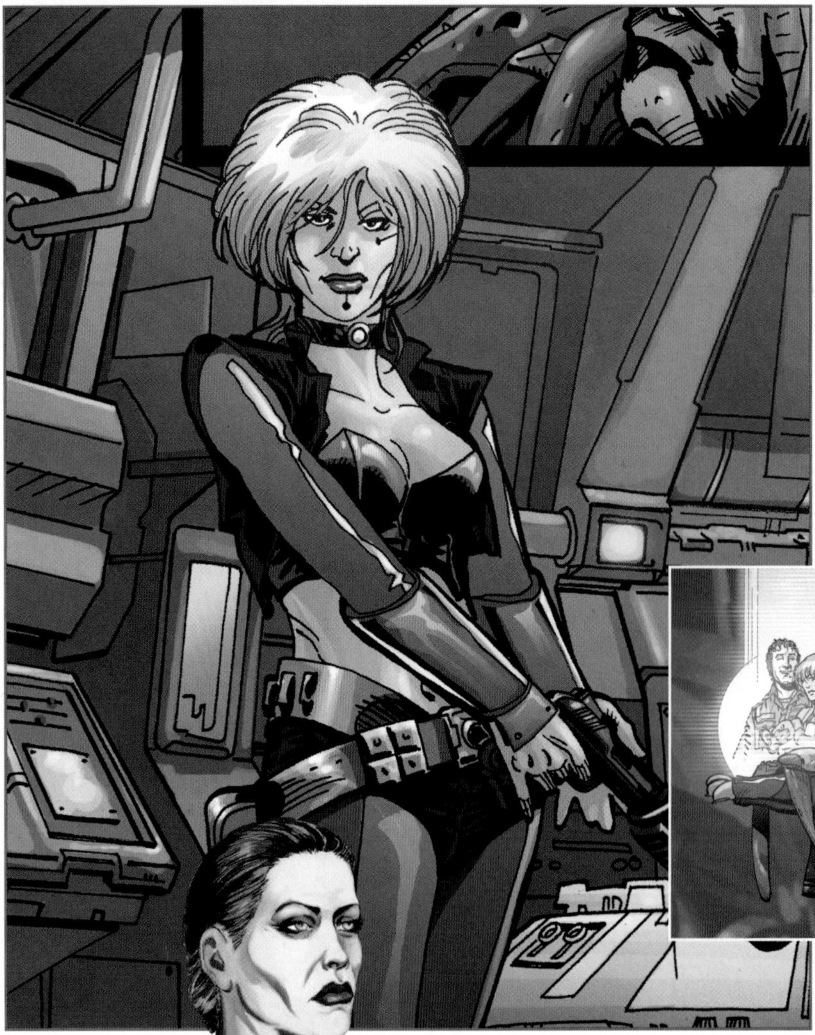

MORRIGAN CORDE

Moff Nyna Calixte's top agent from the days before the Sith took power, and the only one that Calixte can still trust. While Corde can be counted on to complete the most dangerous missions, she has her own secrets and her own agenda: she was once secretly married to Kol Skywalker—then head of the Jedi Order—and is the mother to his son. Though estranged from her child, she will do almost anything to protect him.

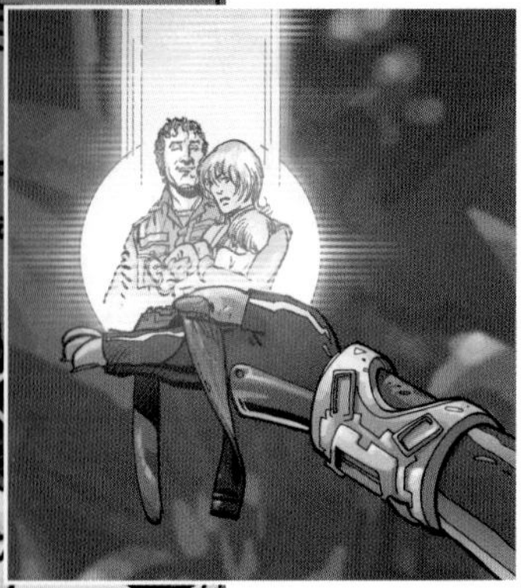

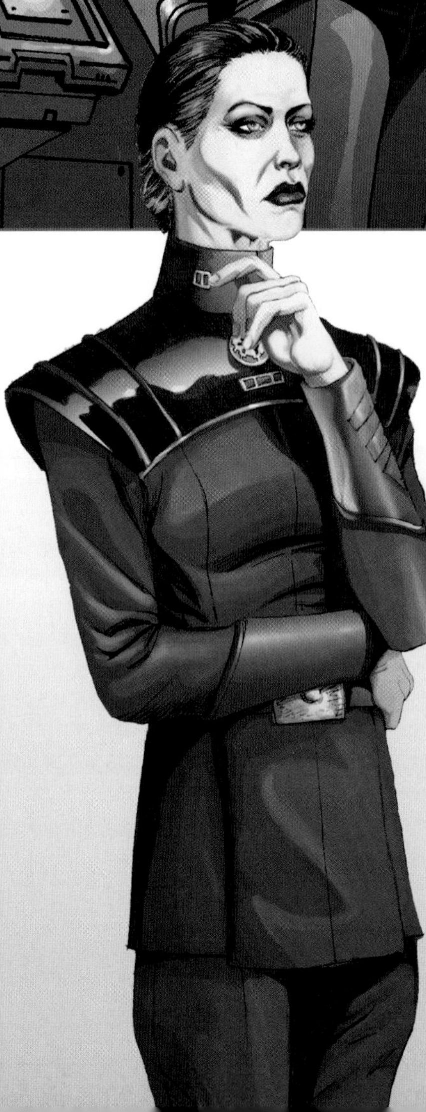

MOFF NYNA CALIXTE

In charge of Imperial Intelligence, Calixte is Morlish Veed's partner in every sense. When the Sith first approached the Empire, it was through Calixte.

Some claim that Calixte has not gained her position as Moff by sheer merit, and view her with disdain. But in doing so, they seriously underestimate Calixte—a deadly mistake.

IMPERIAL MISSION

The Imperial Mission began as part of the first Emperor Fel's "Victory without War" initiative—a way to spread Imperial influence by offering help and support to planets after the Yuuzhan Vong War. The Mission has stations on planets throughout the galaxy. The Missionaries dedicate themselves to the highest principles of service, believing that is what truly embodies the Empire.

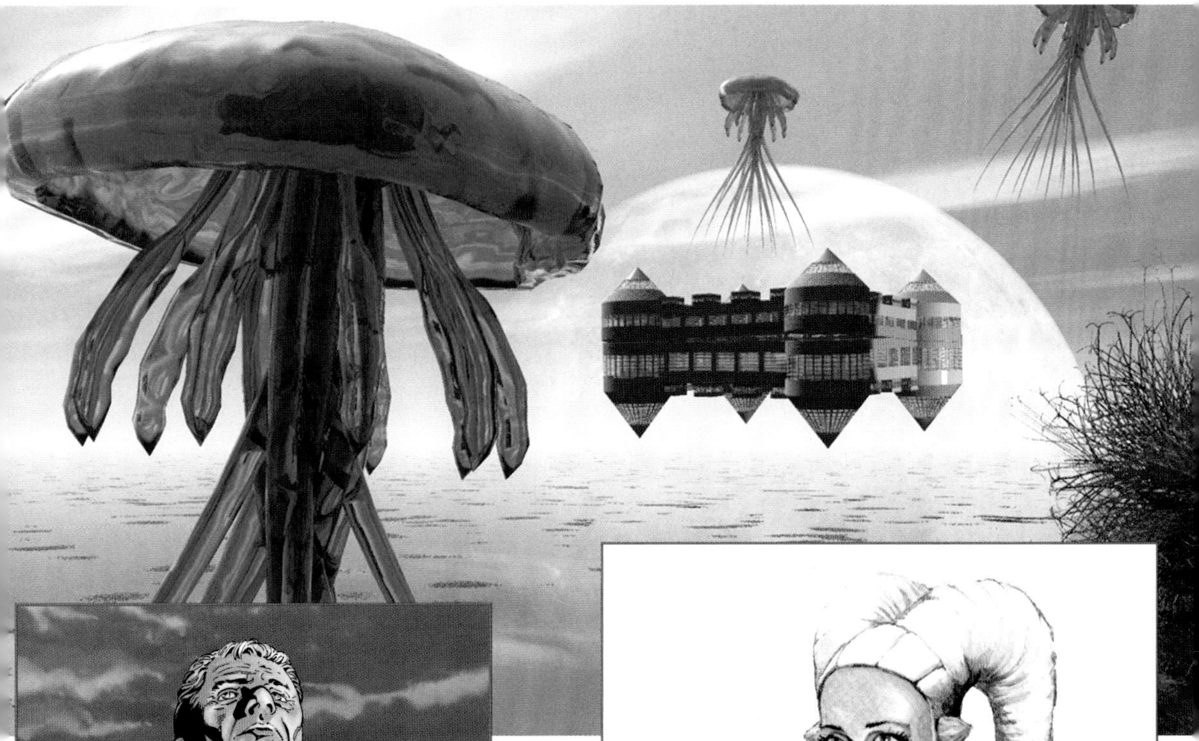

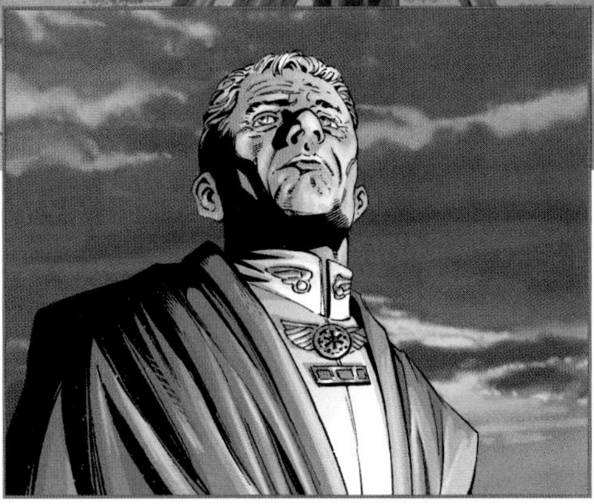

MOFF KONRAD RUS

Konrad Rus currently heads the Imperial Mission. Outwardly, Rus is a quiet man of peace, but he has had to be politically adept in the face of hard-liners among the Moffs who prefer to wage war to expand the Empire. Following the takeover of the Empire by the Sith, he has been forced to find new ways to justify the Mission's existence.

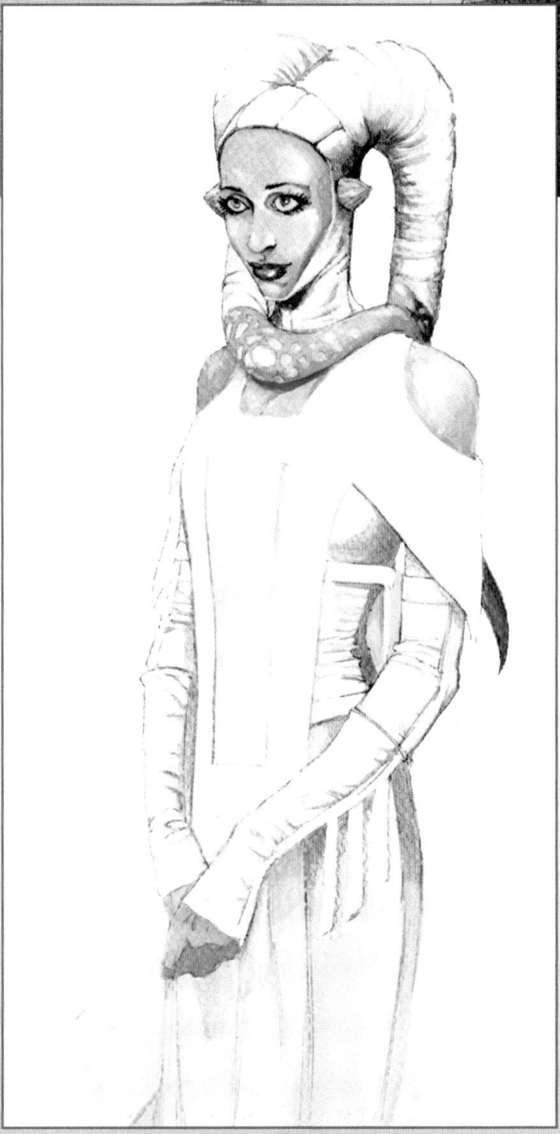

ASTRAAL VAO

Orphaned as children, twins Astraal and Shado Vao were found and helped by the Mission. Shado was recruited for Jedi training, but Astraal believes her destiny lies with the Mission.

IMPERIAL FORCES

STORMTROOPERS

The backbone of the Imperial Army, stormtroopers still serve as everything from advance scouts to shock troops. The bulk of them are raw recruits, taken and shaped to service. For some, the armor represents several generations of the same family that have worn it in service to the Empire. Some legions, such as the 501st, have been in service since the Clone Wars and from their ranks are drawn elite units—the first to hit the ground, the last to leave.

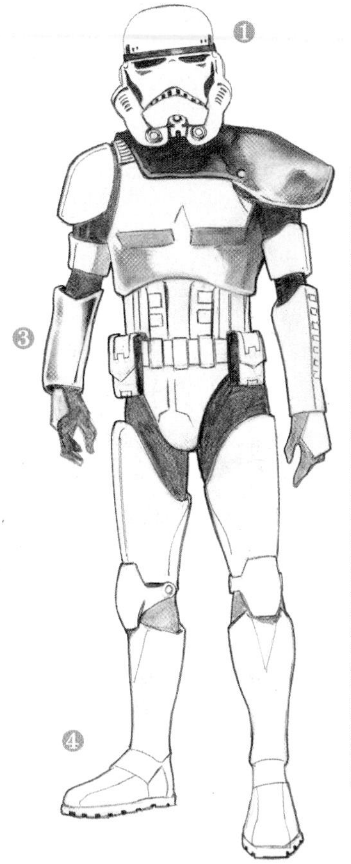

1
3
4

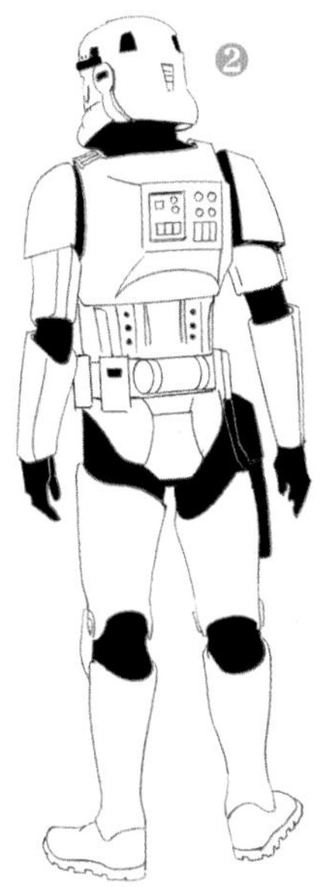

2

1 A stormtrooper's helmet still inspires fear in much of the galaxy. For many, they are literally the face of war.

2 Helmet sensory devices and communications gear have been improved.

3 Armor strength has been upgraded to absorb and diffuse a blast.

4 All-terrain boots have rugged construction.

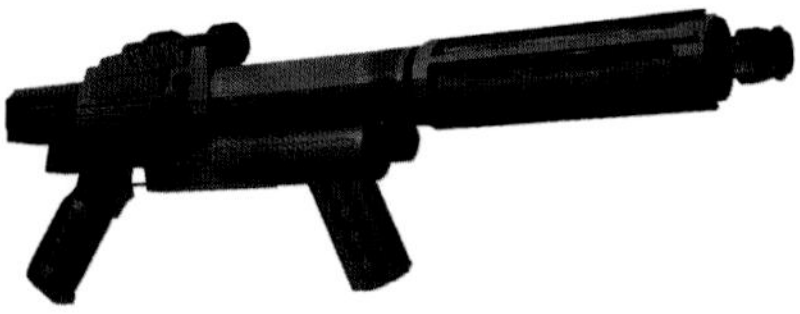

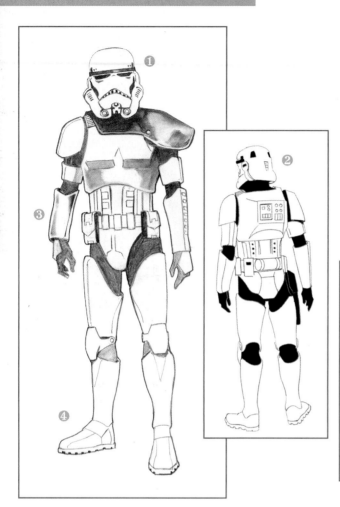

ARC-9965 BLASTER

In the new Empire, nonhumans can also serve and have helmets and armor adapted to fit their alien physiques.

IMPERIAL PILOTS

Fighters are only as good as the pilots who fly them. The Empire has some of the best.

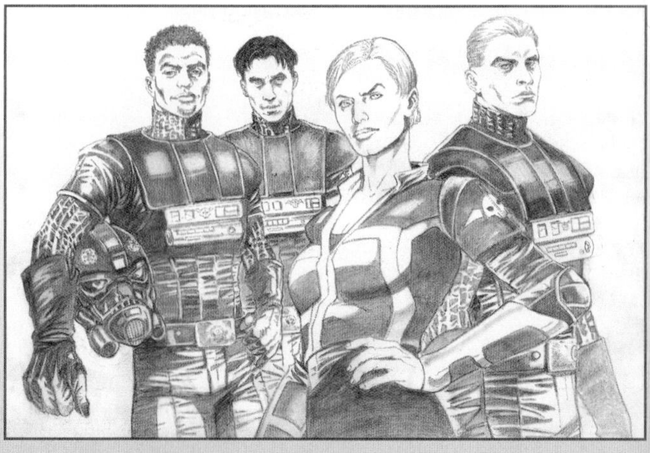

Pilots (*left to right*)
Tev "Crasher" Rimon
Jae "Storm" Akura
Brodie "Cannon" Coburn

"GUNNER" YAGE

Captain Gunn "Gunner" Yage is one of the Empire's top pilots. Her father, Moff Rulf Yage, a crusty hardliner who was proclaimed the Hero of Ossus, wanted a boy and raised her like one.

Gunn has come up through the ranks, receiving no special treatment along the way, and not asking for any. Everything she has she has earned—including her father's grudging respect. Gaining her mother's approval, however, is unlikely—as her mother is Moff Nyna Calixte.

Gunner's squadron, especially her wingmates, are as tough and loyal as their captain and would fly into a black hole for her. She is the leader of Skull Squadron.

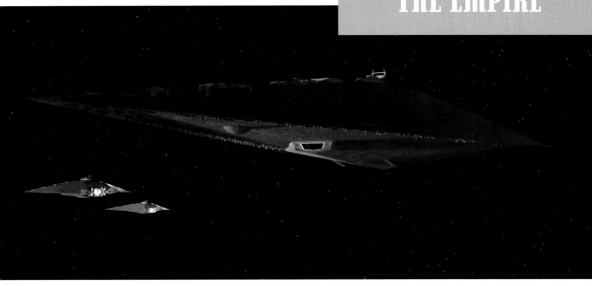

PELLAEON-CLASS STAR DESTROYER

Like its predecessors, this Star Destroyer is the mainstay of the Imperial fleets. Armed with massive turbolasers and planetary bombardment systems, *Pellaeon*-class Star Destroyers also carry wings of fighter squadrons, stormtroopers for rapid deployment throughout the galaxy, and companies of assault vehicles.

Built at the renowned Kuat Drive Yards, this generation of Star Destroyers' sleeker profile offers better protection and greater shielding of its command section.

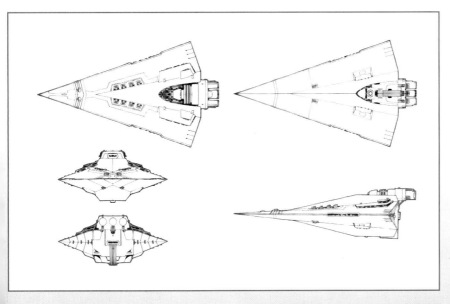

IMPERIAL FAST FRIGATE

At only about a quarter of the size of the Star Destroyer, the Empire's frigates are often the spear point of any action. Designed for rapid response, the frigates sacrifice shielding and armor for speed and unexpectedly heavy weaponry. Many Imperial officers have made names for themselves at the helms of these doughty vessels.

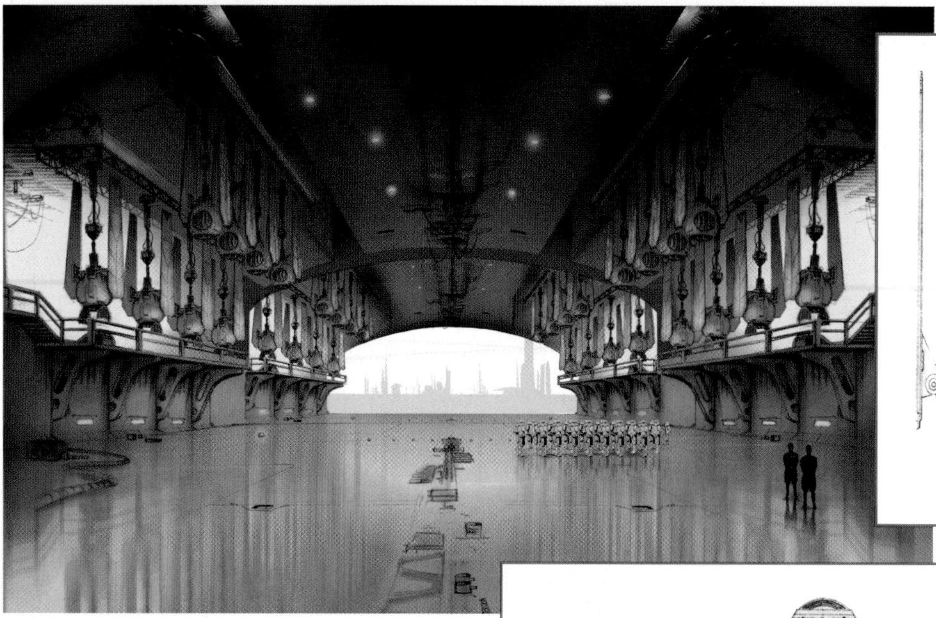

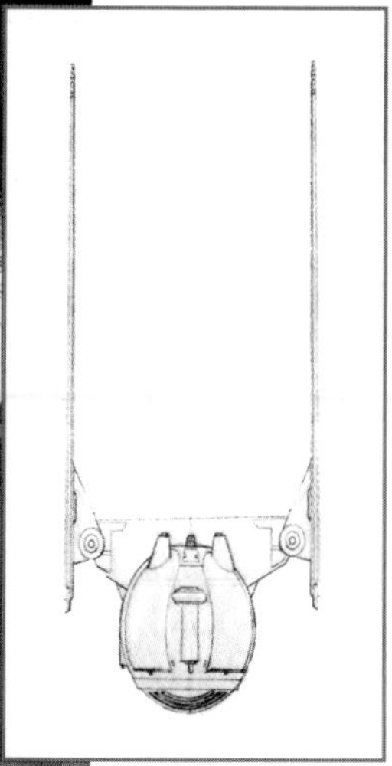

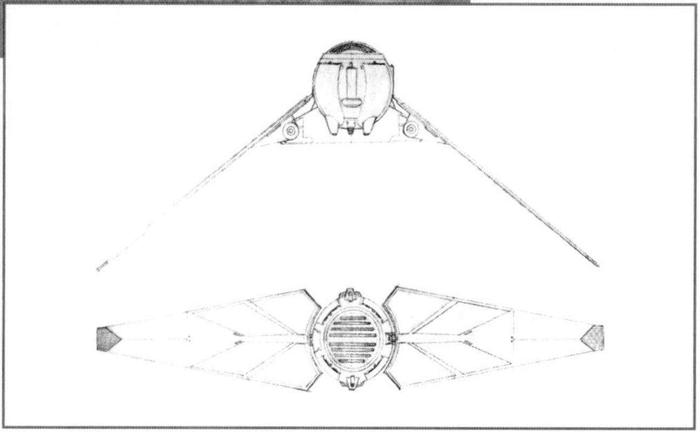

PREDATOR-CLASS FIGHTER

A product of the Sienar shipyards, the *Predator*-class fighter offers several improvements over the old TIE fighter. It boasts hyperdrive capability (with limited preset destinations), shield generators (built into the dagger-shaped wings), and (much to the relief of its pilots) a life-support system. Its multiposition wings make the Predator one of the most maneuverable fighters in the galaxy.

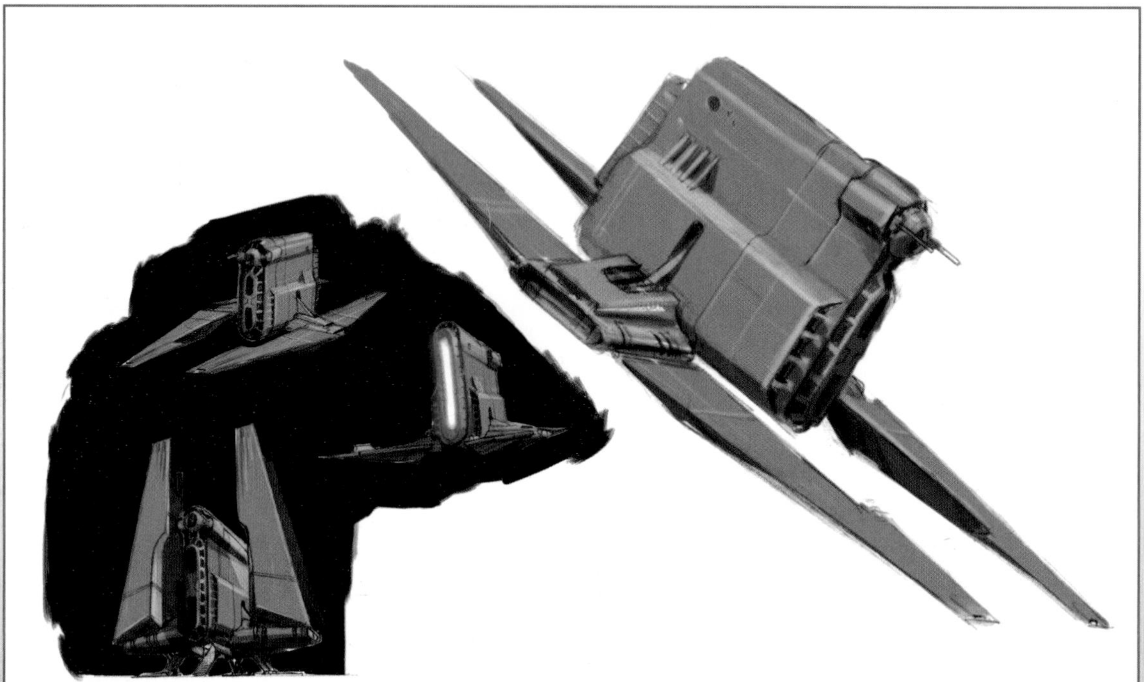

NU-CLASS IMPERIAL SHUTTLE

The workhorse of both the military and the diplomatic arms of the Empire, the *Nu*-class shuttle comes in two standard variants: the armed and armored military shuttle, and the unarmed, more passenger-friendly diplomatic version.

THE "TRUE" EMPIRE

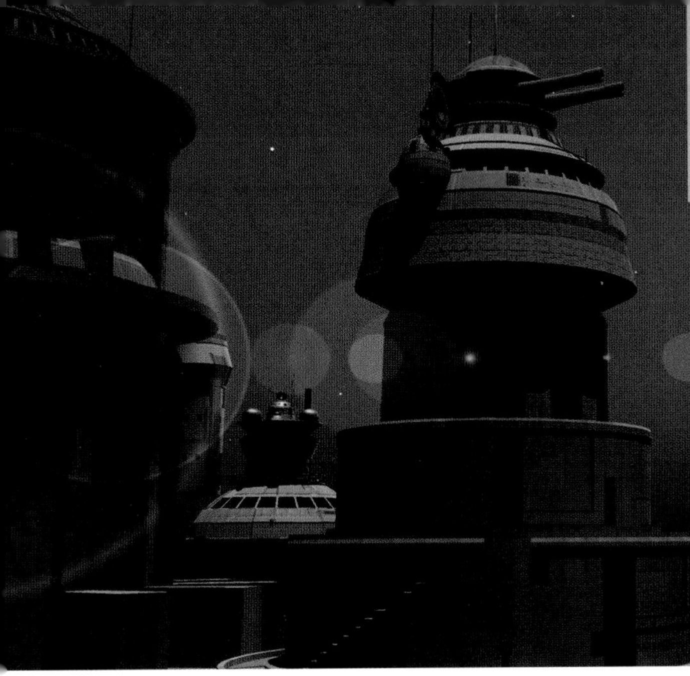

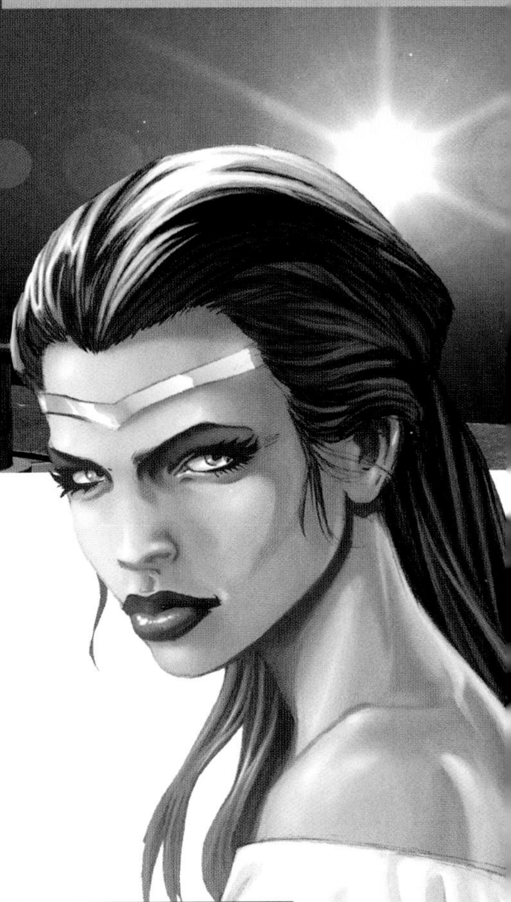

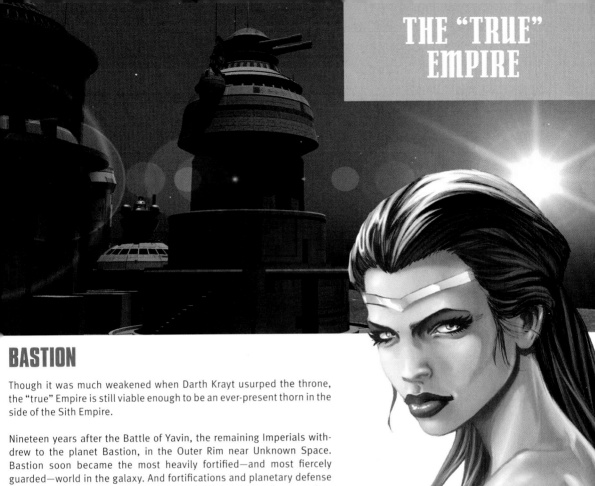

BASTION

Though it was much weakened when Darth Krayt usurped the throne, the "true" Empire is still viable enough to be an ever-present thorn in the side of the Sith Empire.

Nineteen years after the Battle of Yavin, the remaining Imperials withdrew to the planet Bastion, in the Outer Rim near Unknown Space. Bastion soon became the most heavily fortified—and most fiercely guarded—world in the galaxy. And fortifications and planetary defense systems have been continually improved and updated in the more than one hundred years since, to the point where launching a successful assault on Bastion would leave the attacker so debilitated than none will even consider it.

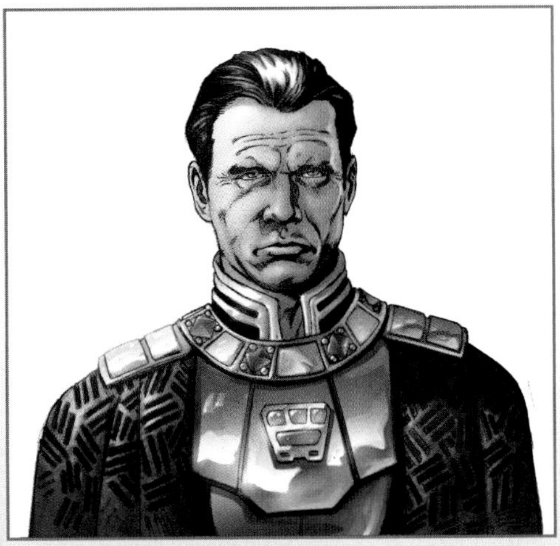

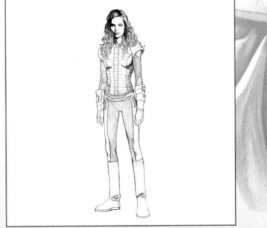

EMPEROR ROAN FEL

Roan Fel is the third emperor of the Fel dynasty to sit upon the Imperial throne. He is a fully trained Imperial Knight. Known for his political acumen and strategic thinking, Fel tried to keep the Empire on the course his grandfather set for it. He could not, however, foresee the coming of the Sith nor the impact they would have on his throne—and his family. Even in exile, Fel has maintained a persistent campaign against the Sith.

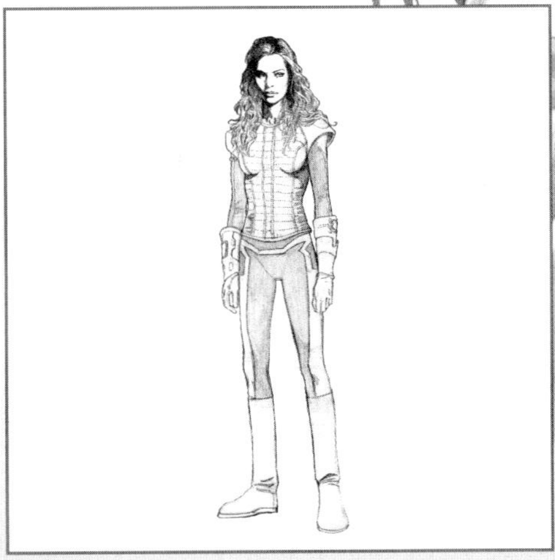

PRINCESS MARASIAH FEL

Known to those closest to her simply as Sia, she is the emperor's only child. Before their exile, there were many Moffs who openly questioned allowing Roan Fel to name a woman as his successor, but Marasiah's qualifications for the position have been proven under fire.

She has recently completed her training as an Imperial Knight, and has been formally knighted.

IMPERIAL KNIGHTS

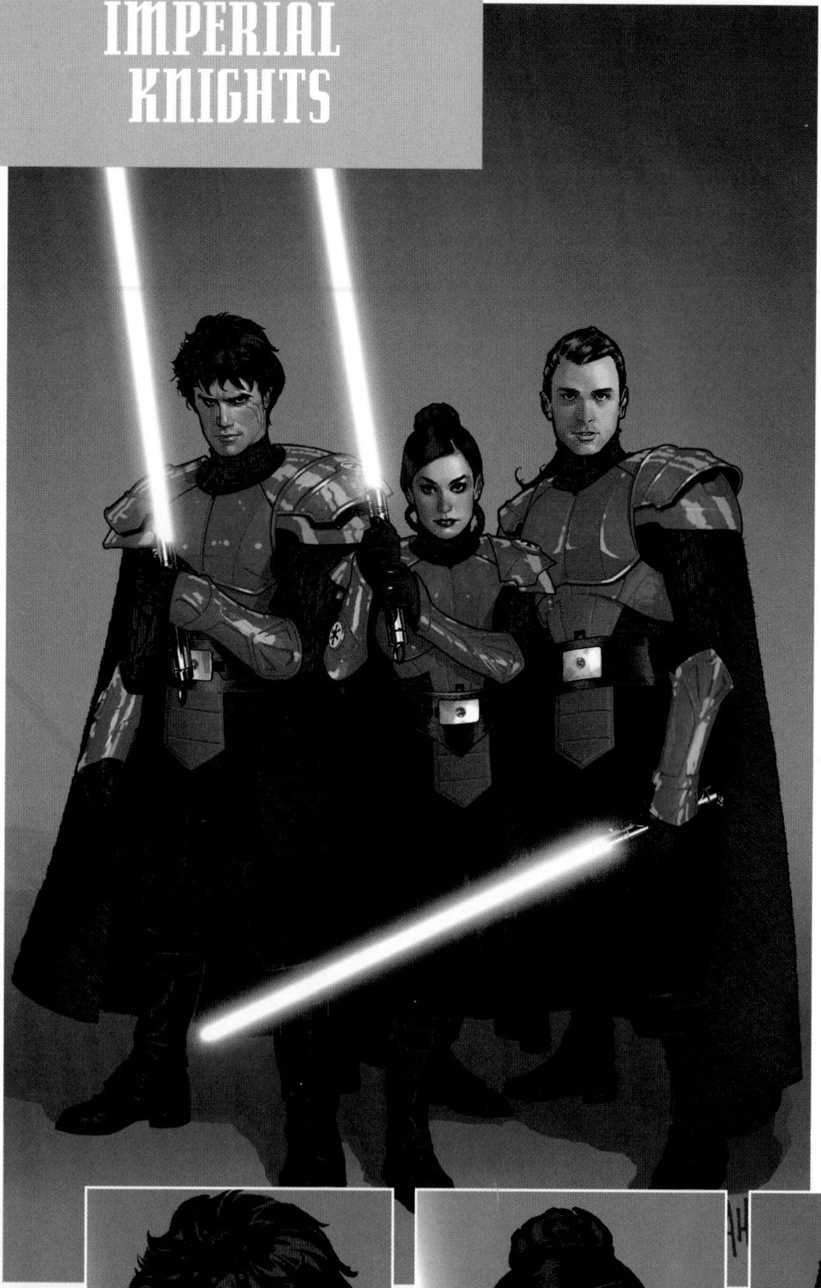

Though their numbers are small, the Imperial Knights are fully trained Force users, with all the skills and abilities of a Jedi. However, unlike their Jedi counterparts whose allegiance is to the Jedi Order or the Force, Imperial Knights have sworn themselves to the service of the Empire as personified in Emperor Roan Fel.

As a symbol of their unity and how each individual is less than the Empire they serve, the Imperial Knights all use lightsabers of the same design.

The Jedi view the Imperial Knights as "gray"—though the Imperials do not seek to draw on the dark side of the Force, neither do they strictly follow the light side. While there is often friction between the Imperial Knights and the Jedi, the Sith are a common enemy to both groups.

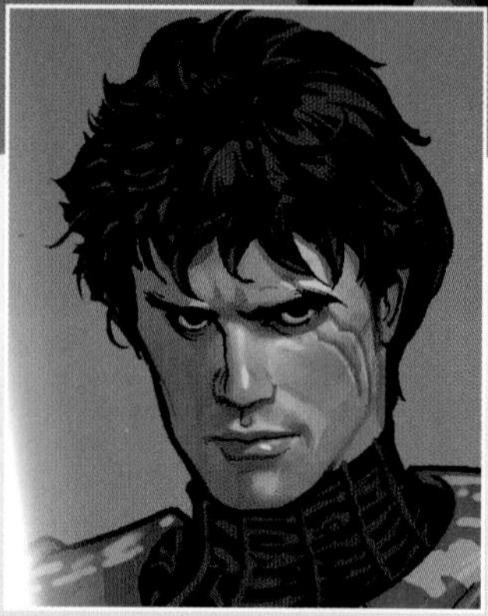

ANTARES DRACO

The second in command of the Imperial Knights (after Emperor Fel), and equally formidable with a lightsaber or behind the controls of a fighter, Draco would give his life for the emperor. He is also in love with Princess Marasiah.

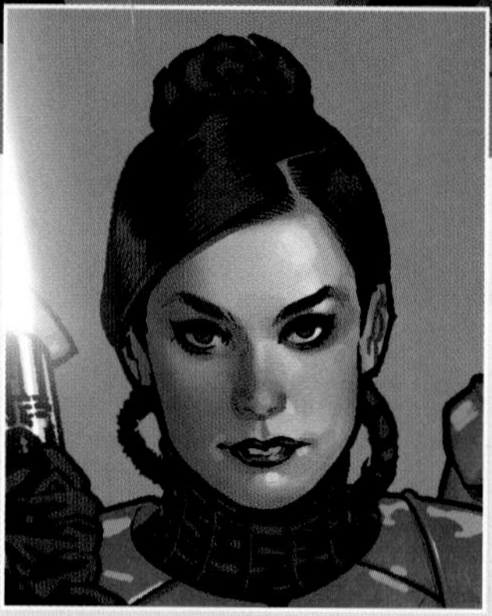

SIGEL DARE

Cold as ice, dutiful and rigid in her thinking and approach. She never liked the Sith, but has no use for Jedi, either.

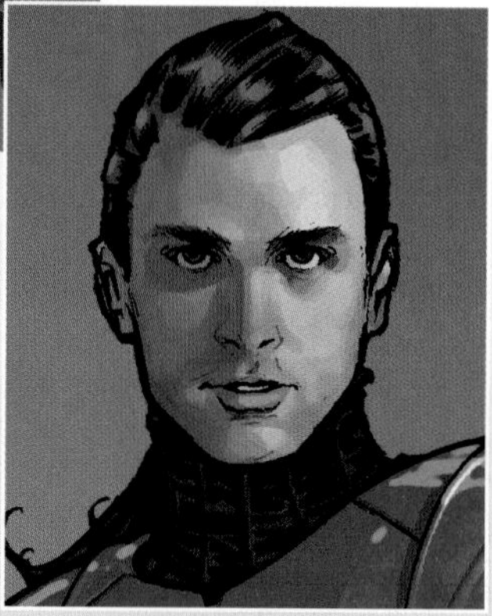

GANNER KRIEG

Calm and serious, Ganner is Antares's most trusted friend. Though he does not always agree with Antares, he is always ready to stand beside him.

THE GALACTIC ALLIANCE

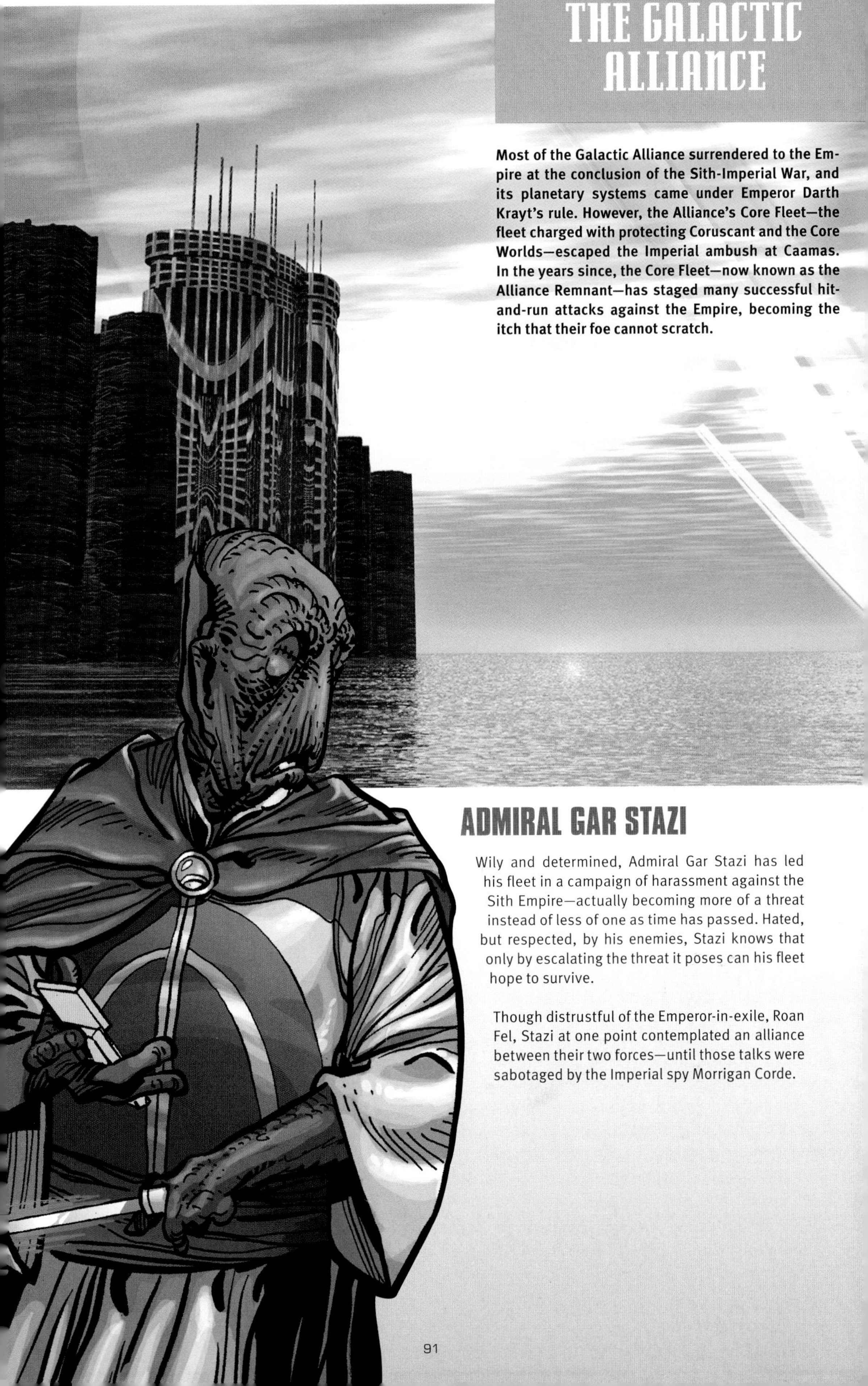

Most of the Galactic Alliance surrendered to the Empire at the conclusion of the Sith-Imperial War, and its planetary systems came under Emperor Darth Krayt's rule. However, the Alliance's Core Fleet—the fleet charged with protecting Coruscant and the Core Worlds—escaped the Imperial ambush at Caamas. In the years since, the Core Fleet—now known as the Alliance Remnant—has staged many successful hit-and-run attacks against the Empire, becoming the itch that their foe cannot scratch.

ADMIRAL GAR STAZI

Wily and determined, Admiral Gar Stazi has led his fleet in a campaign of harassment against the Sith Empire—actually becoming more of a threat instead of less of one as time has passed. Hated, but respected, by his enemies, Stazi knows that only by escalating the threat it poses can his fleet hope to survive.

Though distrustful of the Emperor-in-exile, Roan Fel, Stazi at one point contemplated an alliance between their two forces—until those talks were sabotaged by the Imperial spy Morrigan Corde.

SHIPS OF THE GALACTIC ALLIANCE

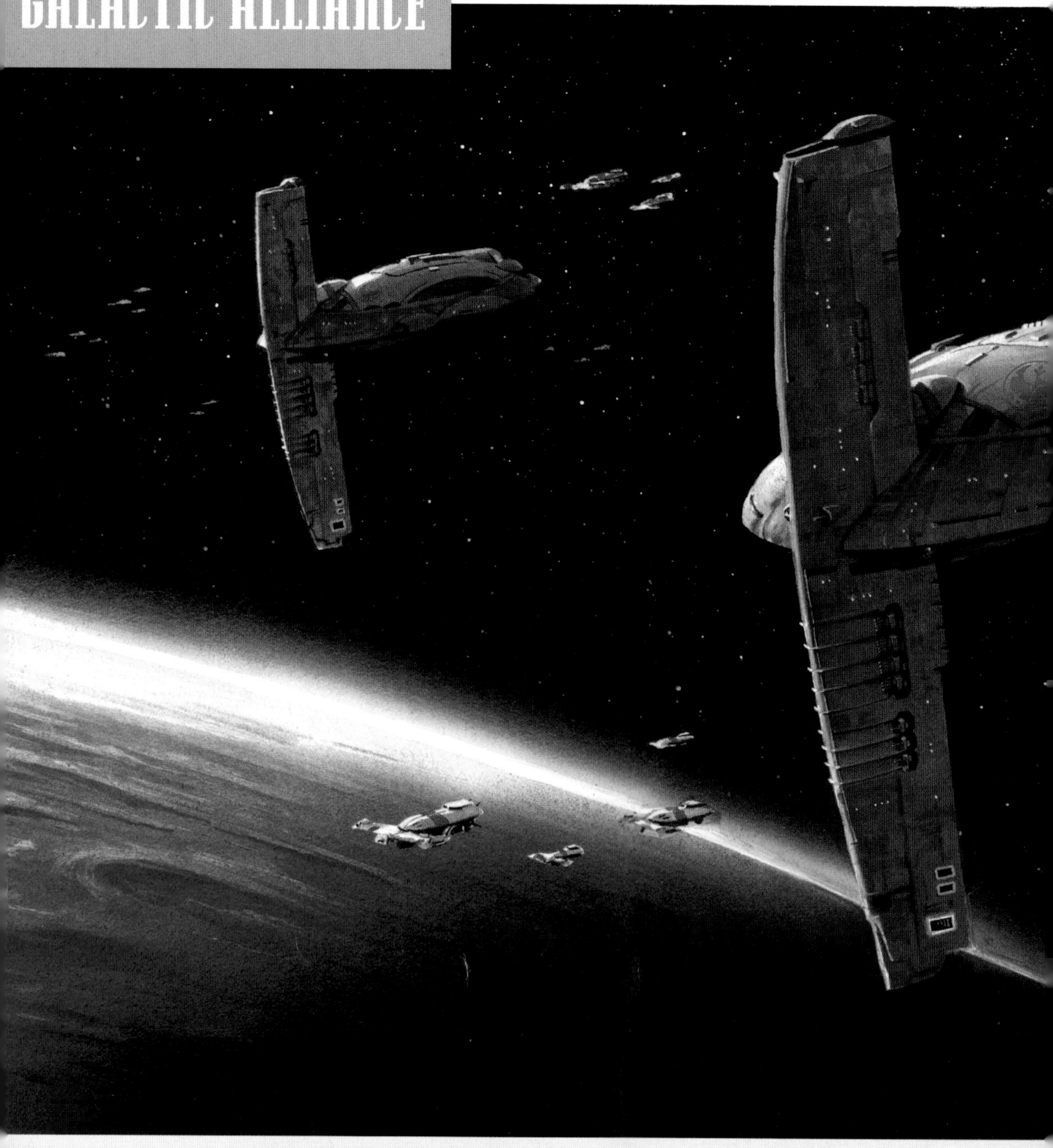

SCYTHE-CLASS BATTLE CRUISER

Though only about a third of the size of an Imperial Star Destroyer, the *Scythe*-class battle cruiser is faster and more maneuverable than its Imperial counterpart, plus its leading edges—both horizontal and vertical—are packed with torpedo tubes and turbo-laser batteries. Few Imperial captains have lived to describe what it's like to be at the center of the "cross of fire" (as the intersecting arc of the Scythe's weaponry is known).

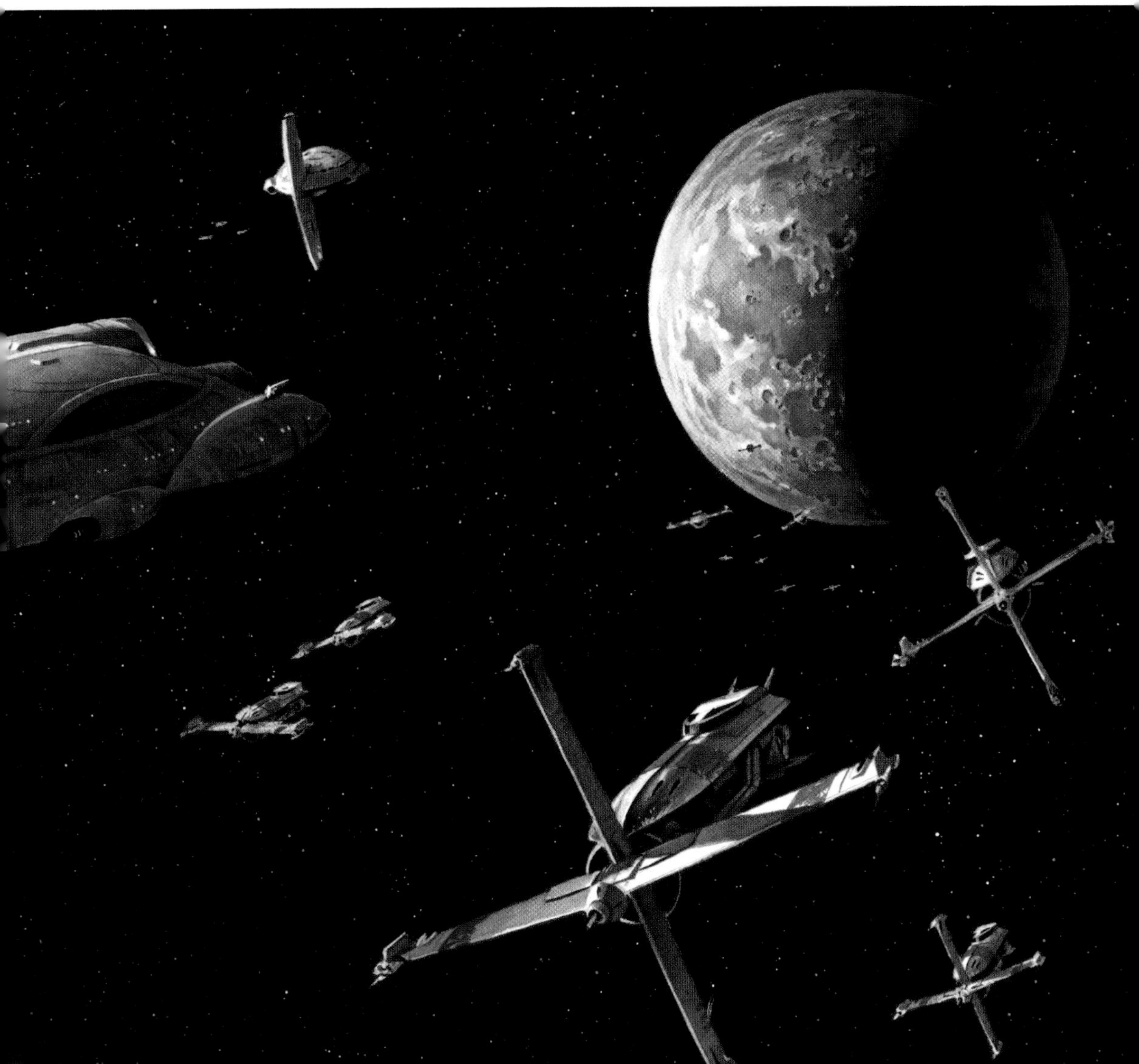

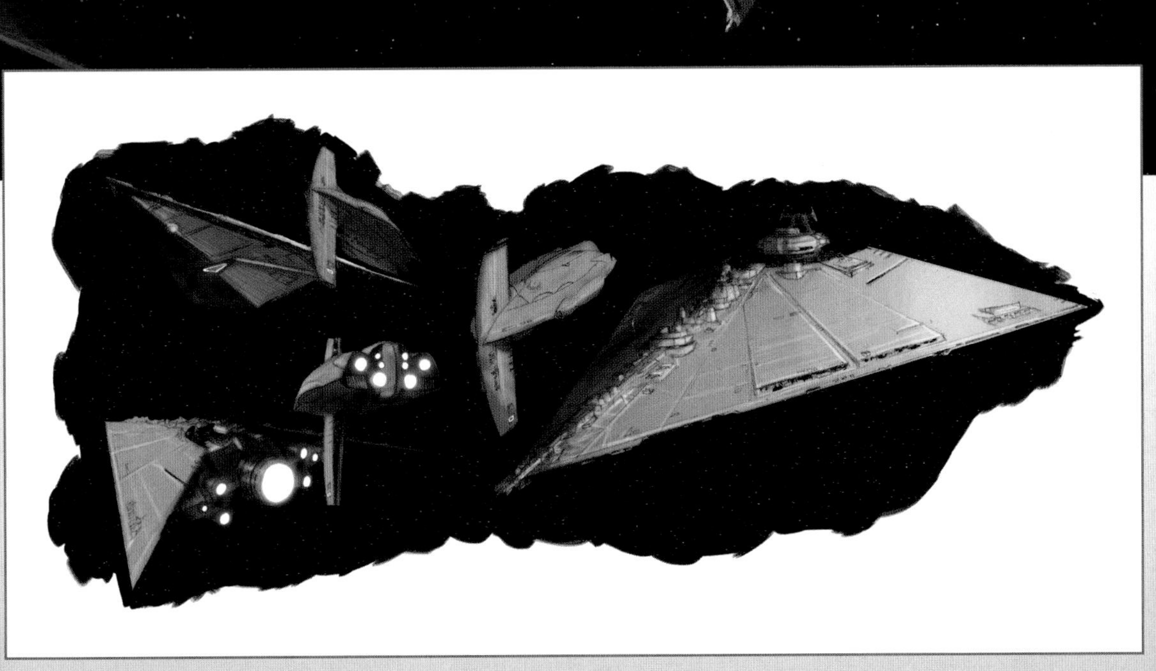

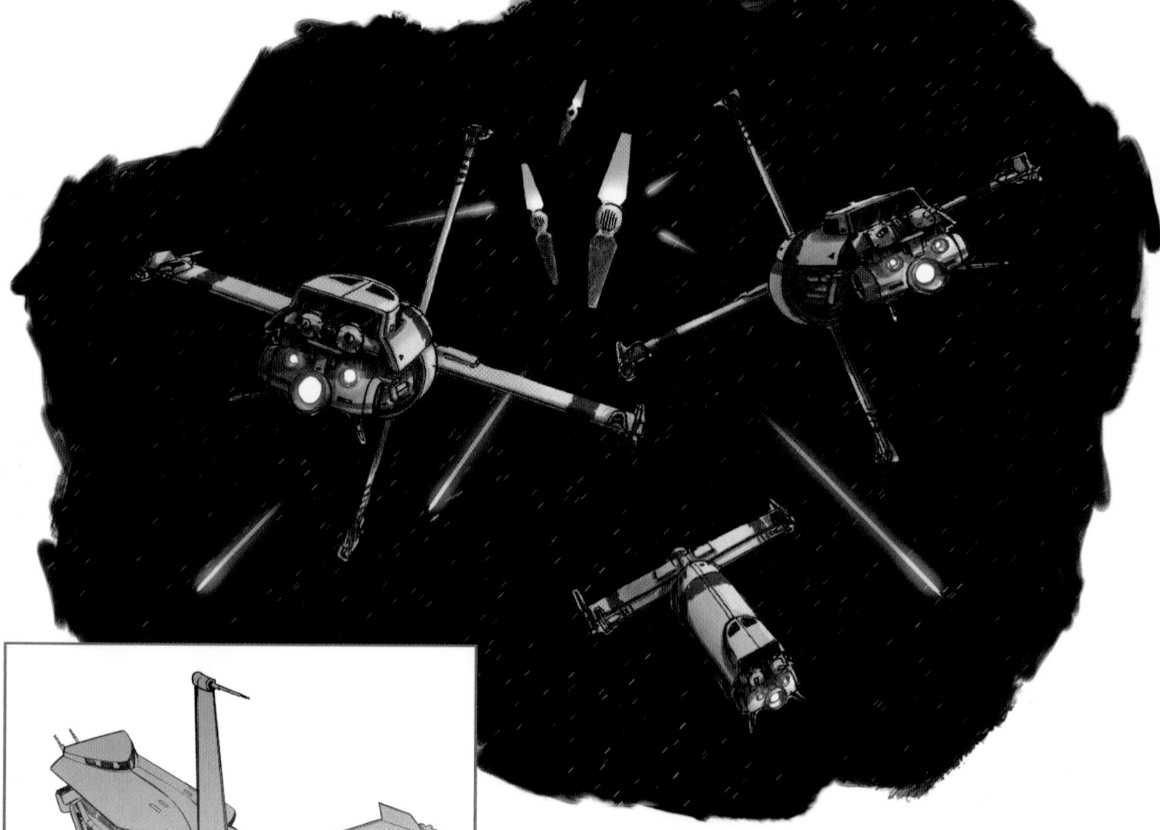

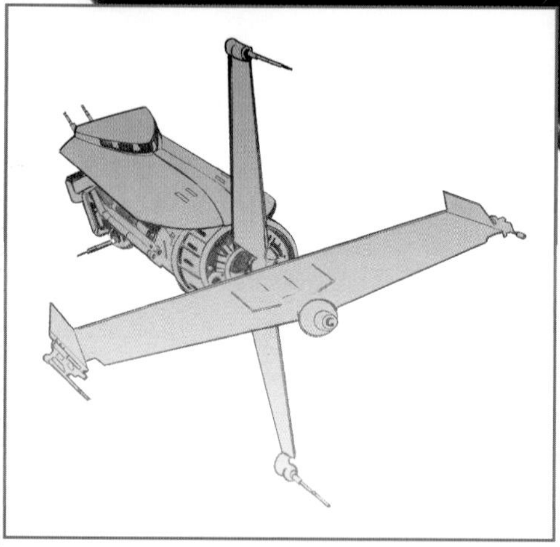

CROSSFIRE FIGHTER

Whereas the Imperial Predator relies on speed and maneuverability, the Crossfire is designed to cross long distances to reach its target, pack a devastating punch when it arrives, take all the punishment the enemy can dish out, and still return home in one piece. In flight mode both of the wing sections are horizontal; in fighter/attack mode, the rear wing section rotates to the vertical.

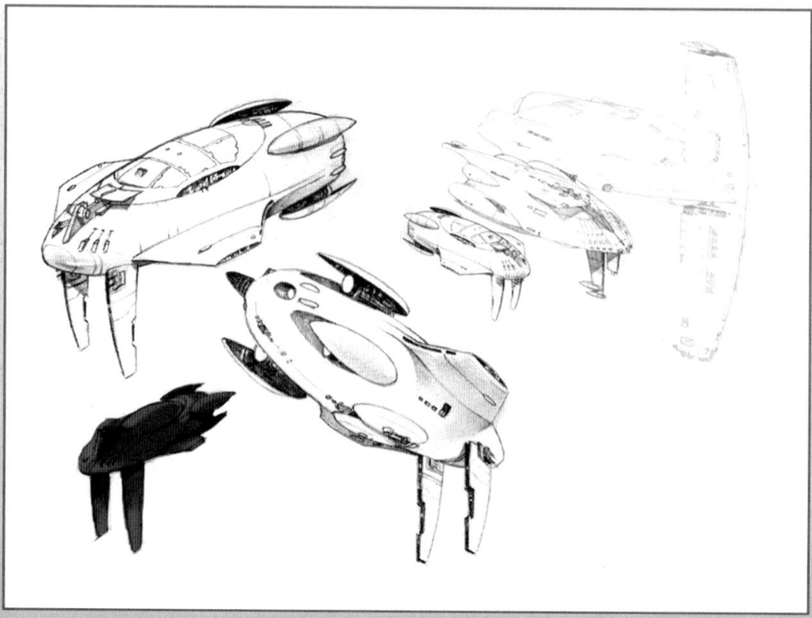

SABERTOOTH-CLASS ASSAULT/RESCUE VESSEL

With its grapple-equipped "teeth" able to swivel and adjust to almost any angle, the Sabertooth is designed to latch on to larger ships. When it's attached to an enemy vessel, the Sabertooth's crew can quickly breach the enemy's hull and disgorge squads of assault troops directly into the opposing ship. When latched on to a friendly ship, the Sabertooth can move a damaged ship out of harm's way or rescue its crew.

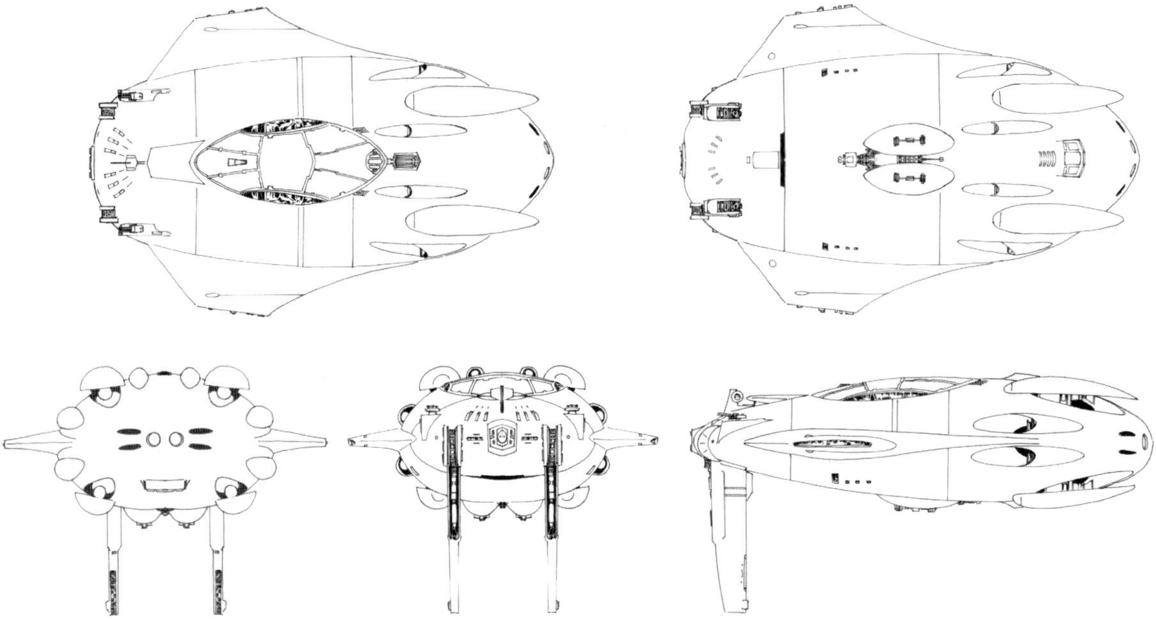

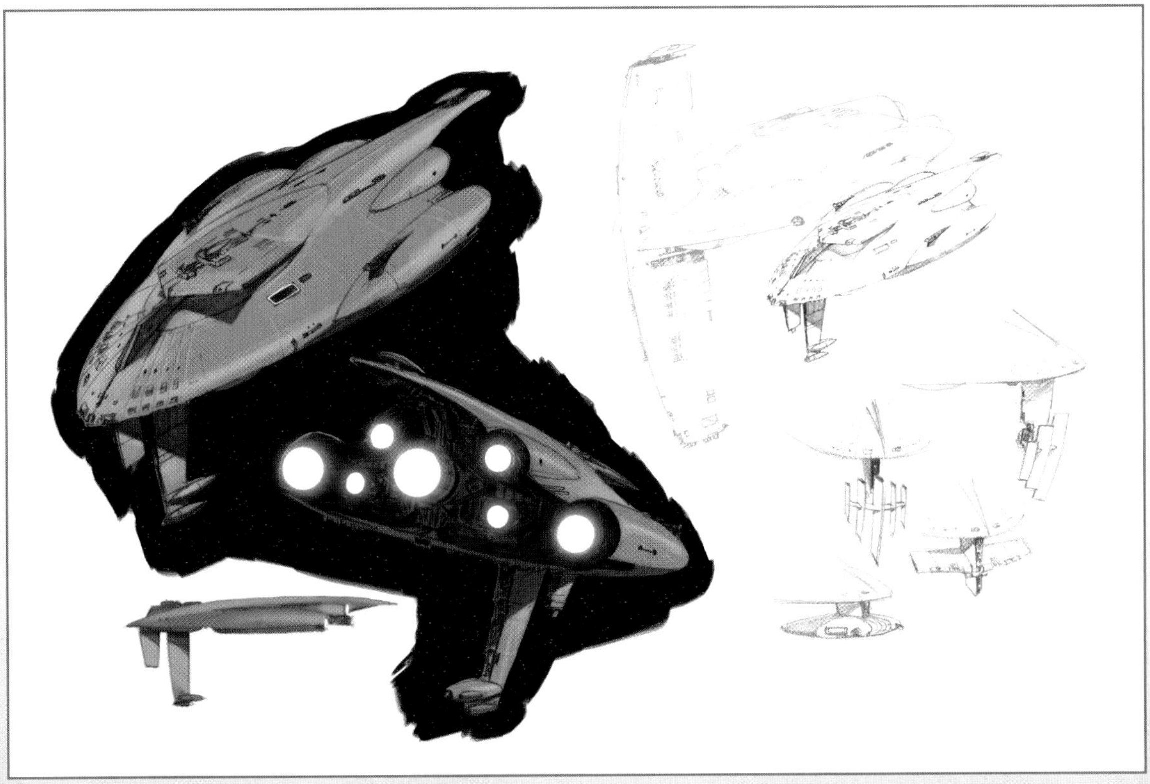

GALACTIC ALLIANCE FRIGATE

While it usually serves the same function as the Imperial ship of the same class, the Galactic Alliance's frigate can also adapt to other roles. The front "blades," which normally house the traditional turbolasers and torpedo tubes, can be switched out for long-range sensor pods, communications jammers, or barrage missile launchers.

THE JEDI

The Jedi, always a force for peace, had tried to broker a reconciliation between the defeated Yuuzhan Vong and the rest of the galaxy, but the Sith fomented war between the Galactic Alliance and the Empire. After the main forces of the Galactic Alliance surrendered and the Academy at Ossus was attacked, the Jedi scattered, leaderless and with few allies. Today they are hunted by the Sith Empire and its agents.

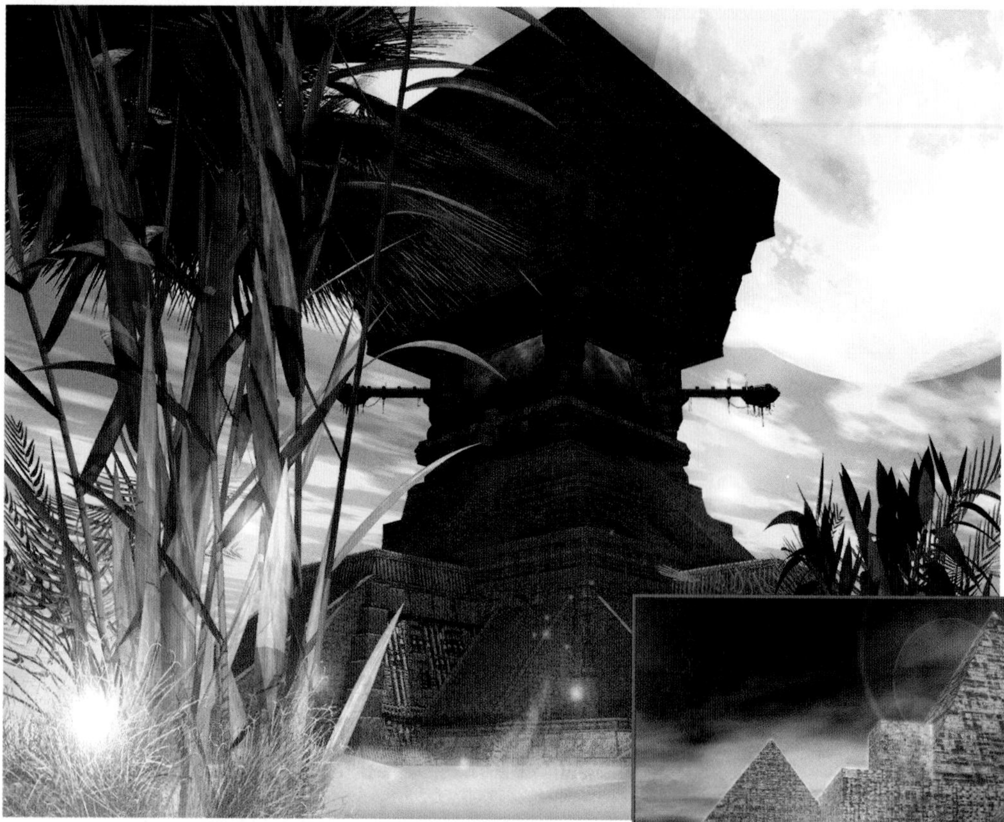

THE JEDI ACADEMY ON OSSUS

Rebuilt from the ruins of an ancient structure on Ossus by Luke Skywalker, the Jedi Academy produced several generations of new Jedi—before its destruction by the Sith.

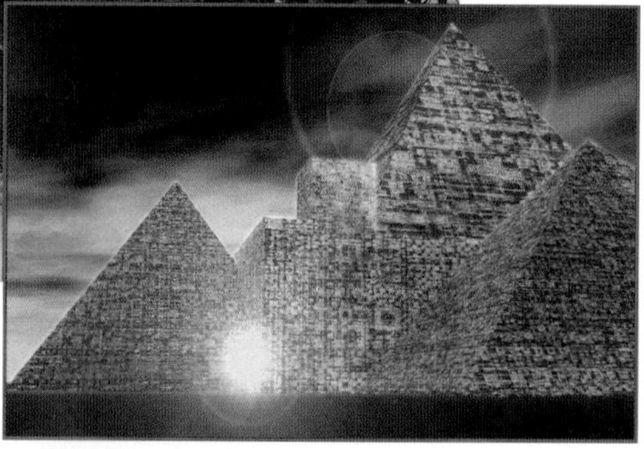

THE JEDI TEMPLE ON CORUSCANT

Prior to the Sith-Imperial War, the rebuilt Jedi Temple on Coruscant was considered among the most beautiful buildings on the city-planet. Constructed of hundreds of thousands of transparisteel panels, it was a symbol of hope for a troubled galaxy. Now it has been replaced by the dark edifice of the Sith Temple.

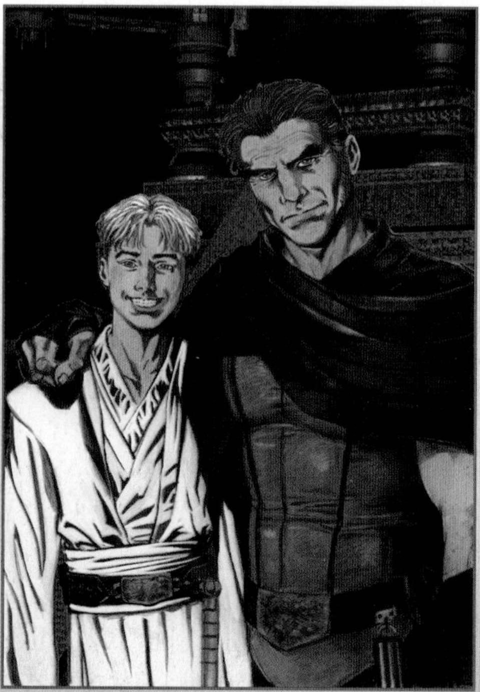

KOL SKYWALKER

A descendant of Anakin and Luke Skywalker, honor bound and driven, Kol was one of the leaders of the Jedi Council. Disliking politics, he preferred to spend more time at the training facility on Ossus than at the more formal temple on Coruscant.

A master tactician, Kol made sure the new Jedi understood that defending the peace was preferable to winning a war. In the end, though, sabotaged by the Sith and abandoned by the defeated Galactic Alliance, the Jedi were unable to do either.

He was briefly married to Morrigan Corde, who left him shortly after she gave birth to their son Cade.

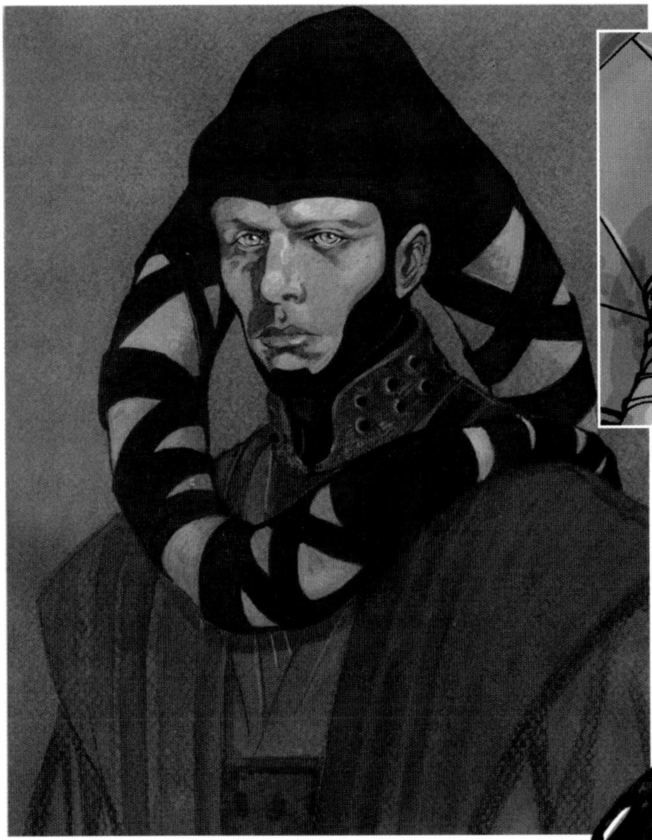

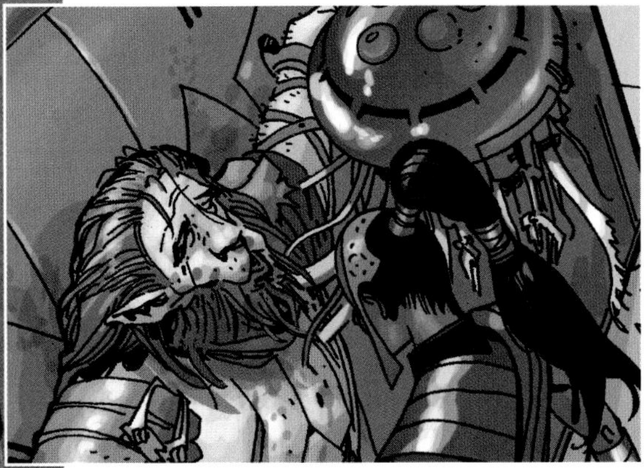

HOSK TREY'LIS

Captured by a group of bounty hunters led by Cade Skywalker, Trey'lis was turned over to the Sith—where his expected fate would be torture and eventual death. But Hosk Trey'lis never gave up hope in the young Skywalker . . .

SHADO VAO

Kol Skywalker's former Padawan, Shado has honed his martial skills and has yet to find his equal with a lightsaber. The Twi'lek and Cade Skywalker were boyhood friends.

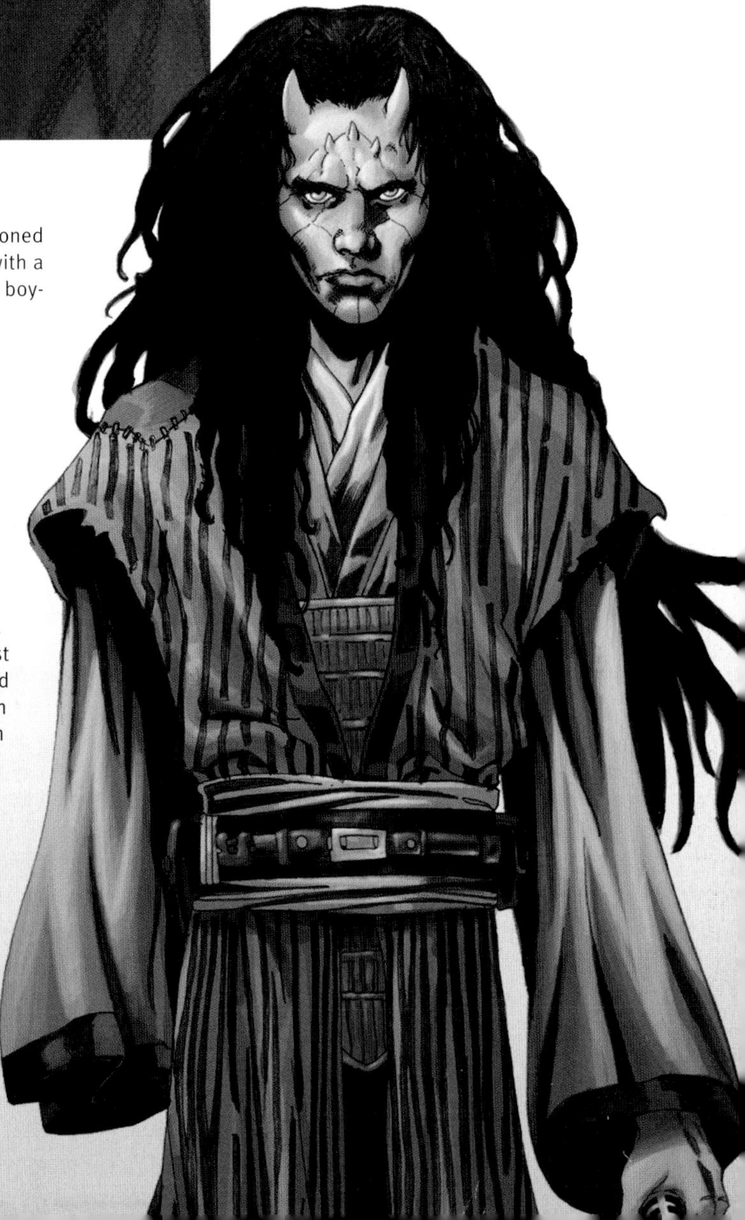

WOLF SAZEN

Kol Skywalker's former apprentice and Cade's Master. Contemplative and serious, Wolf follows the living Force and had hoped to teach his Padawan to do the same. Wolf was present at the fall of Ossus and Kol Skywalker's death. He lost his right arm in the battle and nearly lost his life. He has since retrained himself to wield his lightsaber with his left hand, keeping an empty sleeve rather than replace his right arm and hand.

While many Jedi have lost hope, Wolf believes the return of a Skywalker to the Order's head could unite the Jedi and enable them to defeat the Sith. Wolf's vision of hope for the galaxy means finding his former apprentice and convincing him to assume his legacy.

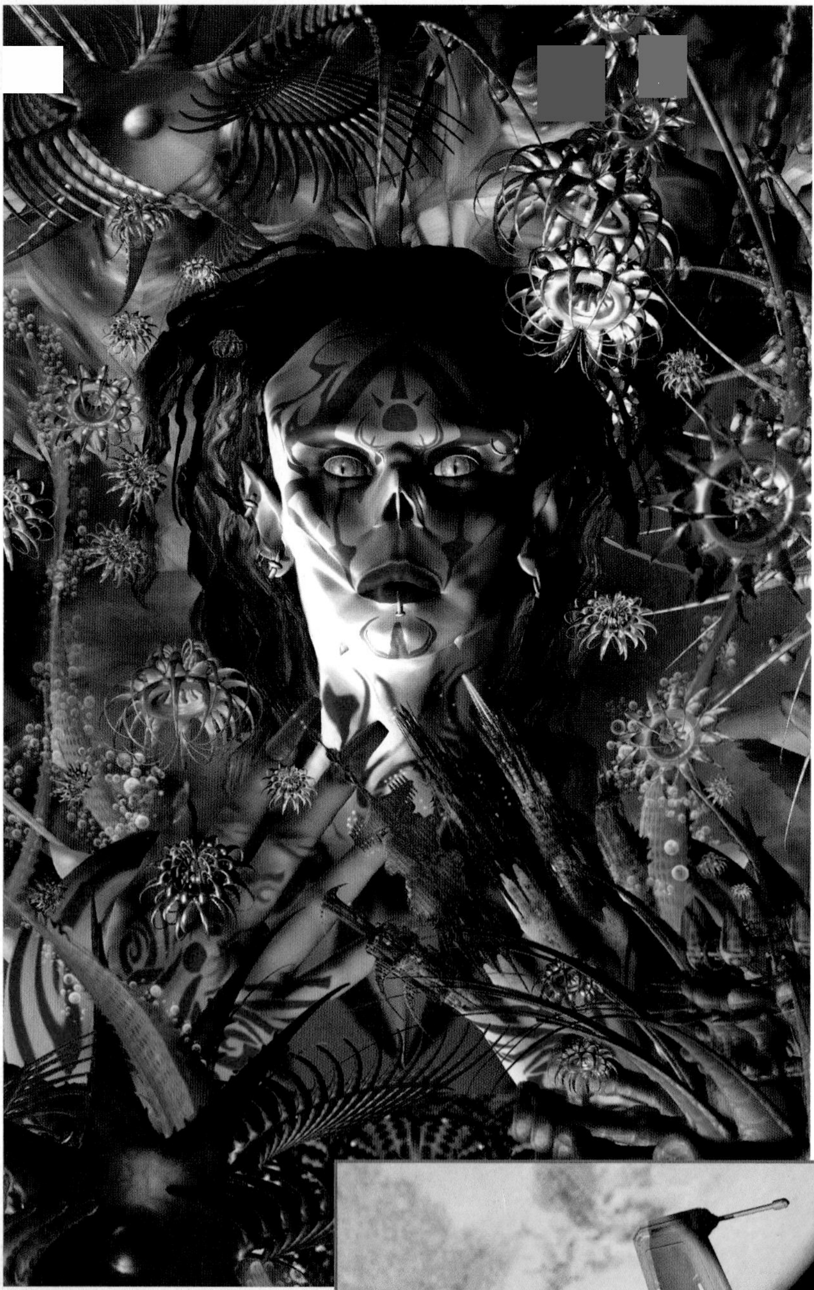

YUUZHAN VONG

Still hated by many in the galaxy for their species' destruction of so many worlds, the surviving Yuuzhan Vong honor the Jedi—especially the Skywalkers—for allowing them a chance to atone for their actions. Likewise, they hate the Sith for sabotaging their attempt to repair the damage they had done.

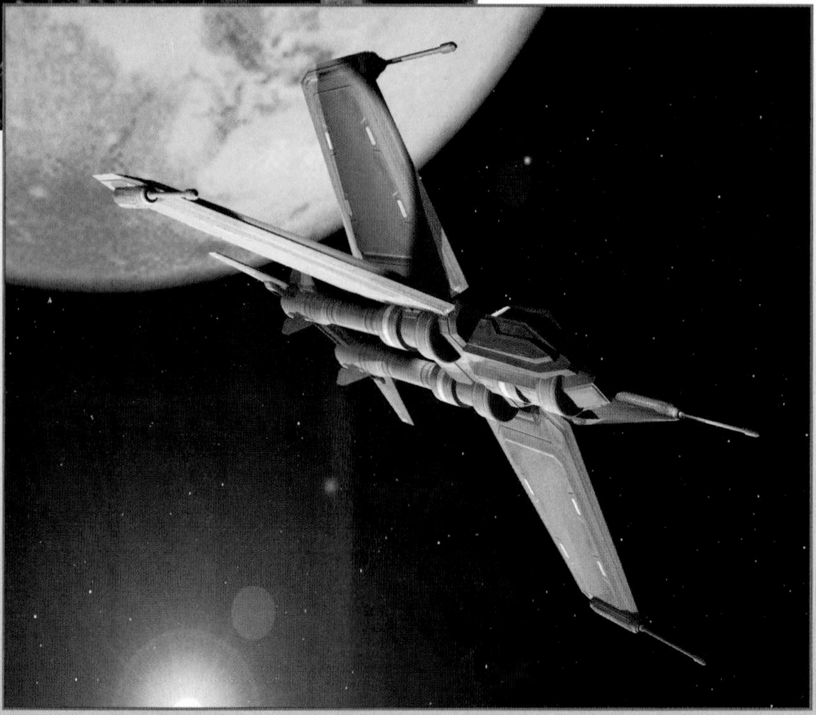

X-83 TWINTAIL FIGHTER

The latest permutation of the famous X-wing fighter, the TwinTail is favored by the Jedi for its unparalleled maneuverability in deep space as well as in atmosphere. These fighters have hyperspace capability, and the astromech is hardwired in the X-83 itself, giving each ship its own "personality." The X-wing battle configuration allows the four laser cannons to fire together or in sequence.

The galactic underworld flourishes at this time. Some well-known criminal organizations—like Black Sun—still exist, but many more unaffiliated pirate bands and smuggling cadres operate independently of one another, supplying black-market goods and contraband to the galaxy.

THE UNDERWORLD

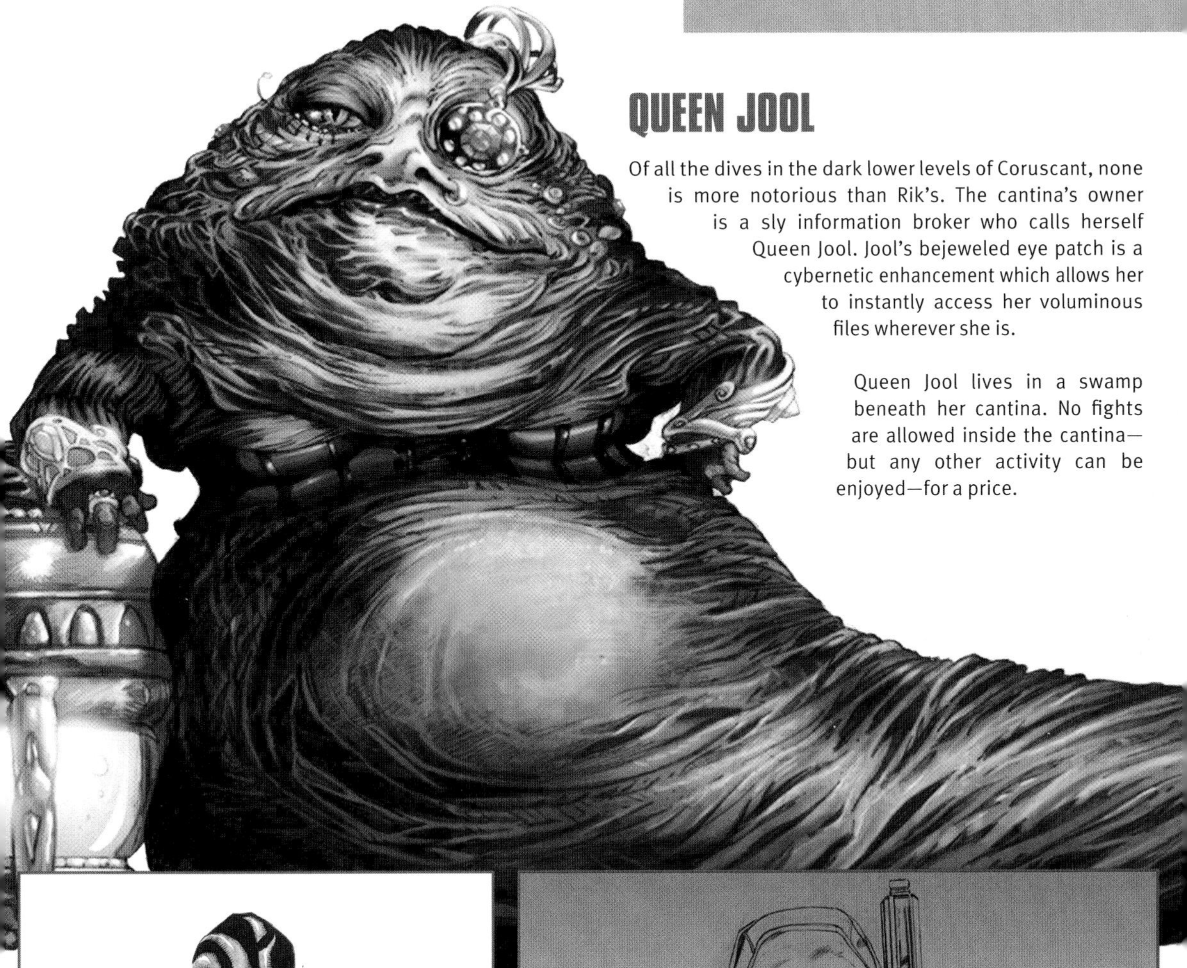

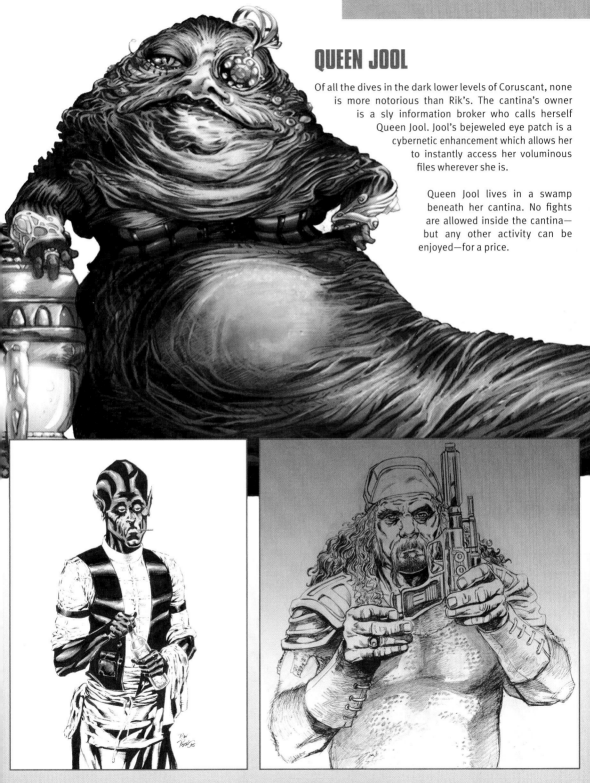

QUEEN JOOL

Of all the dives in the dark lower levels of Coruscant, none is more notorious than Rik's. The cantina's owner is a sly information broker who calls herself Queen Jool. Jool's bejeweled eye patch is a cybernetic enhancement which allows her to instantly access her voluminous files wherever she is.

Queen Jool lives in a swamp beneath her cantina. No fights are allowed inside the cantina—but any other activity can be enjoyed—for a price.

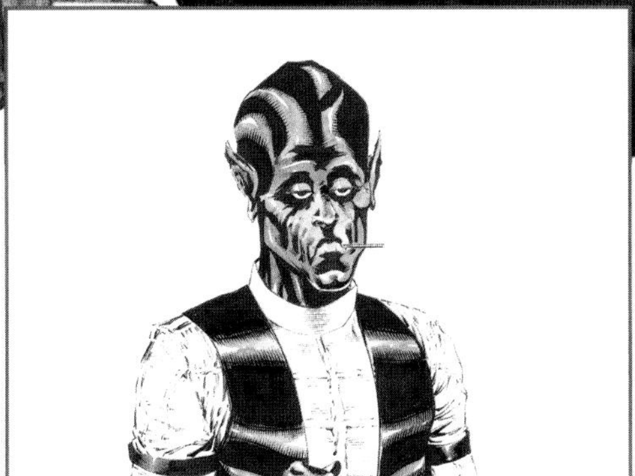

FINN

The bartender at Rik's is also its chief enforcer. Finn can take your head off with a drink, with a blaster, or possibly with his fist. Unimpressed by anything, he has heard it all, brother.

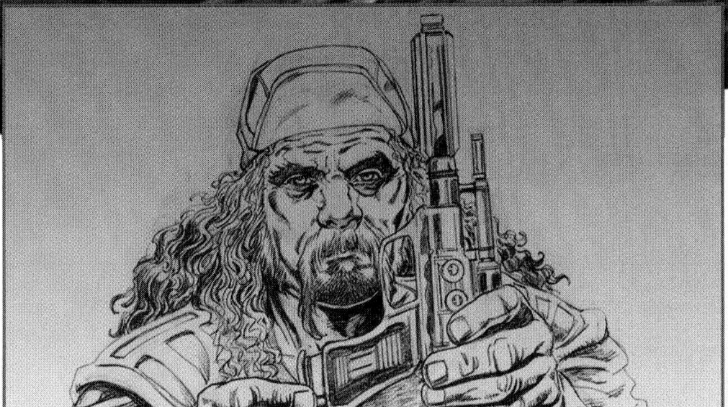

"BANTHA" RAWK

A chief mechanic at the Selonian shipyards, "Bantha" Rawk has a lucrative side business creating and modifying weapons for bounty hunters and others in need of reliable armament.

RAV

A former pirate, Rav runs a bounty clearing-house on Socorro. Rav provides services and supplies for bounty hunters, ranging from engine parts to spice—which keeps many in debt to him despite the high bounties they are given for their prey.

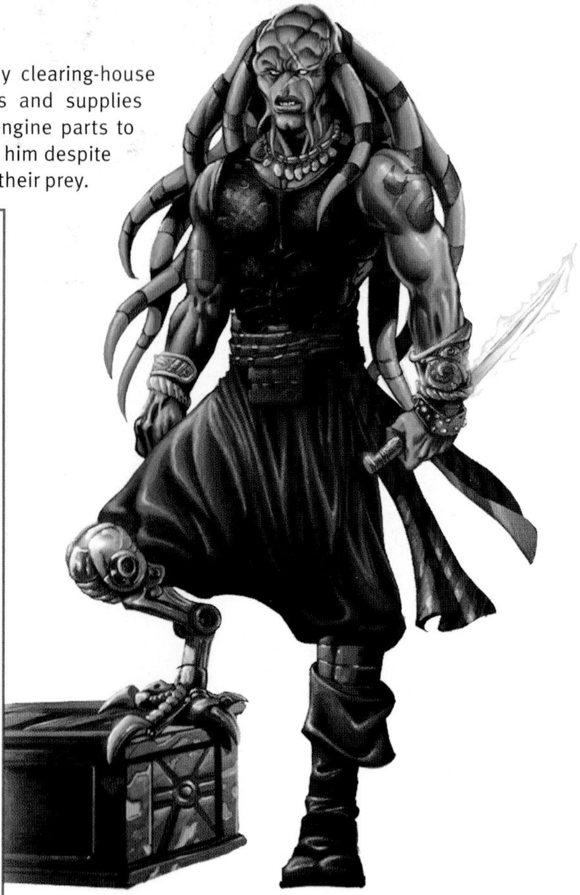

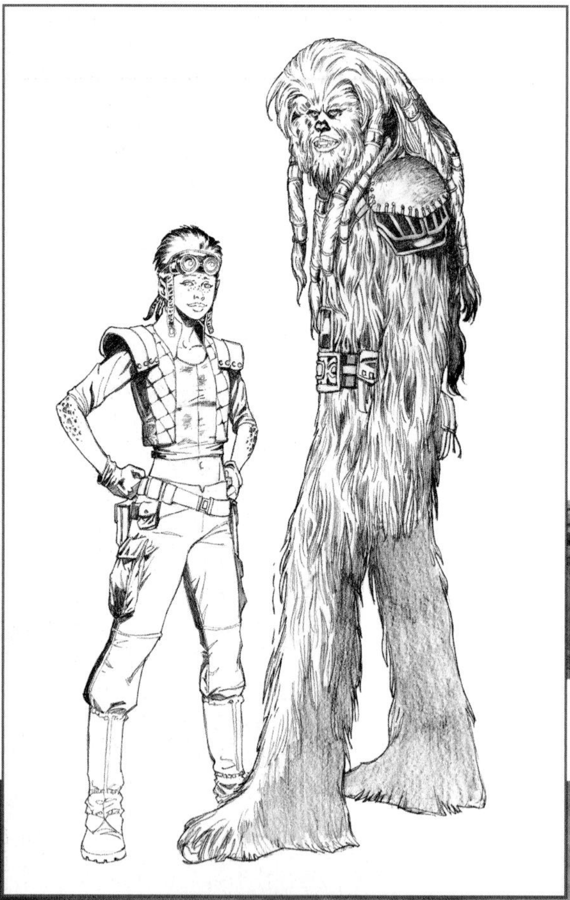

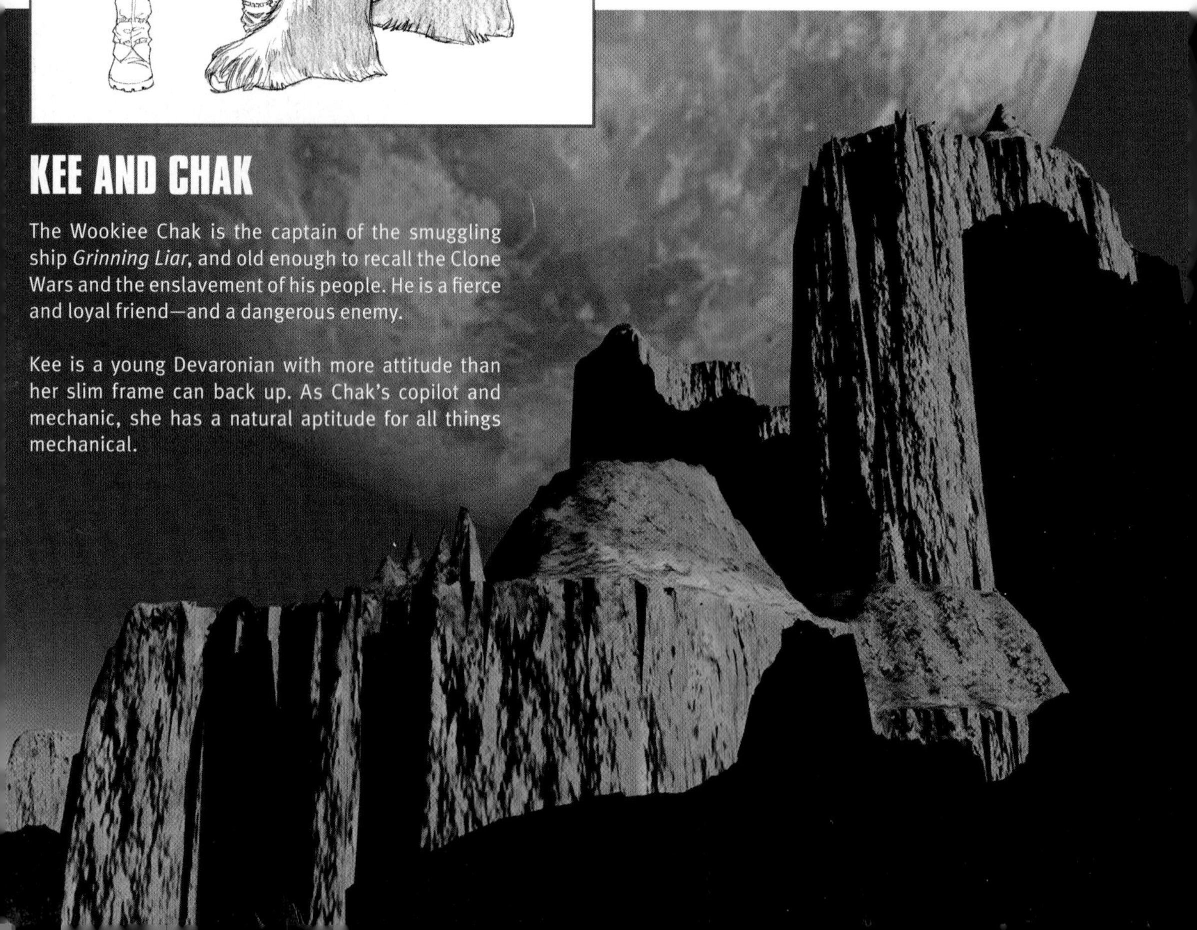

KEE AND CHAK

The Wookiee Chak is the captain of the smuggling ship *Grinning Liar*, and old enough to recall the Clone Wars and the enslavement of his people. He is a fierce and loyal friend—and a dangerous enemy.

Kee is a young Devaronian with more attitude than her slim frame can back up. As Chak's copilot and mechanic, she has a natural aptitude for all things mechanical.

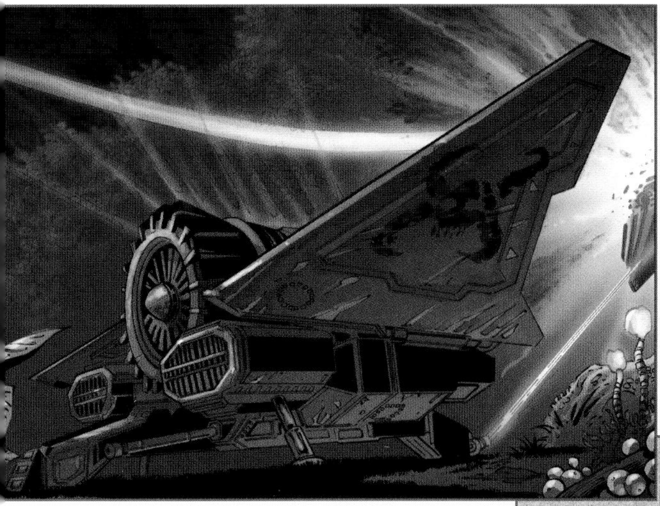

BOUNTY HUNTERS

Existing in a gray area between the rigid laws of the Sith Empire and the utter lawlessness of the galactic underworld are the bounty hunters. For a price they enforce the will of the Sith, tracking down fugitives—especially Jedi, for whom the Sith harbor a special hatred—with little regard for the safety or property of bystanders (whether those bystanders be innocent, or simply not yet convicted).

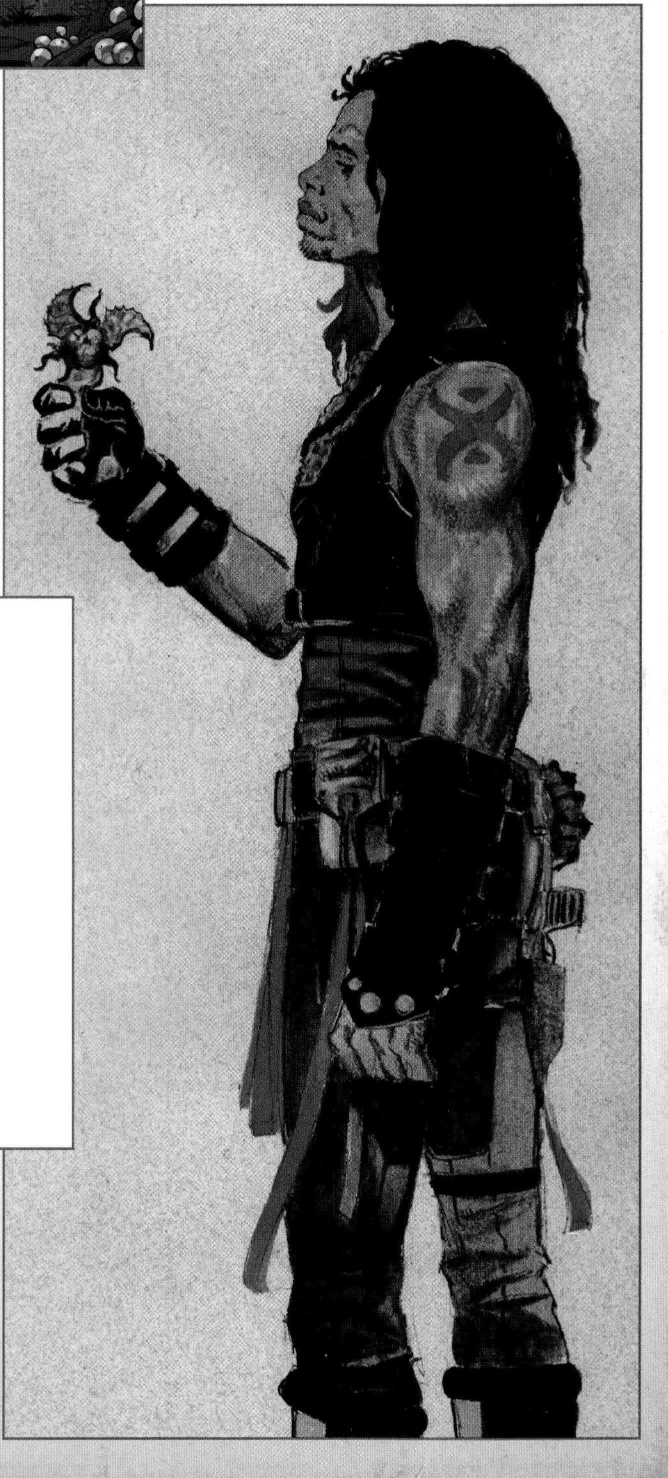

THE *MYNOCK*

Among the shadow caste of bounty hunters is the crew of the *Mynock*, a converted fast-transport vessel now outfitted with numerous "improvements," such as extra armor and shields, and high-powered weaponry. Named for a parasitic vermin common throughout the galaxy, the ship reflects the nature of its crew, who live off the bounty of the Empire and the spoils of the underworld.

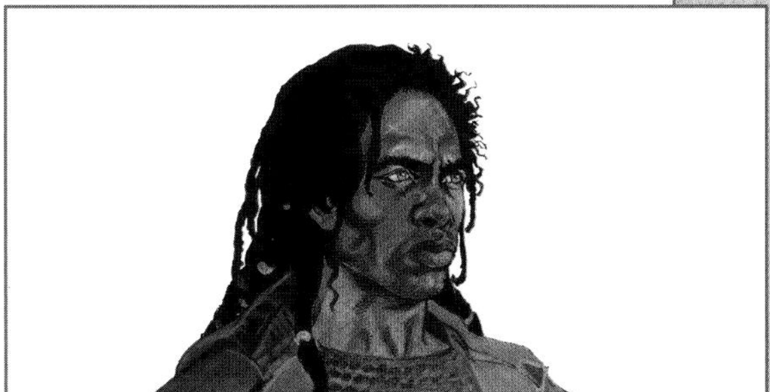

JARIAH SYN

The copilot of the *Mynock*, Jariah Syn is pragmatic and cynical. If a bounty on a fugitive pays the same dead as alive, Syn figures dead is easier. He is a weapons expert with an affinity for outlawed items, such as Yuuzhan Vong thud bugs, razorbugs, and the like. Syn also harbors a long and abiding loathing of Jedi—which has caused trouble between him and his captain, now that he knows the captain's true history.

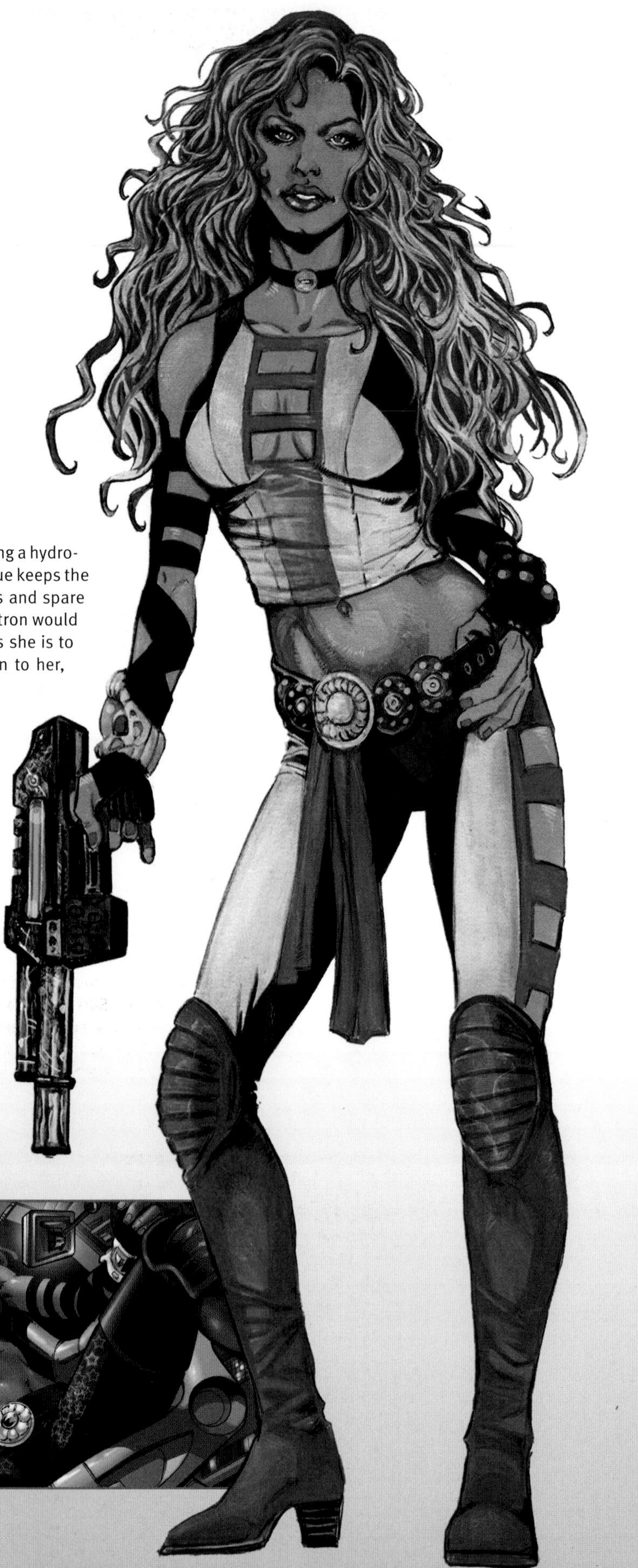

DELIAH BLUE

Able to fix almost anything mechanical using a hydro-spanner and a few choice words, Deliah Blue keeps the *Mynock* running despite a dearth of funds and spare parts. Once a dedicated party girl, the Zeltron would now like to stay as close to her captain as she is to his ship. Something in him seems broken to her, and you can't fix what you can't reach.

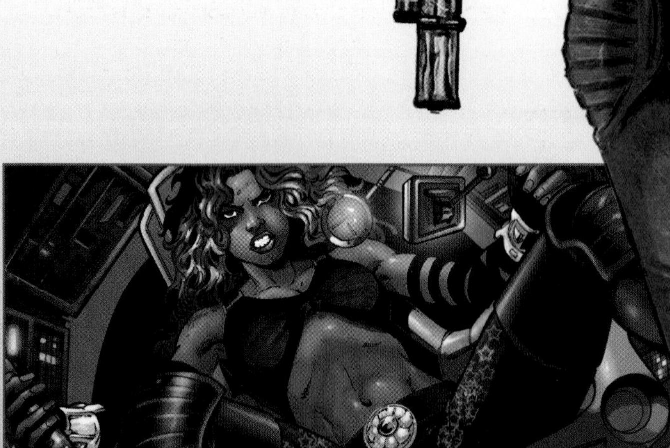

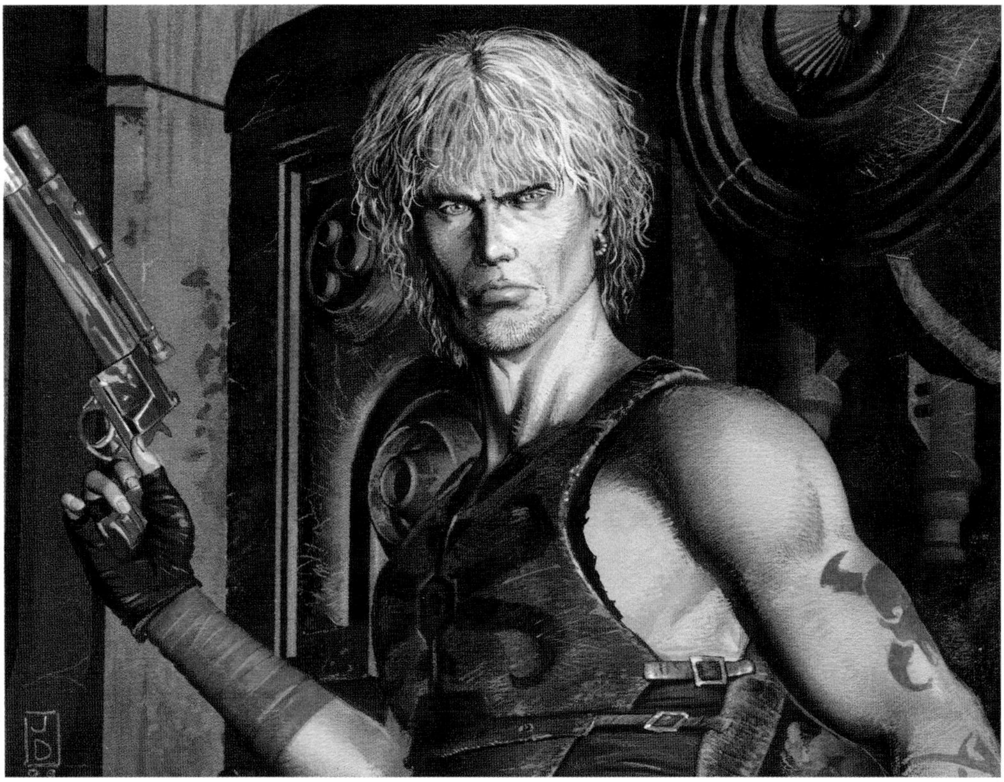

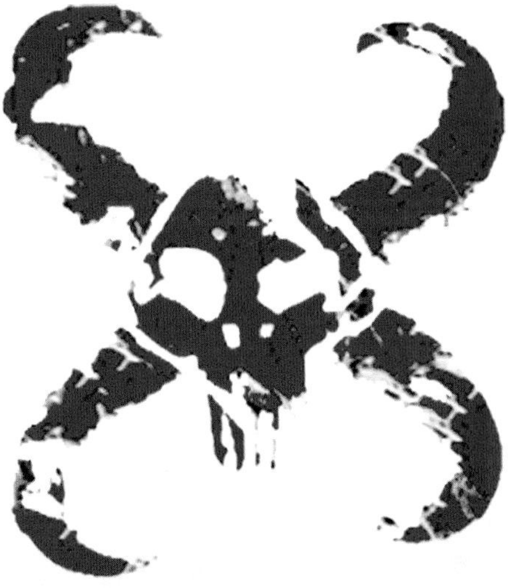

CADE SKYWALKER

After seeing his father killed by the Sith and witnessing the sacking of the Jedi Academy on Ossus, Cade Skywalker turned his back on his Jedi teachings and the Jedi Order. Believed dead by most of the surviving Jedi, Cade dropped the surname "Skywalker" and joined a pirate crew led by Rav. It was during his time with the pirates that he met and bonded with Jariah Syn.

Eventually earning enough to strike out on his own, Cade purchased the *Mynock* and he and Syn became bounty hunters. It was while pursuing a lucrative bounty on Princess Marasiah that Cade rediscovered the ruthlessness of the Sith, and became reacquainted with his former Jedi teacher Wolf Sazen and his friend Shado Vao. Inspired by their actions—and repulsed by the Sith—Cade took up his lightsaber again for the first time in decades. Now elements within the galaxy at large are aware that Cade is a Skywalker—by all accounts, the last Skywalker—and he finds himself on an uncertain path that may take him to redemption, or his doom.

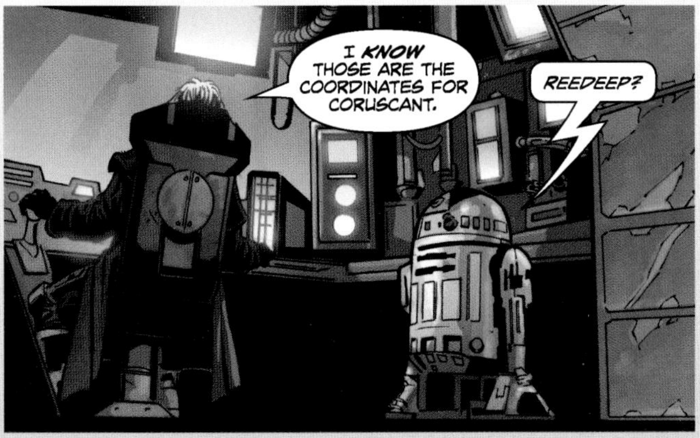
I KNOW THOSE ARE THE COORDINATES FOR CORUSCANT.
REEDEEP?

R2-D2

A battered old astromech droid, R2-D2 has been a companion to a number of different Skywalkers through the years. Hidden in a secret subbasement of the Academy on Ossus and serviced by the Yuuzhan Vong in honor of Cade's father, the plucky droid was made a gift to Cade after he returned (at least partially) to the Jedi fold, and is now a fixture onboard the *Mynock*.

LUKE SKYWALKER

The legendary hero of the Rebellion and the re-progenitor of the Jedi Order, the ghostly visage of Luke Skywalker sometimes appears to Cade, giving the young Skywalker advice (which is usually unwanted and often ignored). Since Luke's appearances often coincide with Cade's regrettable consumption of hallucinogenic "deathsticks," there is some question as to whether the visitations are truly those of the actual "Force ghost" of Luke Skywalker or figments of Cade's own mind.

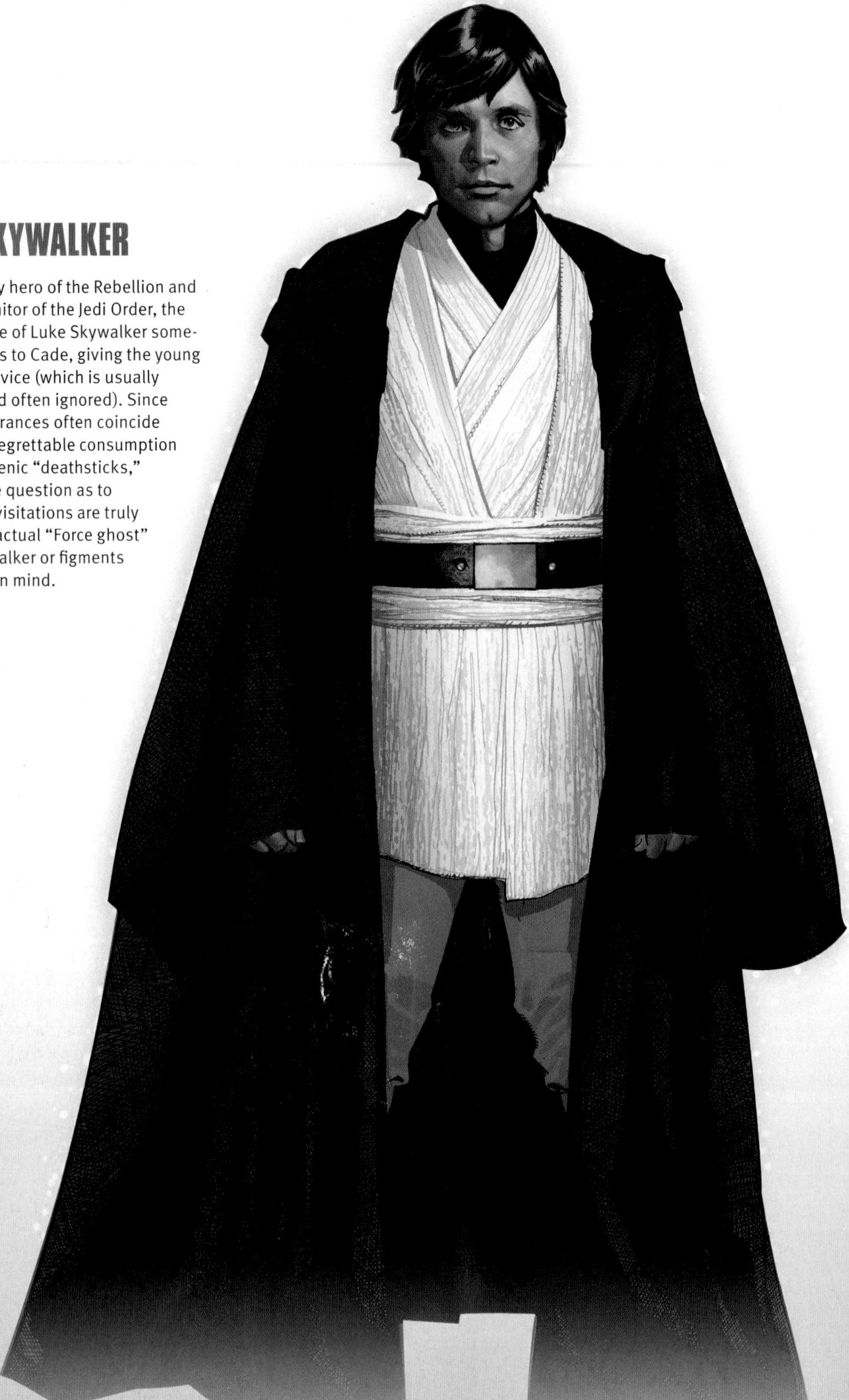

LEGACY HANDBOOK ADDENDUM

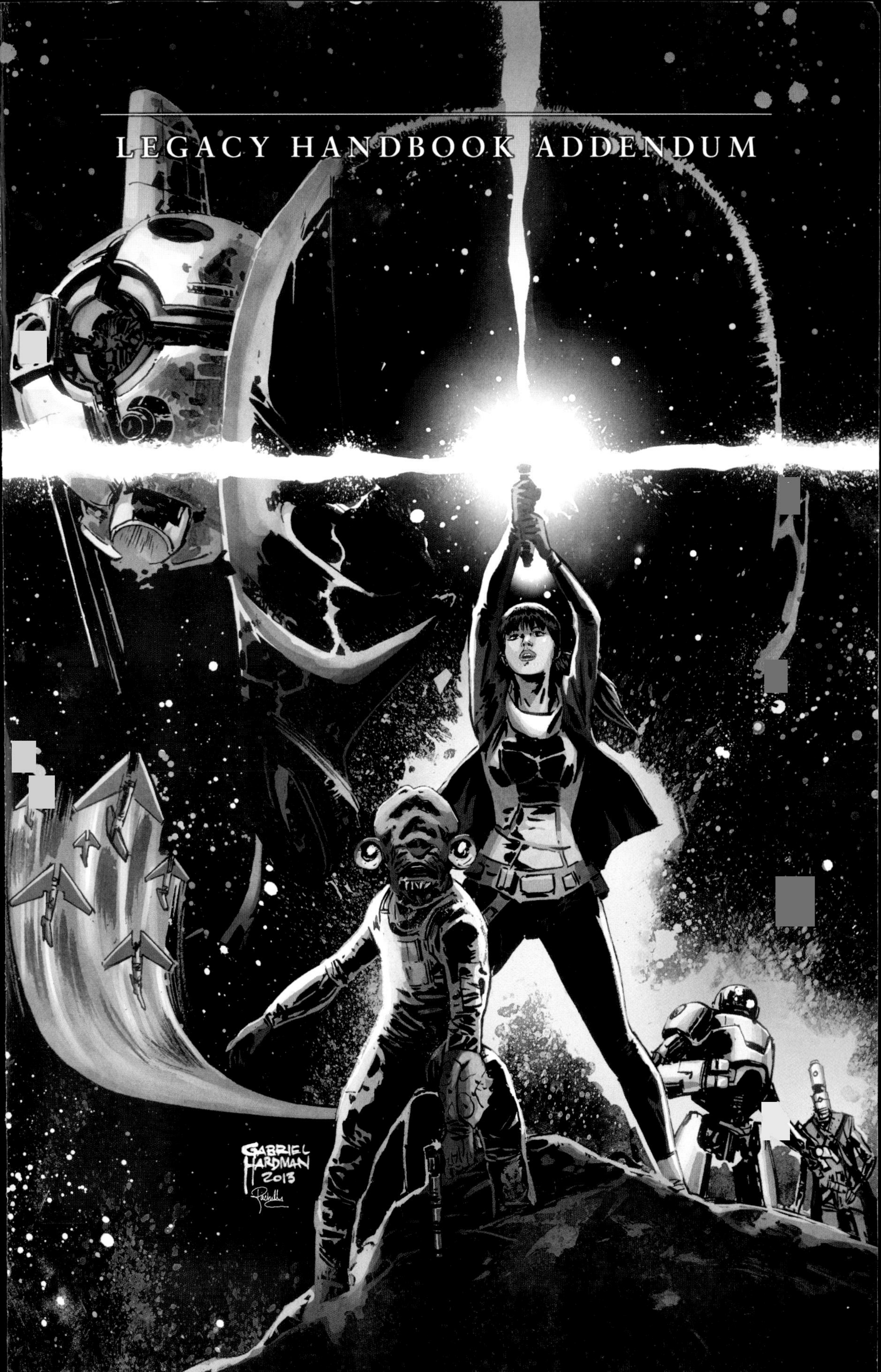
GABRIEL
HARDMAN
2013

ILLUSTRATION BY GABRIEL HARDMAN COLORS BY RACHELLE ROSENBERG

TEXT
RANDY STRADLEY

ART
GABRIEL HARDMAN

THE GALAXY FREED

Eight years after it began, Darth Krayt's Sith Empire was overthrown by the combined forces of Emperor Fel's loyalists, the remnant of the Galactic Alliance, and the resurgent Jedi Order. Krayt's undying body was sent hurtling into Coruscant's sun by Cade Skywalker, and the surviving members of the order of the One Sith were scattered. The galaxy was once again free, but splintered.

In an effort to bring unity to the known galaxy, the new Triumvirate government (formed by the victorious allies) established programs to enhance communications and trade among far-flung systems. One mission, to complete a new communications array in the Shifala system, required an Imperial team to traverse the dangerous Surd Nebula.

With the team was a highly specialized comm droid.

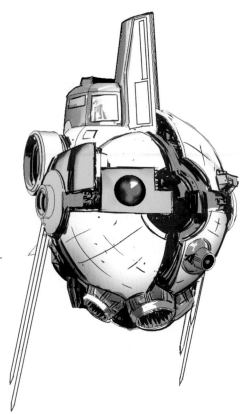

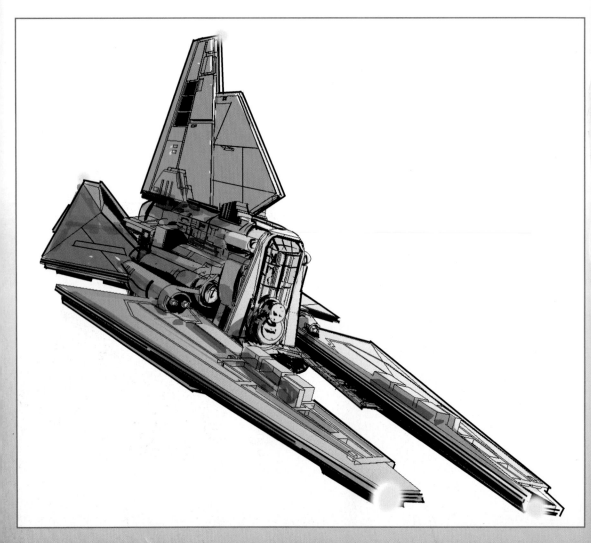

THE SITH THREAT REMAINS

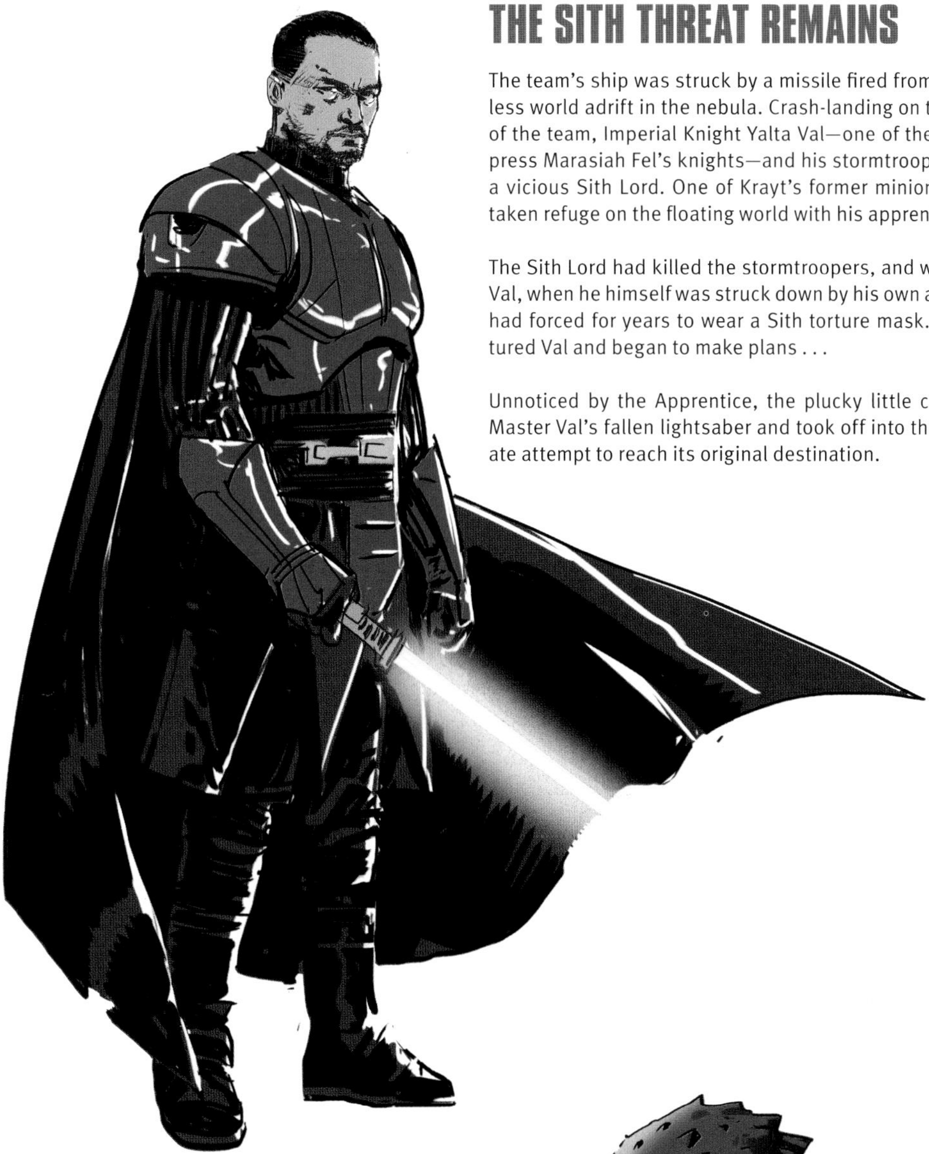

The team's ship was struck by a missile fired from an uncharted, orbitless world adrift in the nebula. Crash-landing on the planet, the leader of the team, Imperial Knight Yalta Val—one of the most trusted of Empress Marasiah Fel's knights—and his stormtroopers were attacked by a vicious Sith Lord. One of Krayt's former minions, the Sith Lord had taken refuge on the floating world with his apprentice.

The Sith Lord had killed the stormtroopers, and was about to kill Yalta Val, when he himself was struck down by his own apprentice—whom he had forced for years to wear a Sith torture mask. The Apprentice captured Val and began to make plans . . .

Unnoticed by the Apprentice, the plucky little comm droid retrieved Master Val's fallen lightsaber and took off into the nebula in a desperate attempt to reach its original destination.

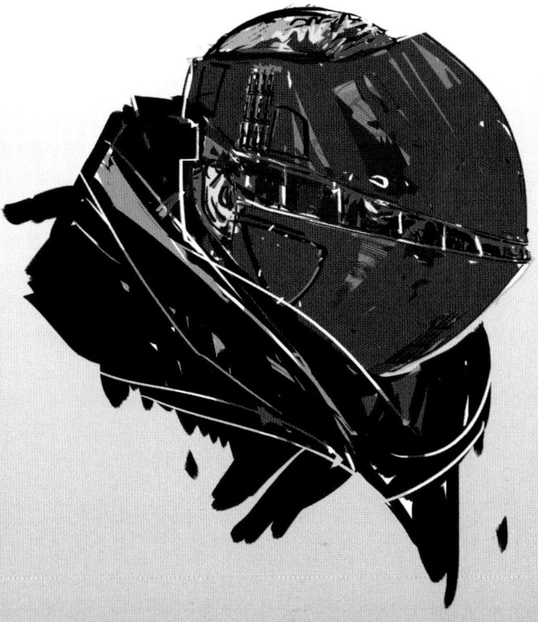

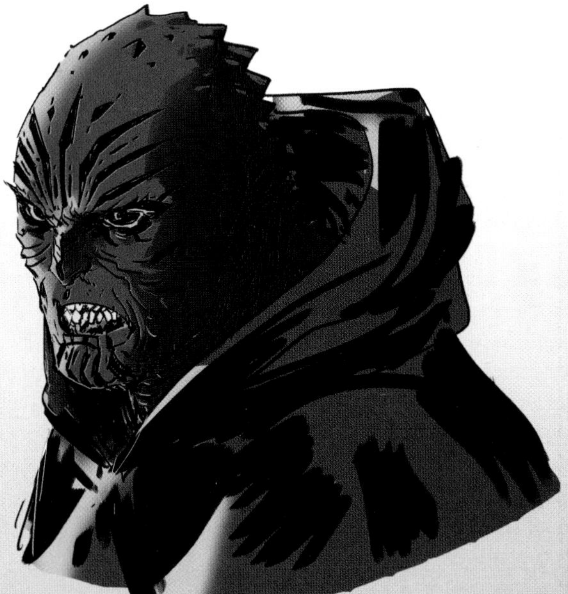

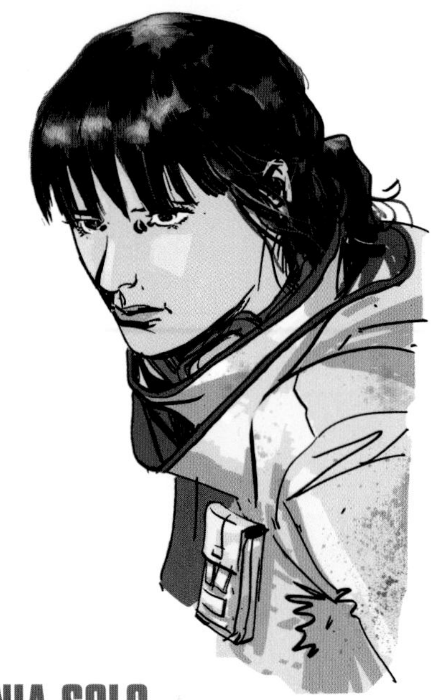

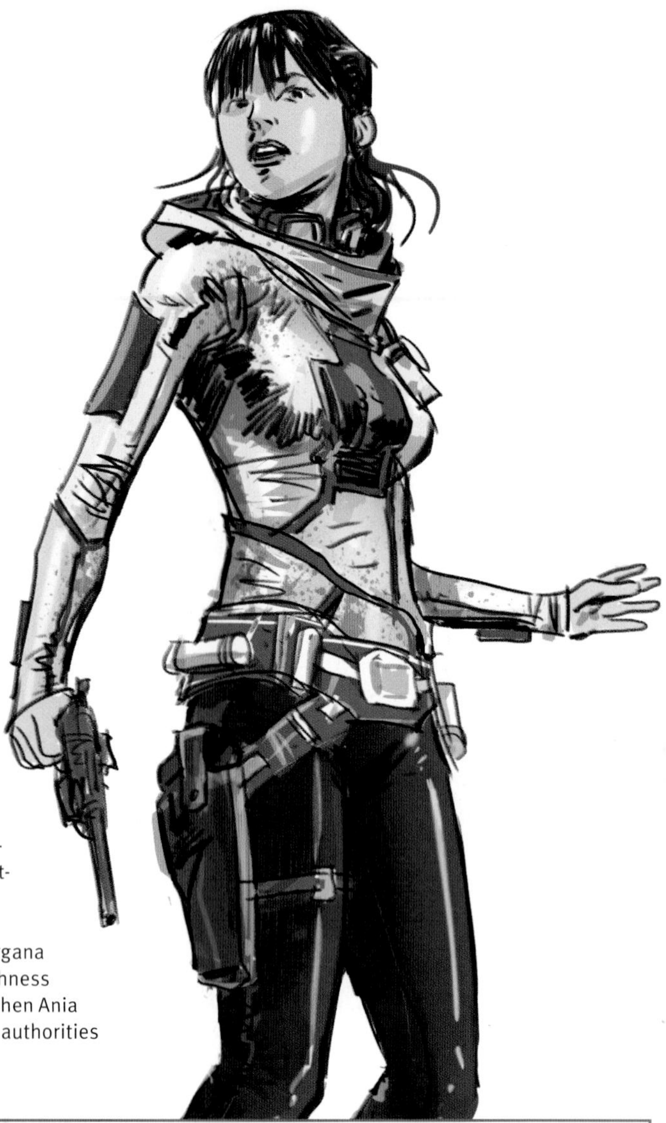

ANIA SOLO, A FORGOTTEN LEGACY

The comm droid, battered and dysfunctional after its passage through the nebula, eventually ended up in the hands of a junk dealer named Ania Solo. She and her friend Sauk, one of the millions of Mon Calamari displaced when the Sith poisoned their homeworld, discovered Yalta Val's lightsaber in the droid's interior compartment.

Ania, a distant descendant of Han Solo and Leia Organa Solo, inherited her great-great-grandfather's brashness and penchant for attracting trouble. Thus it was that when Ania and Sauk attempted to sell the lightsaber, the Shifala authorities moved to arrest them . . .

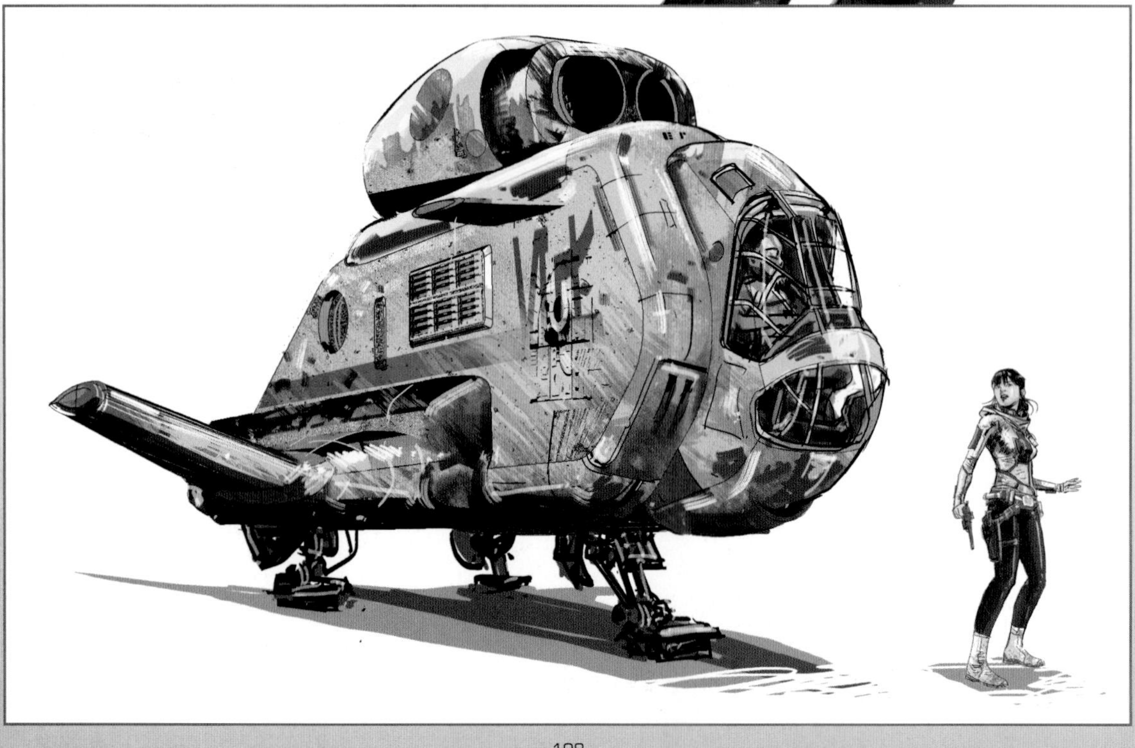

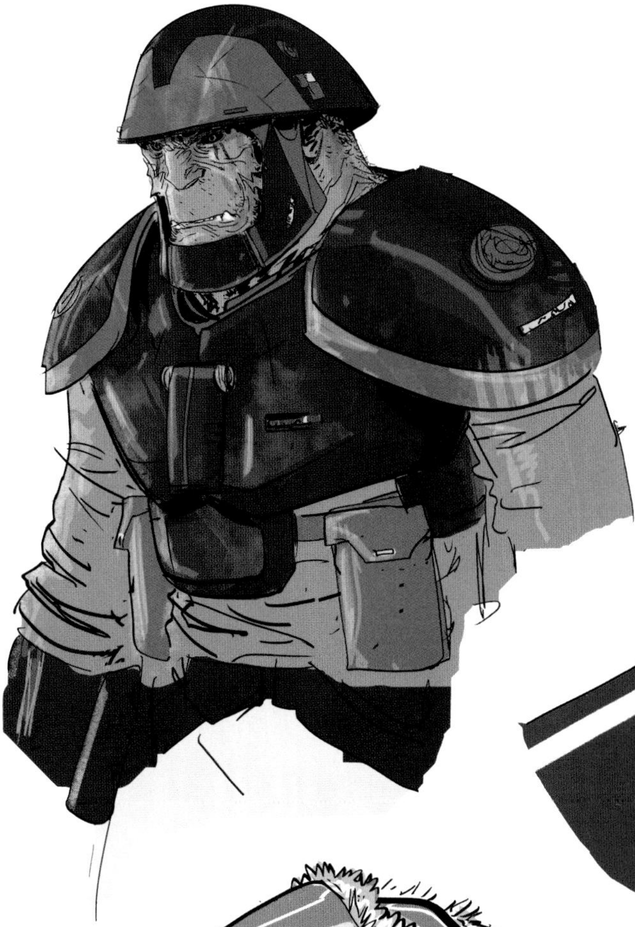

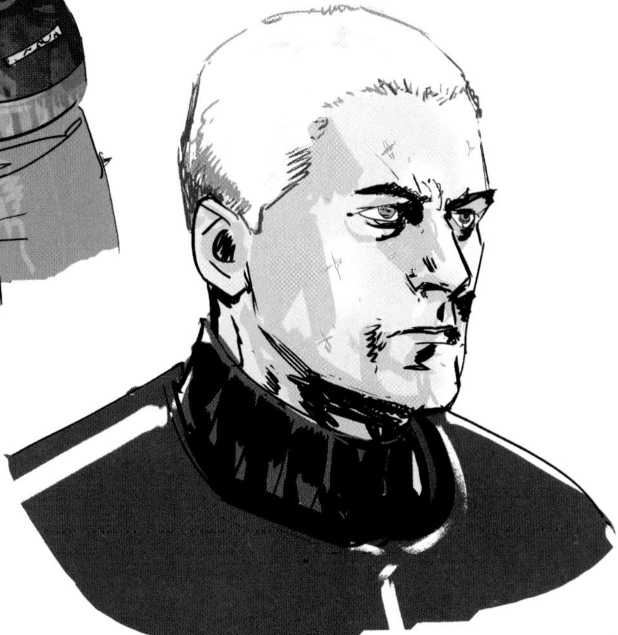

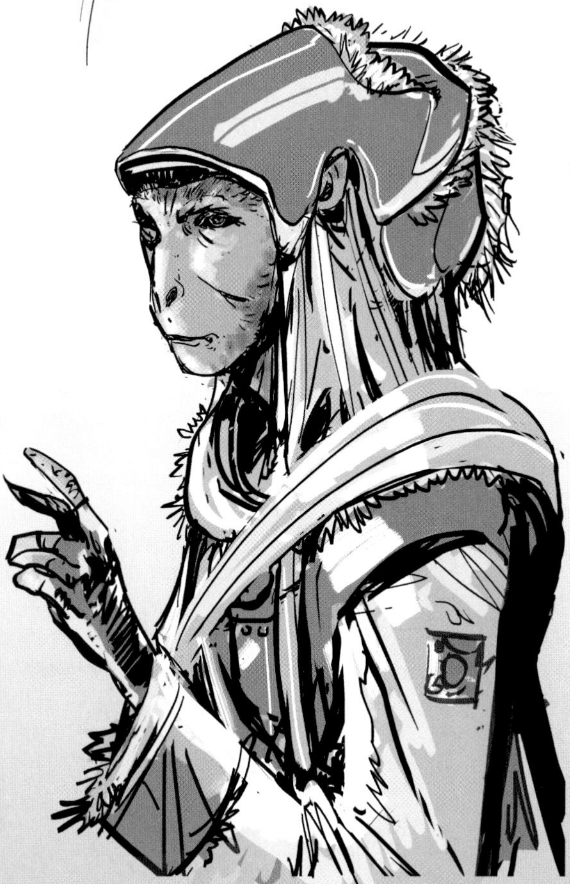

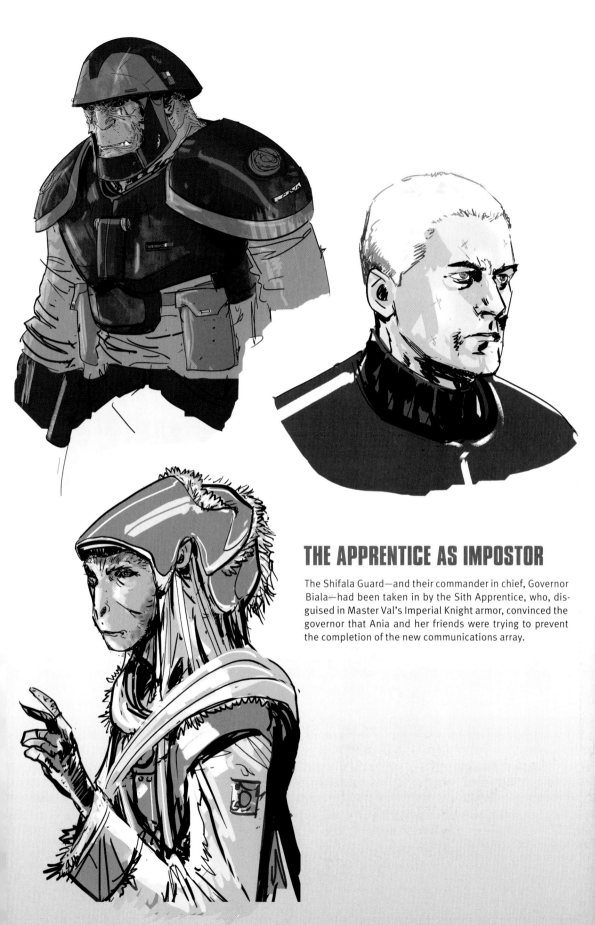

THE APPRENTICE AS IMPOSTOR

The Shifala Guard—and their commander in chief, Governor Biala—had been taken in by the Sith Apprentice, who, disguised in Master Val's Imperial Knight armor, convinced the governor that Ania and her friends were trying to prevent the completion of the new communications array.

THE APPRENTICE REVEALED

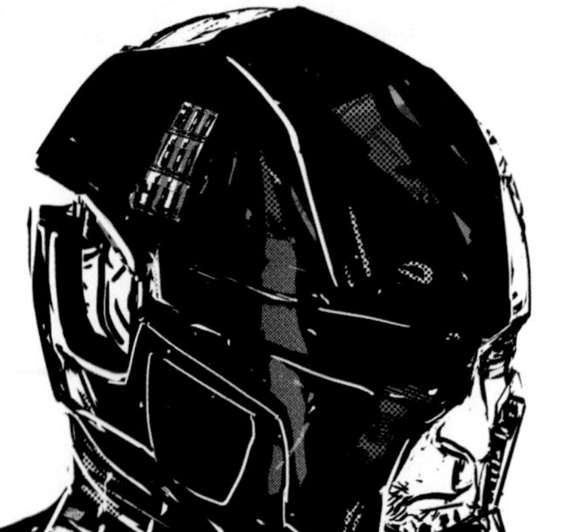

Pursued by the impostor, Ania and her friends encountered Master Val's apprentice, Jao Assam, who helped save them from a monstrous creature on a sulfurous planet—and then joined them in their quest to expose the impostor and locate Master Val.

Eventually the impostor proclaimed himself to be Darth Wredd. He managed to crash the new communications array into the floating world from whence he originated, but not before being disfigured in a duel with Assam. Master Val was rescued, but Darth Wredd escaped.

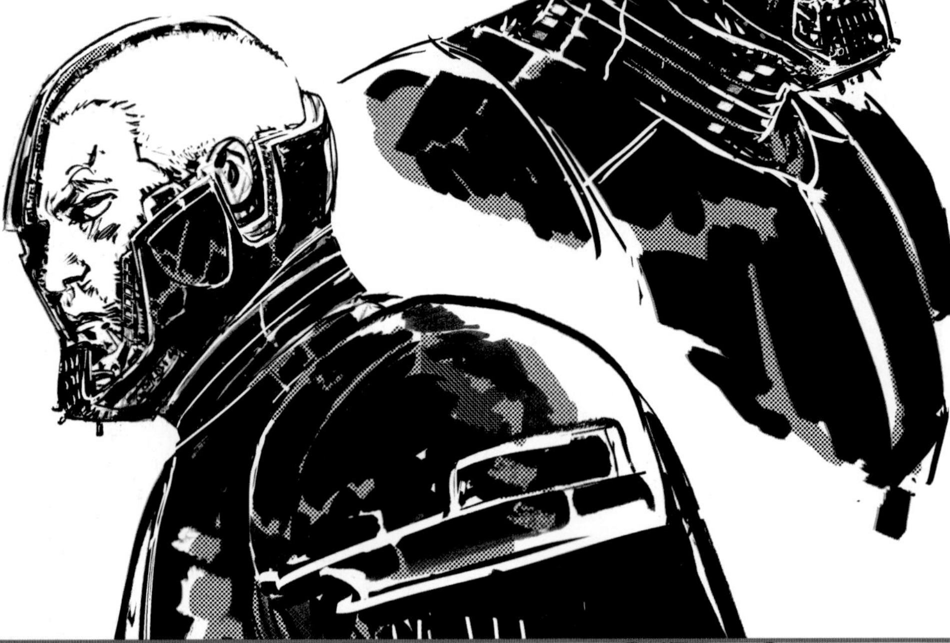

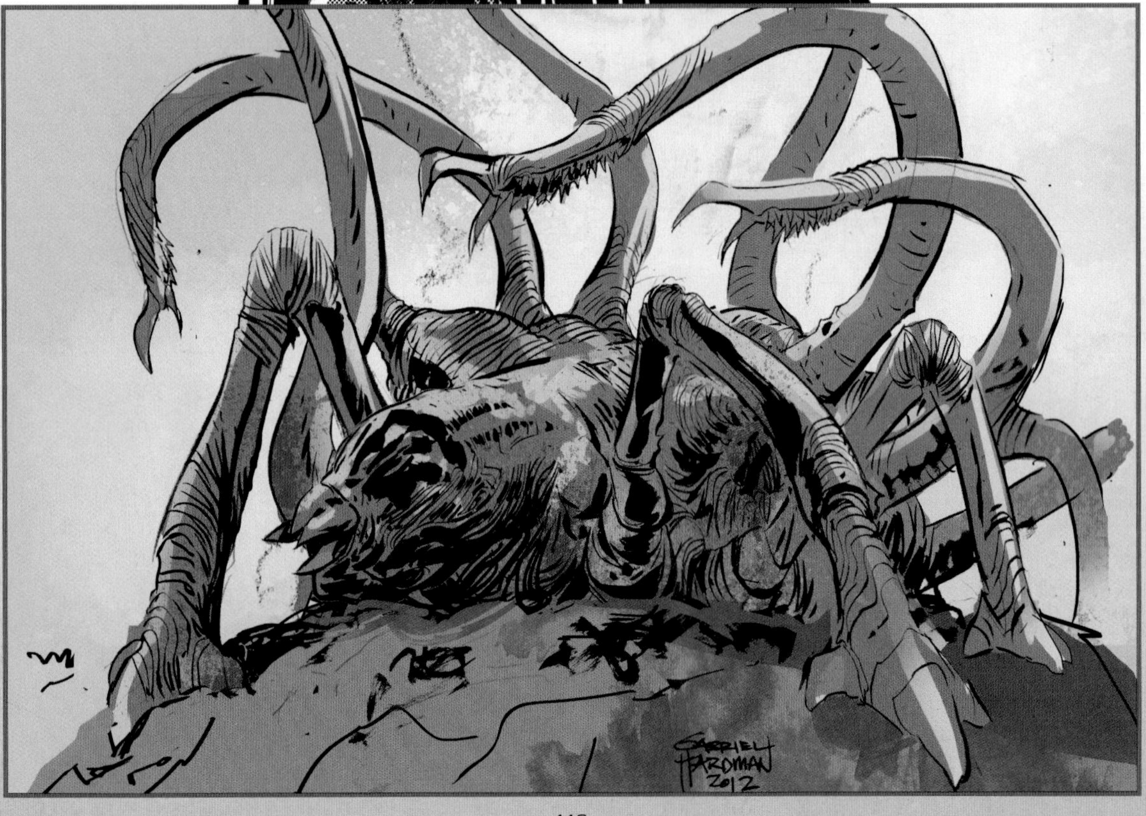
GABRIEL HARDMAN 2012

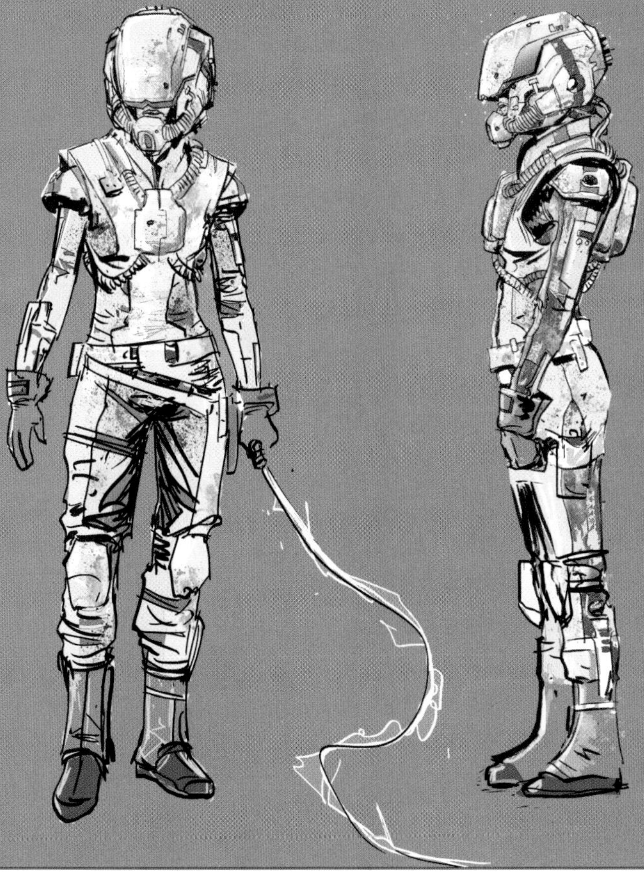

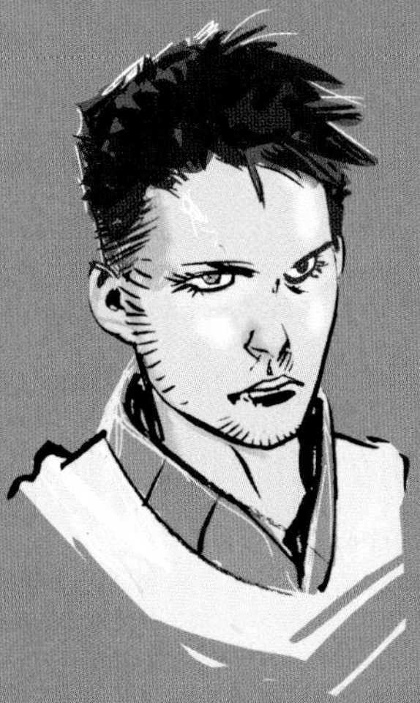

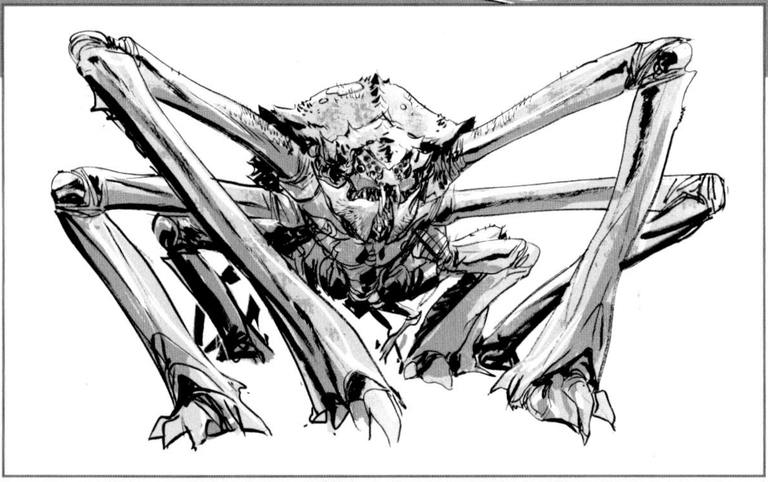

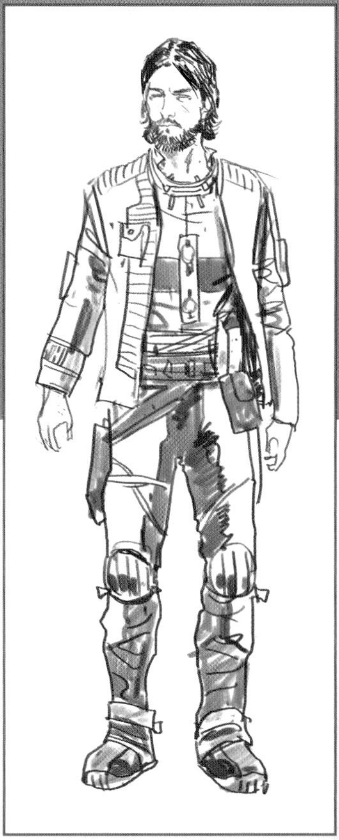

ANIA'S PAST CATCHES UP WITH HER

In their hunt for Darth Wredd, Ania and her companions answered a distress call from a crippled ship commanded by Ramid, one of Ania's former flames. But the encounter was not as chance as it seemed: Ramid and his crew were bounty hunters who had discovered that the Empire had put a price on her head—for murder!

Despite her claims of innocence, Ramid and his crew took Ania prisoner—only to lose her to *another* bounty hunter. By the time Ania's friends caught up with the bounty hunters and rescued her, Master Val had discovered proof that the female bounty hunter was the real murderer and had framed Ania for the crime.

In what looked like it might be their final adventure together, Ania and her companions chased Darth Wredd back to the floating world after he captured Jao Assam. Too late did they realize Wredd's plan was to lure them—and the Empire—into a final showdown with nearly all of the remaining One Sith . . .

TRANDOSHAN STORMTROOPERS

Empress Marasiah Fel's new, more enlightened Empire enlisted more than just humans to serve in its military. A platoon of Trandoshan troopers was instrumental in engaging the One Sith in a final battle.

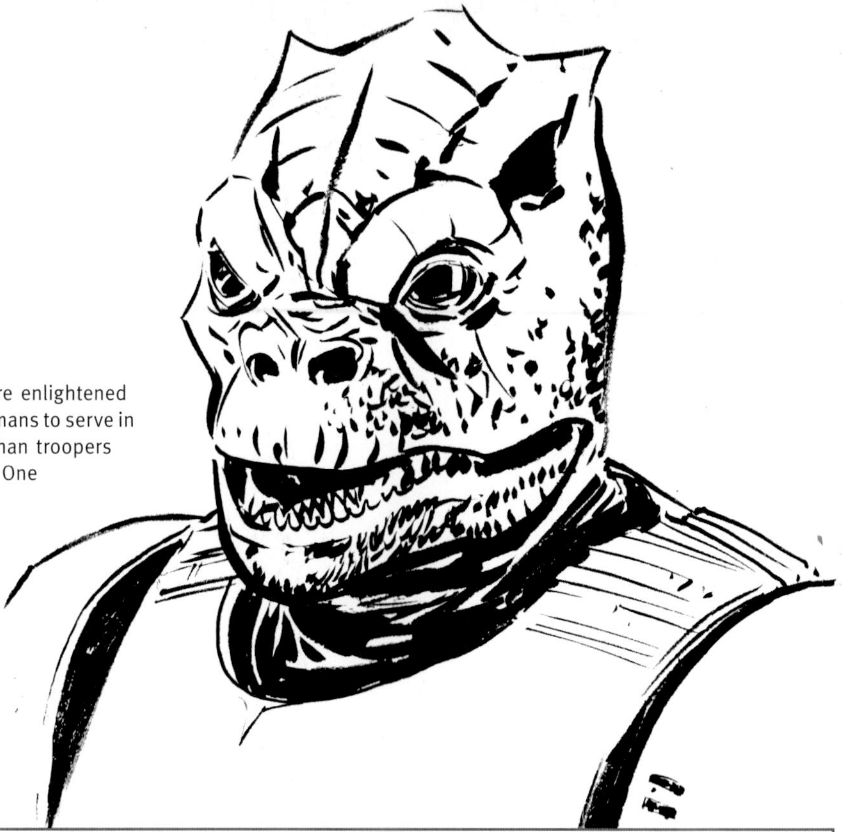

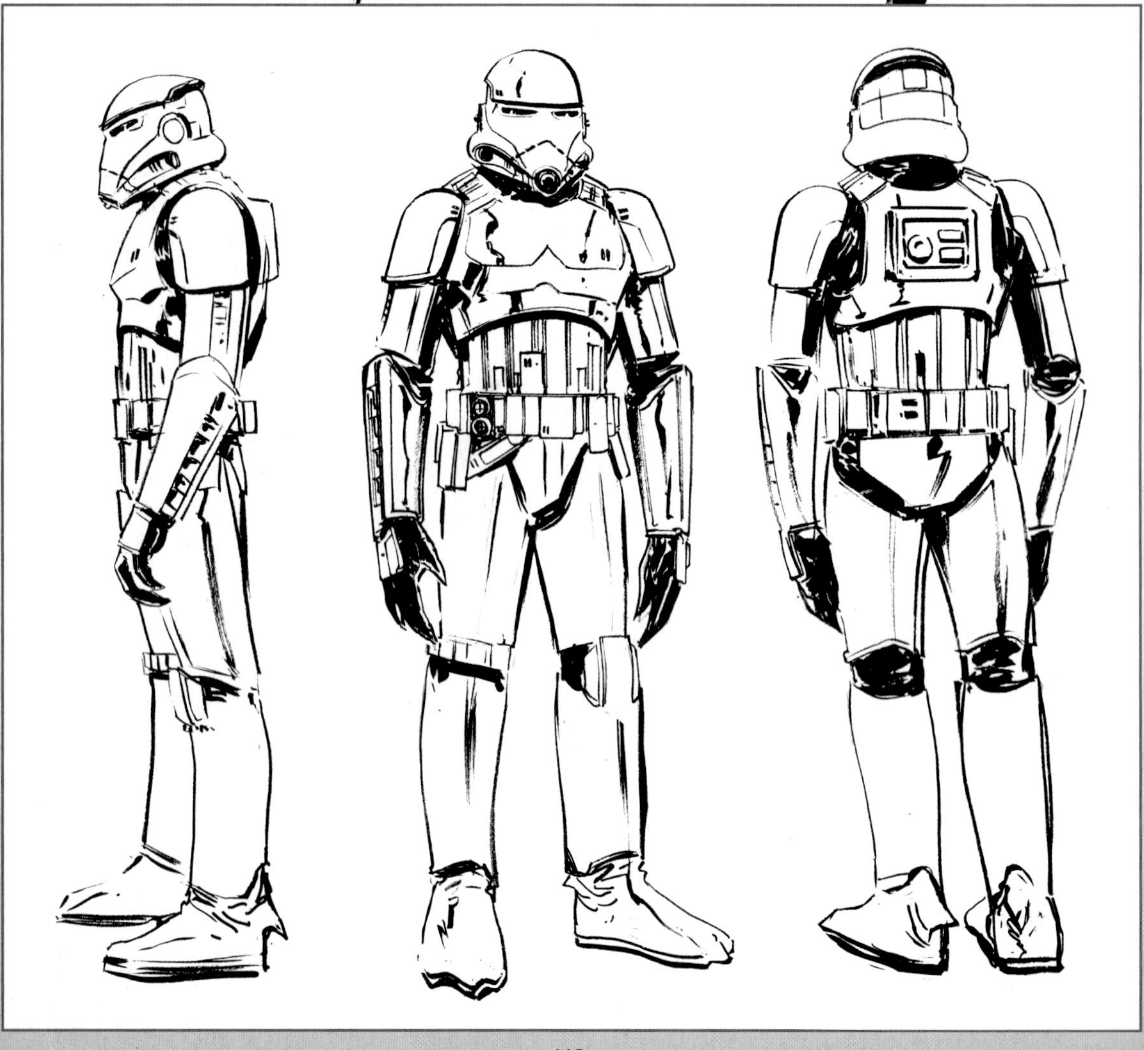